A Gathering of Wonders

ALSO BY JOSEPH WALLACE

*The American Museum of Natural History's
Book of Dinosaurs and Other Ancient Creatures*

The Audubon Pocket Guide to Dinosaurs

The Deep Sea

The Rise and Fall of the Dinosaur

A Gathering
of Wonders

BEHIND THE SCENES AT
THE AMERICAN MUSEUM
OF NATURAL HISTORY

Joseph Wallace

ST. MARTIN'S PRESS · NEW YORK

IN CONJUNCTION WITH THE AMERICAN
MUSEUM OF NATURAL HISTORY

Library of Congress Cataloging-in-Publication Data

Wallace, Joseph E.
    A gathering of wonders : behind the scenes at the American Museum of Natural History / Joseph Wallace.—1st ed.
        p. cm.
    ISBN 0-312-25221-8
    1. American Museum of Natural History.   2. Natural history.
I. American Museum of Natural History.   II. Title.

QH70.U62 N489 2000
508'.074747'1—dc21   00-025481

Book design by Michelle McMillian

Frontispiece photo: The Morgan Gem and Mineral Hall in the 1890s.

First Edition: June 2000

10   9   8   7   6   5   4   3   2   1

For Nora, Gerrie, and Liz,
better friends than they've
known these past few years.

Contents

Foreword

My grandfather, John T. Nichols, was for many years the Curator of fishes at the American Museum of Natural History in New York. One of his sons, my father, David G. Nichols, often worked on small mammal collections for the Museum. My mother, Monique Robert Le Braz, met my father at the Museum thanks to the kindly actions of her uncle through marriage, Trubee Davison, who was once president of the Museum. While in that position, Trubee obtained for my mother a minor research post in anthropology, and that's when she met my dad.

Since I owe my existence to this felicitous confluence of personalities in that great institution, you can see how the Museum would loom rather large in my legend.

When I was a child in the 1940s I got to runkle around in the estuaries and backwaters of the Museum. My grandfather had a messy but fascinating office located somewhere in the musty bowels of the hallowed edifice. I remember a bunch of yellowed publications heaped about in a general state of disarray, and shelves of bottled frogs and fishes. I myself became a devotee of formaldehyde, and went through a stage during my grammar school days where just about anything that slithered

or flapped or croaked or burbled was fair game for my poisonous little vats or for my collecting jars half-filled with naphtha-
lene crystals.

My father set his traps in fields around the old family home-
stead in Mastic, New York, on the South Shore of Long Island.
Many's the time I followed after him carrying my own little
pouch, while he harvested the catch from the night before. Then I
sat at the kitchen table studiously observing as he skinned the
mice and shrews and other elfin bodies, preparing them as
Museum specimens. I also attended the old man when he plucked
small brown bats from behind the green shutters of the family
house, bats that he also sent to the "Happy Myotis Hunting
Grounds" in the name of science. On other occasions, when Pop
had a permit to collect grosbeaks, solitary sandpipers, or red-
eyed vireos, I tagged along to watch him blast them from tree
tops or sand dunes with a .410 shotgun: He rarely missed.

During this same epoch, my grandfather, John T. Nichols, was
an inveterate collector of box turtles at the Mastic estate. No, he
neither pickled them in formaldehyde nor dropped them into
pots of soup, but rather marked their shells with numbers and
dates and recorded their existence in notebooks. Often we found
turtles that had been caught and released decades earlier, and this
provided quite a thrill.

The whole point of these exercises was to become familiar
with the natural world, and thus to venerate it. I swallowed that
theme song hook, line, and sinker, and have been an amateur
naturalist ever since, unequivocally enamored of just about
everything that lives, eats, propagates, and defecates around the
globe, except, perhaps, for humanity, which on occasion can
sorely try my patience.

When I reached the age of fifty-one, and my grandfather had
been dead for thirty-three years, I gave a talk at the Museum for

the seventy-fifth anniversary gathering of the American Society of Ichthyologists and Herpetologists, an organization founded by Grandpa in 1913. After the speech, a friend in the audience took me back into the clandestine innards of the institution to a dank and cavernous room with hundreds of shelves housing bottles of weird preserved fishes. We went up and down the aisles, looking for creatures that my grandad had bagged, and I must say we found a fair number: That was exciting. We even took a few over to some sinks and drainbords and had a closer look. Many of the critters that John T. gathered for posterity were fairly bizarre: They had threatening teeth and bulging eyes. I was impressed.

Unfortunately, that's the last time I was able to visit the Museum, a moment already nine years in the past. Unfortunately also, is the fact that my father died two years ago, in April 1998. With his passing I lost an intimate connection to eighty-one years of knowledge of, and great curiosity about, life on earth. That's a connection I will keenly miss.

Whenever I visited Pop during the last years of his life in Smithville, Texas, we drove around looking for caracaras, discussing Houston toads, or remarking on the great blue herons at Beuscher Lake, a body of water that he checked in on daily. From his childhood until the end, my father regarded the natural world from a perspective of awe and obligation. We talked about the past, his early days as a naturalist, and the future of the planet. He was discouraged about all the human-made perturbations of ocean, coral reef, and rain-forest canopy, yet ever hopeful that people might one day get it together before the species self-destructs.

In 1935 my father had a spider named after him: *Xysticus nicholsi*. This creature appeared on his neck one buggy afternoon while he was bogged down in a swamp in Alaska. Dad popped it in a bottle, and sent the bottle to the New York Museum for identification. I suspect that spider is still located somewhere in the Museum, on a shelf gathering dust. One day I must fly to the Big Apple and try to find it. I'll have to hurry, though, because I've got a bum heart and my longevity is problematic. Mind you, I'm not complaining; we all wind up as dust.

What is wonderful about the American Museum of Natural History is that it speaks to eternity. So much *life* is there, captured as it were in a bottle; life from millions of years ago . . . life that is touted in current headlines . . . life that may still be percolating a billion years hence. Anyone who ever walks through the doors to gape at a whale or a dinosaur or at a diorama of Pleistocene shenanigans, can't help but be enriched by the experience. The American Museum of Natural History is one of the seminal and most energetic museums on earth, and my point (at last!) is that the book in your hands certainly proves it.

I can't begin to enumerate all the riches, tidbits, stories, information, personalities, gossip, and love of science embraced by this fascinating volume about the Museum and its collections, its history, and all its backroom maneuverings. For me, it was as pleasurable to tag along with Joseph Wallace (and all the curators, anthropologists, archeologists, paleontologists, geologists, entymologists, ornithologists, ichthyologists, astronomers, oceanographers, taxidermists, mammalogists, titi monkeys, Komodo dragons, pectinoids, bowerbirds, coelacanths and velociraptors found in these pages) as it had been, back in my wondrous childhood, to cavort behind Pop and Grandpa as they revealed to me the secrets and mysteries of the natural world. In fact, Joseph Wallace upholds the scientific and humanistic traditions that motivated my dad and grandfather, and shaped my own sensibilities and destiny. That is no small matter in today's chaotic world, and a valid reason to rejoice. Mr. Wallace *cares* about small mammals and weird fishes, bats and box turtles, and everything in between, including the future of our planet.

In these pages you will find the straight skinny about barosauruses, Indian canoes, Cuban ammonites, tricerotops, passion flowers, the oldest known bees, the fattest catfish in the Western Hemisphere, and Mary Cynthia Dickerson, a woman fascinated by snakes. The stories travel all over the place, back and forth in time, and make for a wonderful colorful gumbo reflecting the macroscopic details of the museum soup itself.

Sadly, I searched in vain for that dusty bottle containing *Xysticus nicholsi*. Happily, I came across just about everything else imaginable stashed in the back rooms, huddled in corners, festering under wooden palettes, or sequestered in forgotten closets. And what *fun* I had making all those discoveries and also learning about the swarms of bold and thoroughly eccentric adventurers who scoured the continents to unearth the items that eventually wound up in Manhattan.

I'll admit this book may not be quite as immediate as being inside the actual museum, gawking at the exhibits or poking around in the wings among all the fossils, pelts, and skeletons, but it sure comes close. Truth to tell, *A Gathering of Wonders* is a great animated guidebook and history to read before you go to New York.

In fact, it will make you *want* to go—I promise.
Avanti!

John Nichols
Taos, New Mexico
February 10, 2000

Introduction

The World in a Natural History Museum

When I was a child, my parents held out the hope that I would grow up to be cultured, enriched by the artistic glories that New York City offered. But Impressionist paintings failed to excite me, my legs grew weary at the thought of Greek statuary, and I didn't begin to understand Picasso. Confronted with even the greatest masterpiece, I would always be hopelessly cranky—until my parents would finally relent and take me to my favorite place on earth, the American Museum of Natural History.

There I would stand spellbound before a diorama illustrating an African rain forest, North American plain, or Andean mountaintop scene. And though I liked the mounted gorillas, bisons, and condors, what intoxicated me were the painted backgrounds, the vast, mysterious jungles, and endless plains stretching off into the unimaginable distance. With an intensity that I still remember clearly, I yearned to step through the glass into these backdrops, to visit those marvelous environments for myself.

I grew up on crowded big-city streets, navigating a maze of noise and clutter and smog and buildings so tall they blocked the sun. The American Museum of Natural History was my oxygen, a doorway to green worlds that I otherwise could not have imagined.

Today, the same exhibits that entranced me as a child still affect me in exactly the same way. I can wander among the magnificent displays of African and North American mammals, exotic birds, and ocean life, and still want to leave my real life behind and head for the wilderness.

In recent years, the museum has unveiled a superb collection of equally inspiring new halls, ones that communicate important scientific concepts while also showcasing fascinating specimens. The Hall of Human Biology and Evolution, for example, utilizes holograms, murals, and frequently updated computer databases to keep us informed of ongoing research into human origins. The vast new vertebrate paleontology halls use *Tyrannosaurus,* fossil horses, and ancient fish to teach us about cladistics—the revolutionary classification system that has turned long-held evolutionary theories on their heads.

Meanwhile, the Hall of Biodiversity reveals the vast panoply of species that exists on earth and how that remarkable abundance is under grave threat from human activity. The Rose Center for Earth and Space, which includes the new Hayden Planetarium, brings the stars and planets closer than ever before. And the Hall of Planet Earth details the geologic processes that not only gave us the gems and minerals on display elsewhere, but provide the essential basis—the bedrock, as it were—for everything else on display in the Museum, for all life on earth.

I once assumed that the exhibits at the American Museum sprang fully formed from my own yearnings for adventure and escape. In researching this book, I had the pleasure of learning about the remarkable people who built its collections and exhibits. For more than 125 years, the Museum has been home to a nearly endless procession of brilliant, witty, often eccentric, and always interesting scientists and collectors—men and women who at every turn have taught us invaluable lessons about the world we live in.

What wonderful role models these men and women were! Frank Chapman risking his life to save Florida's beautiful herons and egrets from the depredations of hunters. Roy Chapman Andrews facing the harsh conditions of the Gobi Desert with unfailing aplomb, even joy, and bringing back some of the most exciting fossils ever found. Carl Akeley, ill and worn out, taking one final trek in his beloved African rain forests, where he had done so much to preserve the rare mountain gorilla. Margaret Mead proving over a long lifetime the value of anthropological research that did more than collect artifacts and memorialize vanishing cultures.

Nor is that spirit of scientific discovery a thing of the past. Through expeditions (to remote mountains of Venezuela, the Gobi Desert in Mongolia, a village in India, and fossil deposits in New Jersey, for example) and painstaking research (such as in the Molecular Systematics Laboratory where researchers are studying DNA sequences for clues to the process of evolution), the Museum's scientists are providing fascinating insights into ourselves and our world.

Nearly every biologist at the Museum is engaged in intensive research into the systematics of living or extinct animals. Systematics is an attempt to determine relationships between different animal groups, and in doing so to learn, in the words of Museum Provost Michael J. Novacek, "the organization of the living planet." As Novacek adds in a 1992 book called *Systematics, Ecology, and the Biodiversity Crisis*, "The biological world is a delicate web of connections, a network of species reproducing, growing, feeding on one another, competing for the same resources, evolving, and ultimately going extinct. The building blocks of these finely tuned and, as we are increasingly aware, highly vulnerable systems, are the species themselves." Only through systematics can we understand the diversity of these species and begin to comprehend the impact of their extinction.

The research is equally ambitious in departments not involved in biology. Edmond Mathez curator in Earth and Planetary Sciences, is hoping to unravel the mystery surrounding the bizarre electrical phenomena that occur before earthquakes, while that department's Martin Prinz is using meteorites to learn about the origins of distant planets. Anthropology Curator and Museum Dean of Science Craig Morris is studying the style of the ancient Inka empire, particularly how changes in style reveal how the Inka rulers exercised their great power. And Laurel Kendall, another curator in Anthropology, is exploring the rites and rituals of Korea, where an urbanized society clings to some of its most time-honored traditions.

No book can match the impact of a well-designed museum exhibit. Many of the treasures described here—the towering mother *Barosaurus* defending her young from a marauding *Allosaurus*, the spectacular dioramas of gorillas and coral reefs, and others—must be seen up close to be fully appreciated. What I've tried to do in the chapters that follow is to show that even exhibits in a museum can have a life, a resonance, that stretches far beyond their surface beauty or grandeur. They can be windows into a world that remains complex and diverse almost beyond imagining. Both they and we are richer when we listen to what they teach us.

This book could not have been written without the help of a myriad of busy members of the Museum scientific staff. Nearly three dozen curators, emeritus curators, and others took time away from their real work to talk to me, and they all deserve mention: Laurel Kendall, Craig Morris, Ian Tattersall, David Hurst

Thomas, Stanley Freed, and Lorann Pendleton (Anthropology); James Webster, George Harlow, Edmond Mathez, and Martin Prinz (Earth and Planetary Sciences); Robert DeSalle, David Grimaldi, Lee Herman, Jim Miller, and Norman Platnick (Invertebrate Zoology); Mark Norell, Niles Eldredge, Neil Landman, John Maisey, Malcolm McKenna, Michael Novacek, and Mick Ellison (Paleontology); Charles Cole, Charles Myers, and Lily Rodríguez (Vertebrate Zoology—Herpetology); Melanie Stiassny, James Atz, and Ian Harrison (Vertebrate Zoology—Ichthyology); Darrin Lunde, Nancy Simmons, Ross MacPhee, Robert Voss, and Clare Flemming (Vertebrate Zoology—Mammalogy); George Barrowclough, Mary LeCroy, and Paul Sweet (Vertebrate Zoology—Ornithology).

Many of the above also took time to read portions of the manuscript for scientific accuracy. I owe them for every error they caught, and take full responsibility for whatever errors remain.

I must also thank Museum President Ellen Futter for inviting me behind the scenes. Sigmund Ginsburg, Senior Vice-President for Finance and Business Development, and Rena Zurofsky of the Department of Licensing, Retail, and Special Publishing hammered out the details that made this book possible. Maron Waxman, director of Special Publishing, helped get the ball rolling again and made several important editorial suggestions. And Paul Gottlieb, publisher and editor-in-chief of Harry N. Abrams, was the best advocate any writer could hope for.

In the Museum's superb library, Nina Root, Valerie Wheat, Roscoe Thompson, Lisa Stock, Joel Sweimler, and Tom Baione all provided help beyond measure. Special thanks go out to Mary DeJong, who was working in the library when I first met her. I owe Mary more than I can express for her insights, her sense of humor, and her support during this book's extended evolution (an example of punctuated equilibrium if ever there was one). I'll miss those Thai lunches as well.

I also met Jennifer Fischer, superb teacher and thoughtful student of history, at the library. We discussed our research during several snowy winter days, and these discussions led Jennifer to introduce me to Gordon and Leslie Van Gelder. Gordon and Leslie gave me perspectives on life at the Museum that I couldn't have gotten anywhere else—and then Gordon went on to become my sharp-eyed editor at St. Martin's Press. If Jennifer hadn't taken an interest in my work, I would never have met the Van Gelders, and this book might still be drifting in manuscript purgatory.

Lastly, and as always, I'm grateful to Sharon, Shana, and Jacob, for their extraordinary patience and support. Their names don't go on the front cover, but my books couldn't get written without them.

1   The Specter of Extinction

INTO A WILD WORLD

> It was extraordinary how quickly that rhino was on his feet.
> More than that, he no sooner was up than he was charging.
> I can see him yet. His head was down and he snorted like a
> switch engine. His tail was up and his short, heavy legs were
> pounding along furiously. . . . It certainly took that rhino a
> very few seconds to cover half the distance to us, but it
> seemed more than long enough to me. He seemed to be the
> size of a freight car, and his snorts were actually terrifying.
>
> —*Museum preparator James L. Clark, describing*
> *a 1909 encounter in* Lives of the Hunted *(1929).*

James L. Clark wasn't alone among the early employees of the
American Museum of Natural History in risking his life for
science. Again and again, Museum scientists gloried at the opportunity to confront the largest, most untamable, most dangerous
animals in existence. This thrill of the chase (bordering on
machismo but thankfully leavened by humor and even self-
deprecation) shines in the letters, field journals, and published

writings of nearly all of the Museum's explorers during the institution's first fifty years.

The need to challenge the unknown is what drove Roy Chapman Andrews ("I was born to be an explorer. . . . I couldn't do anything else and be happy," he said) to spend years on pitching boats in frigid northern seas, studying whales. It's what sent Carl Akeley into the African wilds again and again, even after his notorious (and almost fatal) encounters with a charging elephant and a wounded leopard. And it's apparent today to anyone who walks through the Museum's magnificent halls of North American, Asian, African, and marine mammals, with their lions, grizzlies, walruses, and other spectacular creatures.

Joel Asaph Allen (1838–1921), the first curator of the then-joined Department of Mammalogy and Ornithology, would seem an unlikely choice to hire such a group of risktakers. By the time the forty-six-year-old Allen joined the Museum in 1885, he was plagued by a variety of physical and emotional ailments, illnesses that bedeviled him for the rest of his long life. A mild-mannered, shy man (though often witheringly forthright in his written opinions), Allen spent most of his time at the Museum or convalescing at home, not in the field.

But before joining the Museum, Allen had participated in some memorable surveys of the wildlife of the American frontier—expeditions that reveal why such adventurers as Andrews and Akeley would later feel at home in the Museum. Undoubtedly the most remarkable of all was an 1873 engineering and scientific exploration of the Yellowstone River area in Dakota territory, a journey that ranks among the most dangerous expeditions of all time.

This region harbored dangers above and beyond those posed by wild animals and disease-bearing insects, Allen later recalled. The resident Sioux Indians, having clashed frequently with federal soldiers, were naturally suspicious of any visitors from the East. "Hence a heavy military escort was this year provided for the protection of the engineers," Allen recalled. "The escort comprised the famous Seventh Cavalry, with Gen. George A. Custer in command, and parts of the Eighth and Twenty-Second Infantry, and a company of Indian scouts."

Allen, employed at the time by the Harvard Museum of Comparative Zoology, sought to capture and collect specimens of as many bird and mammal species as possible. But the difficulties of this task became clear once General Custer—whose reputation for brutality against Indians preceded him—and the local Sioux began skirmishing. "Indians were first seen watching us from neighboring bluffs near the mouth of the Powder River; they soon became bolder and were seen daily, when orders were given forbidding straying from the line of march, or the use of firearms without permission from the commanding officer," Allen wrote. "This compelled us to abandon bird collecting and side excursions for several weeks."

Soon the standoff broke into open fighting, in which both sides sustained casualties. Although the remaining expedition members eventually made it to safety, these were not the last confrontations between Custer and the Sioux. "It was only three years later, and about sixty miles south of Pompey's Pillar, on the Little Big Horn, that General Custer and his whole command were massacred in a fight with this same band of Sioux Indians," Allen pointed out.

Given his experiences, no one would have blamed Allen for turning his back on field research forever. Instead, he saw such threats merely as challenges to be overcome. "The opportunities for natural history collecting and field research on this expedition were far from ideal, but we did not return empty handed nor without well-filled notebooks," he wrote later. "To me it was an experience of great value from the naturalist's point of view, and one I have never ceased to recall with much pleasure for its personal associations and its dash of military flavor."

Allen's early exploits also brought him face to face with one of the driving forces behind nineteenth-century science: the decimation of North America's wild game, especially the bison. "In the summer of 1871 the author saw on the plains of western Kansas Buffaloes by the hundred thousand, if not by the million," he wrote in 1902. "Three years later these same plains were covered with the bleaching carcasses of these hundreds of thousands of Bisons, from which merely the hides had been removed and the bodies left to rot."

Allen brought passion for exploration and outrage at the slaughter of wild mammals and birds to the Museum when he arrived in 1885, but at first his new employer's financial problems did not allow him to act on either. The Museum could afford to employ only a few scientists in the 1880s and 1890s. In 1888, for example, Allen's title was "Curator of the Department of Ornithology, Mammalogy, Fishes and Reptiles. Also temporarily in charge of the Department of Invertebrate Zoology." Who had time for fieldwork?

Instead, he was determined to greatly enlarge the mammal-and-bird study collections. With few exceptions, during his early years, this goal was achieved more through donations and purchases than collecting expeditions. And, as early annual reports make clear, progress was slow, with typical donations including "1 Mole; 1 White-Footed Mouse; 1 Bat; 1 Cow; 1 Angora Cat" and "1 St. Bernard Dog"—this last donated by future Museum President Henry Fairfield Osborn.

Eventually, purchases and other acquisitions helped the Museum's exhibit and study collections grow by thousands of specimens. But Allen and Museum President Morris K. Jesup well realized that no Museum can build a truly comprehensive collection by merely accepting what is offered to it. So, when finances allowed in the early 1900s, the Museum began hiring new scientists and preparators, all of whom soon began to build the swashbuckling reputation that would characterize the Museum in the decades preceding World War II.

Roy Chapman Andrews, Carl Akeley, and James L. Clark were joined by a host of other scientist-adventurers, including Herbert Lang, Harold E. Anthony, James Chapin, Rollo Beck, and George Cherrie. Collectively, they spent decades tracking through the uncharted forests, swamps, coasts, and deserts of previously unexplored regions of South America, Asia, and Africa, and added tens of thousands of specimens and a host of indelible stories to the collections of the American Museum.

Oddly, the most colorful, poignant, and influential of all these men, Carl Akeley, was not a scientist at all, but a sculptor and preparator of habitat groups. No matter: Whatever his qualifications, Akeley was the man who first made us familiar with the true character of the animals of what he called "brightest Africa." Most importantly of all, he introduced us to one of our closest relatives, the mountain gorilla, and by helping insure that species' survival, marked himself as one of the world's first great, if unsung, heroes of conservation.

CARL AKELEY'S GREAT DREAM

"The game must go," is the cry of Africa. "This is no longer the world's zoo but an agricultural country." Unfortunately the beasts of the forest are communists. They have no sense of property rights; to them a tilled field is a strip of particularly delectable vegetation, an ideal feeding ground—nothing more.... Add to the bands of hunters officially appointed to protect gardens and flocks those who kill for

food, for gain and for "sport" and it becomes evident that
the wild life of Africa is doomed.

—*Carl Akeley, the* Mentor
magazine, 1926.

The Museum has benefited throughout more than half a
century by high talent among men and women in its service,
but Akeley was the only genius who has been one of us.

—*Museum president Henry Fairfield Osborn,*
after Carl Akeley's death in 1926.

What sort of a man was Carl Akeley? He was a brilliantly innovative sculptor and preparator, a man who *knew* what a wild
creature should look like in a museum, and who revolutionized
the field of taxidermy to bring his vision to life. He was an expert
hunter who was thoughtful enough to shrug off society's expec-
tations and abandon hunting for "fun." He was a tireless self-
promoter whose story is still familiar today, more than seventy
years after his death.

But mostly, Carl Akeley was this: A man who, upon realizing
that the wilderness and the animals he loved were threatened
with destruction, engaged in a lifelong battle to ensure that this
catastrophe did not happen.

Carl Akeley was born in 1864 in rural New York. "By all rules
of the game, I should have been a farmer," he recalled, "but for
some reason or other, I was always more interested in birds and
chipmunks than in crops and cattle." At the age of thirteen, he
also became interested in the field of taxidermy, an enthusiasm
that would never leave him.

Before his twentieth birthday—and before contacting any
museum or professional taxidermist—Akeley was already beginning to stretch the boundaries of what a museum exhibit should
include. "I went so far as to take a few painting lessons from a

lady in Holley, New York, a village near my father's farm, in order that I might paint realistic backgrounds for my stuffed birds and animals," he wrote many years later. "So far as I know, my early attempts in this direction were the first experiments with painted backdrops for taxidermic groups. At least one of them is still in existence, but I have been a bit afraid to go see it."

After a stint as a taxidermist at Ward's Natural Science Establishment (a then-famous supplier of mounted animals, fossils, meteors, and other objects to museums and collectors), Akeley moved on to a museum in Milwaukee and then to the famous Field Museum in Chicago. There he honed his vision of animal preparation, rejecting the old method of stuffing skins with straw, a technique that resulted in lumpy, unnatural specimens.

Instead, Akeley's method, developed during his years at the Field Museum, involved modeling a lifelike clay mannequin of the specimen on a rough wood-and-wire armature, casting the life-sized clay model in plaster, and then molding a final image over the plaster model out of cheesecloth, papier-mâché, shellac, and wire. The plaster was removed, and the prepared skin of the specimen was then cemented to the model, resulting in a far more realistic mount than was ever possible before.

In 1896, Akeley visited Africa for the first time, on an expedition to Somaliland with the great zoologist Daniel Giraud Elliot of the Field Museum. By the time he returned, Akeley recalled, "I had determined upon Africa as the country whose superb animals I would re-create through museum groups for the benefit of the American public. I was so bewitched by the beauty and splendor of Africa that it seemed to me inconceivable then that I would not immediately return."

Instead, Akeley spent the next nine years improving his mounting technique, teaching his methods to other preparators (including James L. Clark at the American Museum in 1903), and dreaming of his next trip. He finally got to visit East Africa in

1905; it was on this trip that he first made the acquaintance of the African elephant, "the most fascinating of all wild animals," in Akeley's words. Soon after, however, the Field Museum cancelled plans for an African mammal hall, and Akeley took his drive and determination to the American Museum, beginning with a 1909 collecting expedition to East Africa.

This famous African expedition included, at times, James L. Clark, Theodore Roosevelt, and *Chicago Tribune* cartoonist John T. McCutcheon, who not only memorialized the trip's adventures in a lively book called *In Africa* but also shot one of the elephants that now make up the magnificent group that anchors the Museum's Akeley Hall. It was during this expedition that Akeley first envisioned a massive hall that would show many of the animals of brightest Africa.

Akeley spent the remaining seventeen years of his life planning, designing, collecting for, and trying to finance the African halls. He died ten years before they were finally completed under the guidance of James L. Clark and Akeley's widow, Mary L. Jobe Akeley. There's little doubt, however, that he would have been thrilled with the result. More than seventy years after his death, the hall's dioramas of African savannas and rain forests, filled with lions, rhinos, zebras, and dozens of other species, still seem infused with Carl Akeley's unflagging energy. They are lit with the vividness of his memories of the continent he loved so much.

Akeley achieved his goal of displaying Africa's mammals in realistic settings. But he wanted much more. His passion—his mission—was to exhibit animals that he believed would soon be gone from their homelands, driven into extinction by hunting and habitat loss. The goal of the Akeley Hall was always to remind us that such spectacular, irreplaceable animals exist and perhaps to inspire us to help prevent their destruction.

When he was still a young man, Akeley began to have doubts

about the propriety of hunting for sport. During his very first trip to Africa, his 1896 expedition to Somaliland, he collected some specimens of the native donkey called the "wild ass." Shooting one, he was surprised to see it make no attempt to flee. Instead, it stood calmly nearby until, Akeley recalled, "I put one hand on his withers and tripping him, pushed him over. I began to feel that if this was sport I would never be a sportsman."

Akeley's discomfort turned to disgust when he shot another, inflicting a flesh wound that the animal would certainly have recovered from if it had run away. But, like the first, it didn't. "As we got near he turned and faced us with great gentle eyes," Akeley wrote. "Without the least sign of fear or anger he seemed to wonder why we had harmed him."

Again, the hunter was able to approach the animal so closely that it seemed almost tame. The two wild asses, Akeley marveled, "appeared not to realize that we were the cause of their injuries but rather seemed to expect relief as we approached—yet one English 'sportsman' boasted of having killed twenty-eight." As for Akeley himself: "I announced that if any more wild asses were wanted, someone else would have to shoot them. I had had quite enough."

Akeley's scorn for European "sportsmen" runs like a stream of lava through his writing. He blamed them for the fact that, as Museum President Henry Fairfield Osborn put it, "in Africa the remnants of all the royal families of the Age of Mammals are making their last stand, that their backs are up against the pitiless wall of what we call civilization."

Each time he returned to Africa, Akeley could see the results of hunters' depredations with alarming clarity. In 1926, during his final trip to Africa, he found that the plains that had swarmed with game just fourteen years before were now barren. "I have not appreciated the absolute necessity of carrying out the African Hall, if it is ever to be done, as I now do after this painful revelation," he said in an anguished letter home to Museum Director George H. Sherwood. *"The old conditions, the story of which we want to tell, are now gone, and in another decade the men who knew them will all be gone."*

In a remarkable article entitled "Have a Heart," written for the *Mentor* magazine just before he embarked on this final expedition, Akeley excoriated those who hunted African animals for fun. "Two types of so-called 'sportsmen' who have no possible excuse for their slaughter of African game and who might well be controlled are the man who is dominated by blood lust, and the 'game hog,' " he wrote. He described the former as a man who would rather wound an animal and then slit its throat than kill it cleanly with a single shot, and the latter as someone who killed as many animals as his hunting license permitted—even if it meant throwing away the bodies afterwards.

The local tribes could not be held responsible for the disappearance of the game, Akeley believed. "The white man of Africa blames the native for the present depletion. It is true that in places the natives have great drives, using pits, poisoned arrows and such other methods as they have used from time immemorial, and thus occasion the killing of great numbers of animals," Akeley pointed out. "But we must remember that when the white man came the land was teeming with animal life and for generations that game and the natives had been there together. Directly or indirectly, civilized man is responsible for the rapid disappearance of wild life in Africa."

It's clear that Akeley cared deeply about the animals of Africa's plains, rivers, and forests. But it was the mountainous rain-forests of the Kivu region of the Belgian Congo that moved him most deeply, especially one resident of these cold, misty forests: the mountain gorilla.

Akeley's first encounter with the gorillas was in 1921, on the slopes of Mount Mikeno and Mount Karisimbi. He journeyed to the remote forests to collect a family group for the African hall, and he was admittedly nervous as he entered gorilla country for the first time.

The fact that a man who had faced down elephants, lions, and leopards would tread cautiously in the mountain gorilla's haunts is proof of how inaccurate early depictions of the gorilla had been. Early explorers, such as Paul Du Chaillu, published shameful distortions that led the public to believe that the gorilla was a violent, ferocious creature much given to killing local men and carrying away their women.

Once Akeley came in contact with the gorillas on Mikeno and Karisimbi, he realized how unrealistic earlier descriptions had been. "I saw no indication that the gorilla is in the least aggressive or that he would fight even on just provocation," he wrote in 1923. "I have trailed him through his jungles, come on him at very close quarters, and shot him without seeing the slightest intimation on his part of an intention to start a fight."

It became one of the obsessions of Akeley's final years to depict accurately these giant creatures whose gentleness had moved him so much. "The gorilla group in the Roosevelt African hall will be a great disappointment to that portion of the public which has expected and would prefer to see the gorilla made as human and as horrible as the imagination has painted him," he wrote on returning from Africa, "for it will show the gorilla as a great amiable creature in a setting of extraordinary beauty."

If the explorer was determined to mount a revisionist gorilla display in New York, he was fiercely passionate about a goal he considered far more important: preserving the mountain forests of the Kivu country and the gorillas that lived there. As soon as he glimpsed the view that stretched from the slopes of Karisimbi across "a beautiful forested valley to the gorgeous pinnacle of

Mikeno on the right and to the smouldering craters of Nyamla-gira and Chaninagongo in the distance," Akeley knew that this was a landscape he had to fight to preserve, both in the gorilla habitat group and in reality.

Almost immediately upon his return from the 1921 collecting expedition, Akeley began to enlist support for the establishment of a Kivu gorilla sanctuary. Among his ardent backers were John C. Merriam, of the Carnegie Institution and National Academy of Sciences in Washington, and a pair of Belgian government officials, Ambassador to the United States Baron Emile de Cartier de Marchienne and Consul-General James Gustavus Whiteley. Most crucially of all, King Albert of Belgium, the colonial ruler of the Belgian Congo, had toured U.S. national parks in 1919 in the company of Henry Fairfield Osborn, and was receptive to the idea.

As early as September 1922, Consul-General Whitely had encouraging news for Akeley: "I have also had a letter from the Belgian Ambassador Baron de Cartier, in which he says that he thinks the Kivu District will 'be made safe for Gorillas,' " Whiteley wrote. "I hope it can be done, and that 'our poor relations' will be made safe and happy."

But these supporters of the proposed sanctuary, along with Akeley himself, were well aware that powerful special interests would battle the proposed sanctuary. The main threats to the gorillas of Kivu country were the white hunters who saw gorilla hunting as a potential gold mine. Even limited hunting might destroy the small population that lived there, Akeley told Baron de Cartier, pointing out that "the number of animals in the colony is small. I doubt if there are fifty all told and the number should not be reduced unnecessarily."

Unsurprisingly, hunters raced to kill as many gorillas as possible before the proposed park became a reality. One hunter "was permitted to go in and I have partial reports of his work and photographs which show him with four baby gorillas which he captured," Akeley wrote to Baron de Cartier in January 1924. "It is safe to assume that in capturing them, there were four mothers killed and I fear this would be only a part of the story."

Nor were all supposedly "scientific" collectors free from blame, Akeley told de Cartier in the same letter. Referring to an expedition from another natural history museum in the United States, Akeley wrote, "One member of said expedition said to me that they were not worried because of the fact that they had no permit to kill gorillas in the Belgian Congo, because they had every assurance that it was perfectly simple to poach gorillas and get away with it."

By 1925, as plans for the sanctuary neared completion, Akeley was also under public attack for his estimate that fewer than a hundred gorillas lived in the region. "It is possible that we 'alarmists' who are interested in preventing the destruction of the gorilla, have overstated our case—in fact, I hope we have," he told de Cartier in a statement that is as pertinent today as when he wrote it. "If, in the future, it is found that there are, for any reason, too many gorillas, it will be very simple to reduce their numbers; while, on the other hand, if we were some day suddenly brought face to face with the fact that the last gorilla had been killed, it would be a very different story."

Carl Akeley lived long enough to see the establishment of Parc National Albert, one of the first true sanctuaries established on the African continent, on March 2, 1925. Exhausted by his efforts, he insisted on visiting the region one last time in 1926, where, within the boundaries of the new park, he died of dysentery on the slopes of Mount Mikeno. His final mission reflected his twin passions: He was both gathering background material for the gorilla display at the Museum and undertaking an initial survey of the park for the Belgian government. He is buried today on Mikeno, surrounded by the gorgeous mountain forests that he spent so much of his life trying to save.

Even Carl Akeley's death did not end his influence on the Kivu region and its preservation. His strong-willed wife, Mary (an accomplished explorer who had kept the 1926 expedition going after Carl's death), and Belgian scientist J. M. Derscheid (who had also accompanied that final expedition) soon proposed expanding the park tenfold, from its original size of about 50,000 acres to 500,000 acres.

This ambitious goal was realized on May 6, 1929, when King Albert signed a royal decree establishing the larger boundaries, to be divided into four reserves. Within these reserves, the decree announced, it was forbidden "*to pursue, capture, kill, or molest in any way, any kind of wild animal, including animals which are reputed dangerous or harmful.*" In addition, visitors could not take or destroy the nests of wild birds; cut down, remove, or destroy any uncultivated plant; or build or dig in any way.

In his speech inaugurating the newly expanded sanctuary (which today still exists as a network of national parks and preserves in Zaire, Rwanda, and Uganda; together home to most surviving mountain gorillas) King Albert gave credit where it was due. "I cannot omit recalling to mind the great part in the conception of the Parc National that is due to Carl Akeley," the king said. "He gave his life there while engaged in the task to which he devoted himself, but his work has been carried on and completed through the brave efforts of Mrs. Akeley and the zeal of our compatriot, Doctor Derscheid, who, in carrying out the plan of the reserve, exhibited an activity, a devotion, and an ability which I cannot sufficiently praise."

Akeley, the Visionary

Carl Akeley's devotion to the preservation of wildlife placed him among the few forward-thinking scientists of his day. But his sensitivity to the needs of local people living in and near a preserve, along with his understanding of how sanctuaries could serve as essential research sites, mark him as a true visionary. Even today, more than seventy years after his death, we can learn from his ideas.

As he fought to prevent hunting within the Parc National Albert, Akeley was considering other means of ensuring the park's long-term survival. Confronting an issue that is still often ignored by governments and conservation organizations alike when establishing and managing preserves, he argued for flexibility in dealing with the tribes surrounding the park. "I merely beg to suggest that in the beginning the natives be given 'the benefit of the doubt,' " he wrote to Baron de Cartier, Belgian Ambassador to the United States, in June of 1925. "The cooperation of the natives in the protection of the Parc is important, and I feel this is to be obtained through giving careful thought and consideration to their needs and rights."

As it turned out, Akeley's ideas were shared by those who wrote the park's charter. The African pygmies who had lived for generations side by side with the gorillas (with no detriment to either) were allowed to continue as they had, even hunting any animal except gorillas.

Akeley was equally revolutionary in his thinking about the future of field research. During his lifetime, the vast majority of expeditions were designed merely to collect and get out—"smash and grab" science that gathered living animals for zoos or collected specimens for museums. Occasionally scientists took the time to watch or film animal behavior, but the presence of humans (usually equipped with guns) made it unlikely that the behavior being observed was natural.

Akeley realized that a park where hunting was truly outlawed presented invaluable new opportunities for study. "One of the most interesting and important chapters in the results of the study of the gorilla will be . . . getting them accustomed to the presence of man when he appears as a friend and not as an enemy," he wrote to Baron de Cartier in 1923, two years before the park was established. This important research could only take place, Akeley pointed out, "when the gorillas have been immuned from the attacks of man for a considerable period, so that to a considerable extent they have forgotten the enmity of man, in other words, are in a normal primitive frame of mind as regards man, so that we will be able to begin our studies without prejudiced animals."

The arrival of true field research, today practiced by hundreds of scientists the world over, had to wait more than thirty years before following Akeley's lead. Finally, in the late 1950s, biologist George Schaller studied mountain gorillas in Akeley's old haunts on Mikeno and Karisimbi, taking the time to allow the gorillas to get used to his presence and then observing their natural behavior.

Since then, Jane Goodall, Dian Fossey, Birute Galdikas, and others have earned the trust of chimpanzees, gorillas, and orangutans, producing groundbreaking research as a result. There is no doubt that Carl Akeley would have been thrilled to see the peaceful coexistence he'd long dreamed of between humans and gorillas actually become a reality.

Too Late

When the Museum's Harry C. Raven, an anatomist specializing in mammals, journeyed to Australia in 1921, his goal was to collect diverse species of what he called "the strange animals of the island continent." Though he was very successful, there was one mammal he failed to find, the thylacine (also known as the pouched wolf, tiger, and hyena), an extraordinary marsupial predator that at the time inhabited the rocky slopes of back-country Tasmania.

Curator William K. Gregory, who had preceded Raven to Australia, must have known that the collector was likely to miss the thylacine. In a poignant letter, he recommended that Raven, upon arrival in Tasmania, "be sure to visit Mrs. Roberts's collection of living mammals and birds. . . . Mrs. R. will help you get photos of as many as you want, especially pouched wolf ('tiger')."

The thylacine had for decades been the target of a fierce and dedicated extirpation campaign. Since the early 1800s, a series of bounties, offered due to the thylacine's supposed taste for settlers' sheep, had decimated the population. Still, the thylacine hung on until a final bounty was offered in 1887.

This bounty spelled doom for the species. Between 1888 and 1909, government bounties were paid on 2,184 animals, a horrifying number for a species that had never been common. Additional hundreds or thousands of others were killed but not submitted for the bounty, instead being taken to local property owners for an off-the-books "reward" and then tossed in the trash.

The peak year for thylacine bounties was 1900, when 153 were claimed. By 1908 the number was down to seventeen, by 1909 to two, and in 1910 and afterward not a single bounty was paid—a decline of stunning rapidity. The thylacine was not yet extinct by 1910, but the species may already have been so diminished that it had no hope for survival. Today, most experts consider 1936, when the last captive individual died, as the moment that the remarkable thylacine gave up the unequal battle and passed into extinction.

"The modern world is not kind to animals," Raven wrote upon his return from Australia. "Man, and the animals that man has introduced, will most certainly eliminate the major portion of the strange and fascinating creatures that are typical of Australia and the adjacent islands. . . . The time has not yet come for their epitaph, but there can be little doubt that it will be in order before many more generations have passed."

BUILDING THE PERFECT WHALE

> I didn't know I was going to build a whale. Only three or four people in the world have done this, and only two of us are still alive. It isn't something I can recommend. Not too long ago a colleague in Canada called and told me that his museum was planning to build a whale and did I have any suggestions? I had only one—resign now and get yourself a nice university job.
>
> —*Museum mammalogist Richard G. Van Gelder,*
> *in* Curator *magazine, 1970.*

The risktaking, "no guts, no glory" spirit that has gripped the American Museum's mammalogy department from its inception has done more than send explorers to the corners of the globe in search of adventure. The same attitude has led Museum curators to undertake the planning and construction of some of the largest and most spectacular exhibits to be seen at any natural history museum. None has been more ambitious (some would say foolhardy) than the building of a lifesize model of a huge blue whale—a task the Museum has taken on not once, but twice in the past century.

Before Roy Chapman Andrews visited Mongolia for the first time in 1919 and became obsessed with the Gobi Desert's barren beauty, its unusual wildlife, and its fossils, he satisfied his thirst for the thrills and spirit of scientific inquiry by studying and collecting whales. This was challenge enough, as the task of bringing back the skeleton of a full-size whale was about as much as Andrews could handle.

In the winter of 1907, as Andrews related in a 1914 article for the *American Museum Journal*, he and other Museum employees decided to collect the skeleton of a northern right whale that had been brought in by whalers to a New York beach. "The weather was bitterly cold and after the second day's work a gale buried half the body in sand," he recalled. "It took two weeks of the hardest kind of work to get the skeletons partially cleaned and loaded onto a freight car for shipment to the Museum."

Museum correspondence reveals that collecting whale bones had other drawbacks. "Am sorry your work is proving so unpleasant," Curator George H. Sherwood wrote to one collector. "From experience, I can appreciate your difficulty in 'shaking' the odor. Get some olive oil or oil of bergamot, from the nearest drug store. That will give you a change of odor at least."

The efforts of Andrews and others enabled the Museum to put together a superb collection of whale specimens. Today the bones—great knobby jaws, magnificently curved ribs that must have inspired the designers of early sailing ships, mute skulls with enormous empty eye sockets—reside in an attic storage area in the Department of Mammalogy that once served as the Museum's power station.

Though undeniably compelling, these bones lack any spark of life; they seem instead like disembodied pieces of organic architecture or images from an Edward Weston photograph. They can give no sense of the power, grace, and harnessed energy that a living whale possesses in such abundance. Andrews realized this and decided to do something about it.

While whale skeletons can be reconstructed (over the years, several complete skeletons have hung from the ceilings of different Museum halls), there's no way to preserve and mount a complete whale. Not even Carl Akeley with all his genius could devise a method using a whale's skin and bones to produce a diorama exhibit—the size is too large and the skin too fragile.

But that fact didn't stop Andrews, who solved the problem by building a whale from scratch, using an iron framework, iron netting, wood, plaster of Paris, and papier-mâché. His whale, constructed in 1907, was on display for more than fifty years, during which time it never ceased to resemble a gigantic torpedo far more than it did a living leviathan.

Andrews's whale hung from the ceiling of the Biology of Mammals hall, because it predated the construction of the Hall of Ocean Life and was too large to move after that more appropriate home had been built in the 1920s. This "misplaced whale" was an ongoing annoyance to Museum administrators, especially since the Hall of Ocean Life was so sparsely stocked that it desperately needed the excitement a giant whale would provide.

It's hard to imagine today, now that the magnificent, two-leveled Hall of Ocean Life is one of the most popular halls in the Museum, that it was once considered almost an embarrassment. In his *Curator* piece, Richard Van Gelder pointed out that during most of its first forty years in existence, it "had one main attribute—it was the easiest hall to close when there was a shortage of guards, electricity, or heat. It was closed most of the time."

Finally, in 1959, the Museum decided something had to be done to spruce up the hall. That something, of course, was to build a new model of a blue whale—but this task, according to Van Gelder, was far easier to envision than to carry out, as he, ichthyologist Charles Breder, and Gordon Reekie of the Exhibition Department soon came to realize.

The curators' first idea was to hang the new whale model from the ceiling by wires, much as Andrews's whale had done for half a century. But this wasn't acceptable to a Museum administrator Van Gelder dubbed "Stringfellow," who told him that nothing must hang from the ceiling by "strings."

"So I went back to my office, put my feet up on the desk, and tried to figure out how you can get a whale up in the air without strings," Van Gelder recalled. "Make it out of rubber and fill it with helium, I thought, but put the idea aside. Too much like Macy's Thanksgiving parade."

Another administrator suggested a new plan, supporting the whale on a pedestal, with a chromium rod piercing its belly. Unfortunately, the administrator's miniature mock-up of this concept "looked like some of the fighter plane models that I used to have as desk ornaments during the war: a fat-bellied P-40 blasting up into the wild blue yonder," Van Gelder wrote, and the idea was soon vetoed.

Once again, Van Gelder was told to develop a new design. "First of all, I reasoned, we can't have the whale hanging from the ceiling. Secondly, we can't have it off the floor supported by rods. What else is left?"

He began to think about the months he'd spent at sea on collecting expeditions, and about how—in all that time—he'd glimpsed only one whole whale, a humpback that breached near his ship. "But all of the other whales that I saw were nothing more than a bit of fin, a puff of vapor, or a pair of flukes," he wrote. "You just don't see whole whales, except in the air. Also, except dead ones."

Now *there* was an idea. The mammalogist proposed, tongue in cheek, that the hall feature a beached whale. Of course, Van Gelder assumed that this ridiculous suggestion would be laughed off and his idea of having a model suspended from the ceiling would be embraced. But to his shock, "not only was the dead-whale idea accepted, it was received enthusiastically."

Van Gelder watched in dismay as the plan took shape. When he recommended a ten-foot-high form lying sprawled on a rectangular sand-filled base, one Museum higher-up suggested that the whale's midsection be covered by "simulated water," with nothing showing but the head on one end and the flukes on the other. The head poking out provoked Van Gelder to dub this the "gopher plan."

Van Gelder wrote that ichthyologist Charles Breder had his own ideas for how to spice up the dead-whale concept. "We had been talking about lighting the corpse, and he mentioned that in the beached whale that he had seen, phosphorescent bacteria had grown on it so that at night it was outlined in a ghostly glow. We decided that we would have a cycling light over the whale that would change, over a five minute period, from night to day—and in the dark part we would indicate the phosphorescence with ultra-violet light."

Then Gordon Reekie, of the Exhibition Department, suggested that a truly realistic scene would include sounds as well, specifically a tape of the cries of gulls and other seabirds that would come to feed on the carcass of the whale. This seemingly innocent suggestion made it possible for Van Gelder to see a way out of the whole dead-whale morass: "There was one other sense to be catered to, but I saved my idea for a few weeks."

He was saving it for a luncheon of the Women's Committee, a Museum fund-raising group. During his speech, Van Gelder told them about the proposed new whale.

"I waxed poetic with word pictures of the beast. I told how the cries of the sea birds would slowly die out as sunset approached and then the ghostly glow of the bacteria would take over until at dawn, once more, the crash of the waves, and the rising chorus of hungry gulls would again take the fore. And then as they sat enthralled by my description, I dropped my voice to a conspiratorial whisper. "We are even planning something never done before. A gentle breeze will waft the odor of the sea toward the visitors, to complete the attack on all the senses, and we are even going to try to simulate the odor of the decomposing whale, so that all can share in this wonderful experience *in totality*."

The Women's Committee, Van Gelder discovered, was made up of a "strong and brave group of women; not one of them lost her chicken-à-la-king. But some came close." The word soon got back to Museum authorities: This group of influential patrons did not approve of the dead-whale idea *at all*. So, much to Van Gelder's relief, the concept was scrapped, and it was back to the drawing board.

Finally, Exhibition's Lyle Barton came up with the simple, elegant idea that visitors to the Museum can see today: bolting the ninety-foot-plus, plastic-and-steel whale directly to the enormous hall's ceiling. The result is a lifelike model of a living creature, with no pedestals and no strings attached. Finally unveiled in 1968 (after nine years of false starts), the blue whale remains one of the most spectacular and popular displays ever mounted at any museum in the world.

Scientists now know that not every physical detail of the model is completely accurate. The color, for example, isn't blue enough. But without doubt, this superb exhibit comes breathtakingly close to capturing the spirit that animates the real blue whale, the largest animal ever to have lived on earth.

During the years that Richard Van Gelder was struggling to bring his vision of a blue-whale model to life, he must have been well aware of the plight of the great animal he was seeking to celebrate. For of all the great whales that were persecuted for their oil or blubber, few came closer to the edge of extinction than the magnificent blue.

We tend to think that whaling took place in some earlier, more barbaric era, at a time when no voices were raised to protest its excesses. The truth is, by the late 1800s, scientists and others were lamenting the dwindling numbers of many species under the onslaught of well-equipped whalers. "There is no doubt that here as in other countries the pursuit of whales has fallen off enormously in the last fifty years," said the biologist F. A. Beddard in his *A Book of Whales* in 1900. "That there should be this decrease is not surprising, when we learn . . . that during the years 1835–1872 about 292,714 whales must have been either captured or destroyed!"

In his book *Whale Hunting with Gun and Camera* (1916), Roy Chapman Andrews titled one chapter "The Passing of the Whale." "Even if we deny whales the right to live, and disregard the scientific importance of this marvelously specialized group of mammals, it is apparent that, reduced to a sordid standard, our problem demands immediate attention," he wrote. "It is of the utmost importance that while there is yet time the governments of the world should realize that if proper legislation is enacted to regulate the killing of whales, a great and lucrative industry can not only be conducted profitably in the present, but preserved for the future." If not, Andrews added, "commercial extinction is inevitable within a very few decades."

Of course, most of the countries involved in large-scale whaling ignored the warnings given by Andrews and others. During this century, the actions of the leading whaling nations—including Norway, Japan, Russia, and the United States—have included deflecting criticism, ignoring sanctions, swearing to change their behavior, and then lying when caught in the act of breaking their promises.

Between 1851 (when steam-powered ships and explosive harpoons began to allow whalers to pursue the almost mythically fast and agile blue whale) and the 1960s (when their killing was at last outlawed), more than 300,000 blue whales were slaughtered. The year that sent the species to the brink was 1931, when nearly 30,000 were killed in the southern Atlantic alone. "Sometimes the bang-bang of harpoon guns is unceasing on the banks," reported the Museum's Robert Cushman Murphy from these waters in a 1936 documentary film called *The Bottom of the World*. "What chance do whales have? At the rate they are being butchered, they are surely headed toward an end in their last stronghold."

Along with the belated banning of hunting, the main factor in the blue whale's favor was that "commercial extinction" took place before the actual disappearance of the species. Eventually blue whales became so rare, so hard to find, that they were no longer actively pursued. Not that this guaranteed the species' survival. As Andrews pointed out more than eighty years ago, "Enormous and highly specialized animals are usually slow breeders and especially liable to extinction." Even now, doubts exist over whether the blue whale will ultimately survive.

Some of the signs are promising, though. Off the coast of California, blues are being seen more and more frequently by whale watchers and biologists alike. A National Marine Fisheries Service census in 1991 estimated that 2,049 blue whales occupied coastal waters there, a startling increase from the 1,600 individuals estimated to inhabit the entire northern Pacific in 1974.

Other estimates in the same waters have been lower, and populations in other oceans remain little studied. But at least these findings give hope that the great blue whale has escaped the threat of immediate extinction, and that the massive bones and lifelike model in the American Museum will remain merely reminders of a living species, not a memorial for a vanished one.

Gone Forever ... Or Still Here?

The shocking, depressing claims have been heard for years in the environmental and scientific communities and in the mass media as well. Thousands of species of mammals, birds, and other creatures are becoming extinct each year. The earth is in the midst of a new mass extinction, rivaling or even surpassing the famous event that killed off the large dinosaurs and other spectacular species 65 million years ago. This is a mass extinction that will only grow more cataclysmic in the years to come.

These claims are compelling and easy to believe, given such factors as the planet's steady human population rise and the ongoing clearance of tropical rain-forests. But, according to some scientists at the museum, the real question is: Are the claims true?

These same scientists believe that the answer is: Who knows? "The numbers being publicized—such as the idea that three species go extinct each hour—are unverifiable," says Mammalogy's Ross MacPhee. "If they exist at all, those three species are all arthropods. Given how little we know about arthropods, we can't even say if true species are disappearing, or simply populations within more widespread species."

The problem is that no one has yet devised a set of rigorous standards to determine when a species has become extinct. Beyond the obvious examples (the dodo, the passenger pigeon, the Carolina parakeet), the question of what is extinct and what isn't remains frustratingly vague. "I'm not saying that extinction isn't a problem," MacPhee points out. "I'm saying that it has to be a *scientific* problem—and it hasn't been treated that way yet."

The lack of scientific standards in the extinction debate became clear to Mammalogy's MacPhee and Ichthyology's Melanie Stiassny and Ian Harrison in the mid-1990s, when they sought to develop accurate lists of mammal and fish extinctions that have occurred during the past five hundred years. In researching essays for the 1999 book *Extinctions in Near Time* (edited by MacPhee and Clare Flemming), the authors relied on the *Red List of Threatened Animals* by the International Union for the Conservation of Nature (IUCN). This 1996 publication is considered to be the most accurate and scientific gauge of species status yet published.

But when they applied a set of strict, analytical criteria to the determination of whether a species was extinct, the authors found that the IUCN's data wasn't nearly accurate enough. "The *Red List* lists about ninety fish species as extinct, including fifty cichlids from Lake Victoria," Harrison says. "When I went through the data, I found about the same number of species that appear to be extinct. But only about fifty percent of the species appeared on both lists."

MacPhee and Flemming found the same startlingly low overlap when they devised a list of extinct mammals. "We found a 51 percent mismatch between our list and the IUCN data," MacPhee says. "There are a huge number of what I think of as embedded 'just-so stories,' in which people consider a species extinct just because that's what they've heard."

These findings showed that an urgent need existed for a more accurate accounting of extinct and threatened species than currently exists. The result was the formation of the Committee on Recently Extinct Organisms (CREO), an ambitious Museum effort, originally chaired by Ian Harrison, to provide more reliable data on an ever-changing computerized database. "CREO enables researchers to realize what they don't know," says Mary DeJong, until recently a researcher in the Museum's Center for Biodiversity and Conservation who has been involved in the project since its inception. "We're providing a place where scientists can report every bit of relevant data from their research. If a researcher visits an area where a threatened species lives, and never sees the species, that's evidence of possible extinction. But until now, there's been no central place to record such data. It's been a monumental data-collection nightmare."

CREO is an interdepartmental effort whose steering committee has thus far included Entomology's Jim Carpenter, Ornithology's Joel Cracraft, Invertebrates' Paula Mikkelson, and Vertebrate Paleontology's Richard Tedford, among others. Perhaps even more importantly, dozens of scientists from museums, universities, and environmental organizations worldwide have signed on.

"In the past, there's been no consistency in how species were declared extinct," Harrison says. "By providing a place for these scientists and others to report their findings, CREO is giving us our first chance to learn what's really still out there, and what isn't."

MAMMALOGY TODAY: ENDLESS QUESTIONS

Of course we have to be concerned about endangered species, but it's the habitats we really have to worry about. If you don't save the habitat, you might as well blow away the last pandas and mount them at the Explorers' Club, because it really isn't going to matter what else you try to do.

—*Ross MacPhee, Curator in Mammalogy.*

The Riddle of *Xenothrix*

Studying the history of science over a century or more provides a fascinating and revealing view of how the goals, passions, and obsessions of researchers change as the years pass. For Joel Asaph Allen, a chief purpose of mammalogy at the Museum was to gradually enlarge a collection that he saw as weak and arbitrary. For Carl Akeley, G. H. H. Tate, Harold E. Anthony, and other collectors in the first decades of this century, the goal was twofold: to build up a scientific resource by collecting as many specimens as possible, and to memorialize the most spectacular of these disappearing creatures in splendid displays.

More recently, Museum scientists have begun to focus on a more systematic analysis of mammal populations, seeking to identify the characteristics that demonstrate the relationships between different species. Today, this work is more pertinent and more pressing than ever, given the reality of booming human populations and the resulting species-threatening habitat loss.

Curator Guy Musser, for example, has taken on a difficult long-term challenge, studying the rodents of large stretches of Asia and Oceania. Rodents are such a dominant component of the mammal faunas in these areas that much of Musser's work involves identification and description of new species. Only by taking this necessary first step, finding out what's there, will he be able to answer crucial biogeographic questions about rodent diversity, range, and evolutionary relationships.

MacPhee himself believes that the study of living mammals cannot be divorced from those extinct species that were their close relatives. He focuses on the recently extinct mammals of the West Indies, and is especially fascinated by the knotty problem of why these islands (which, isolated from any mainland, would be thought to host only a few mammals) actually had a surprisingly diverse mammal fauna until very recent times. Even today the fossils of previously unknown mammals are being found: MacPhee and Manuel A. Iturralde-Vinent, of the Museo Nacional de Historia Natural in Havana, have recently described a new sloth and rodent from Cuba and Puerto Rico, and are in the process of describing several other new specimens.

For MacPhee, an essential, as yet unanswered question surrounds the methods such mammals or their ancestors used to reach these isolated islands. "Maybe I lack imagination, but I have trouble envisaging pregnant females of all these species floating a thousand kilometers from the Amazon River to the West Indies," he comments. Instead, he believes that lower sea levels during the Oligocene epoch (which lasted from about 35 to 24 million years ago), along with a more closely packed array of islands (gradually separated by movements of the earth's tectonic plates), allowed mammals comparatively easy access to what now appear to be widely scattered islands.

One of the most intriguing mammals that once occupied the West Indies is *Xenothrix*, an extinct Jamaican monkey possibly related to the titi monkeys of South America. The first evidence that this monkey existed—a left mandible (jaw bone)—was found in a cave, not far from a midden and some human remains, by Museum mammalogist Harold E. Anthony during a 1919–20 expedition. Anthony knew that he'd found a bone belonging to a primate, but was so unwilling to accept the idea of a native Jamaican monkey that he discounted his own find. The specimen, he wrote in his field journal, "was not associated with the human remains but not so far from them that the animal must not be strongly suspected as an introduced species."

Anthony's suspicions had a strong basis in fact: Monkeys have long been brought to the Caribbean from mainland South America (as well as Africa) by human settlers. But when the Museum's Karl F. Koopman and Harvard's Ernest E. Williams examined the specimen thirty years later, they found it did not correspond to any other known monkey on the mainland or elsewhere. In fact, Anthony had discovered the remains of a native monkey so unusual, Williams and Koopman wrote in 1952, that "we regard it as a conservative rather than radical judgment to conclude that the Jamaican fossil requires the erection of a new genus to contain it."

In recent years, MacPhee and colleagues Donald MacFarlane and Adam and Alan Fincham have undertaken extensive new field-work in Jamaica. As Anthony did, they have chosen the grueling task of excavating cave floors and walls, realizing that these are particularly rich locations for fossils. "Caves are nature's dustbin," explains Clare Flemming, until recently Laboratory and Special Collections Supervisor in Mammalogy, and a participant in the collecting effort. "They collect bones over a long period of time, including the remains of animals that inhabited them and of prey species left by owls and other raptors that roost near cave entrances."

In early 1995, MacPhee's team found a second *Xenothrix* specimen in a Jamaican cave, another left mandible. A second 1995 field season turned up a third fossil, yet another left mandible. "We were learning about *Xenothrix* in square millimeters," MacPhee comments. Adds Flemming, "*Xenothrix* might have been too large for most Jamaican raptors to handle, which is why it's so rare in caves. But we kept going back, because we were always hopeful that we'd find something else if we kept looking."

During their final field season in October 1996, the team finally found what they were seeking. They were searching in a site called "Lloyd's Cave," reached by way of the difficult-access "mantrap" entrance (so dubbed because MacPhee had gotten trapped there during a previous visit), and at first the results were no more promising than other sites had been.

"We were digging on the cave floor," MacPhee recalls. "After all, we believed that *Xenothrix* had been extinct for at least two thousand years—so any remains would likely be buried under dirt and other rubble." But then team member Donald McFarlane, working in a side room of the cave, came upon a startling sight: a large portion of a skull and jaw, complete with six teeth. One glance from MacPhee confirmed what McFarlane had guessed. They'd finally found something other than a *Xenothrix* left mandible.

"You should have seen us," MacPhee recalls. "We went nuts." But what was most interesting of all was the fact that McFarlane had found the skull lying on the surface of the cave floor. "And it had almost no dirt on it," MacPhee explains. "This skull had never been buried, and it was lying among the remains of rats, which were only introduced to the island after European colonization." In other words, this evidence seemed to indicate that *Xenothrix* hadn't been extinct for two thousand years or longer, but rather for only a few hundred years.

In a 1999 paper published in the *Journal of Human Evolution,* Ines Horovitz of the Museum's Department of Vertebrate Paleontology and Ross MacPhee reach the conclusion that *Xenothrix* is just one of three related monkeys, now extinct, that once inhabited the Greater Antilles islands. All three, the authors demonstrate, appear to be most closely related to the titi monkeys (genus *Callicebus*) of the South American mainland.

"I believe that about thirty million years ago, the ancestor of all three monkeys crossed over from the mainland," MacPhee says. "So did many other mammals, including an insectivore whose bones were found preserved in Dominican amber, a sloth, and others."

While the conventional wisdom holds that mainland mammals colonized these islands by drifting over on rafts of vegetation, MacPhee subscribes to another theory. "It seems clear to me that these animals crossed over on a short-lived land bridge that connected the mainland to what later became the Antilles," he explains. "Once the land bridge was submerged, and the islands became separated as well, the monkeys on each island evolved into separate species, including *Xenothrix*."

A Wealth of Tropical Life

In 1916, with the backing of Henry Fairfield Osborn, Theodore Roosevelt, and other prominent patrons, the New York Zoological Society's Department of Tropical Research founded one of the first rain-forest research facilities on earth: Kartabo Station, located in British Guiana in South America. Here the naturalist and future Museum research associate William Beebe set out to learn as much as possible about the virtually unexplored tropical forests surrounding the station.

Beebe recorded humidity, rainfall totals, temperature fluctuations, and other basic data. But mostly he studied the abundant flora and fauna of this untouched region, which entranced him. In a 1925 report for the Society's publication *Zoologica*, he said that the forest "was impossible to describe in accurate detail, for every square yard, every dense thicket, has a character of its own."

While scientists had collected and identified many of the birds and animals of the Guianan forest, Beebe wanted to actually study the creatures that occupied Kartabo's luxuriant surroundings. Most people, Beebe observed, thought of the jungle as a silent, empty place, and this was true if all a visitor did was hurry through it. "When he is content quite to cease being a traveller, and become a stander, or sitter or squatter, the wealth of tropical life begins to be apparent."

Beebe was unparalleled in his ability to observe while standing, sitting, and squatting. But even after years of studying the fauna of Kartabo, he was far from achieving anything close to a complete inventory of the creatures of his patch of rain-forest, especially when it came to Kartabo's mammals.

According to Mammalogy's Robert S. Voss and Curator-in-Charge Nancy B. Simmons, Beebe can't be faulted for the gaps in his knowledge. Even with more up-to-date methods, very few accurate mammal inventories have been done in any tropical forest, for a very simple reason: Except for a few of the larger species, most rain-forest mammals are exceedingly hard to find.

"Most birds have an interest in being visible, and many are easy to tell apart by sight or sound," Voss explains. "But mammals are a lot more difficult. Most of them are nocturnal. Most are silent. Most have not the slightest interest in being seen. And if you do see them, you frequently can't identify the species, because very few of the smaller mammals are easy to tell apart by sight."

For today's biologists, research usually involves a few weeks collecting in the field followed by months in the laboratory. If they so chose, Voss (who specializes in rodents) and Simmons (who studies bats) could have spent the rest of their careers puzzling out the tangled classification of these two enormous mammalian orders without ever leaving the Museum. "But as we spent time in wonderful tropical environments filled with all these hidden complexities, we realized that we wanted to stay long enough in one place to really understand what was happening there," Voss says.

Completing an in-depth inventory seemed particularly important, he adds, "because as tropical forests are being destroyed very rapidly, we're simply not in a position to evaluate what the impact is on local species. We need to learn more about what's actually living in these forests."

The two mammalogists, along with Scientific Assistant Darrin Lunde, chose to undertake their intensive mammal inventory at a rain-forest research station in Paracou, French Guiana, just a few hundred miles from Beebe's Kartabo Station. Paracou was attractive for several reasons, Simmons points out. "French Guiana is still about 95 percent forested, and the forests around the research station are still largely undisturbed," she explains. "By rain-forest standards, the site was incredibly luxurious: We had showers, and we were only fifteen minutes' drive from a place where we could buy fresh croissants."

The inventory, funded by the Museum and the National Geographic Society, began in 1991 and ended in 1994. "You simply have to do this kind of survey over the course of several years," Voss comments. "Mammal populations can undergo enormous fluctuations from year to year, depending on many factors, so a single season's collecting is guaranteed to miss a large percentage of what's out there."

Another essential component of a successful inventory is the use of a variety of different collecting techniques. By the end of their survey, the researchers had used ground-level mist nets; canopy-level nets suspended in the treetops by lines shot into the crowns of tall trees with a special slingshot; pitfall traps (buckets buried in the forest floor); and baited traps hoisted into the trees. They also hunted at night with a headlamp and shotgun. "Our goal was to try everything," Voss says.

In some cases, the simplest techniques worked best of all. "We discovered that certain species of bats tended to roost near the ground during the day," Simmons recalls. "So I would explore all fallen and hollow trees—which turned out to be a much more effective way of finding them than trying to net them at night."

In any such inventory, both scientists say, it is essential that many of the animals caught be kept as specimens, not released. "Somewhere between forty and sixty percent of all mammals in a neotropical rain forest community are bats, and most may be very similar species belonging to one family," Simmons points out. "Again and again, we'd think we'd captured a species we'd seen before, only to find out it was something new when we studied it in the laboratory."

At the end of their final field season, the scientists had tallied a total of 139 mammal species—one of the longest species lists ever gathered at any site and comprising (they estimate) about ninety percent of the mammal fauna of Paracou. Of the species collected, seventy-seven were bats and twenty-one were rodents; large mammals either seen or recorded based on discussions with knowledgeable area residents included jaguar, red howler monkey, and giant armadillo.

"We appear to have found two bat species new to science, as well as several mammals that were new to French Guiana, a few of which were known only from thousands of kilometers away," Voss says. "Clearly, inventories in other areas will come up with equally significant and surprising results."

Food for Thought

By January 1918, the First World War had been dragging on for four years. Crop failures had begun to cause famine in some areas of Europe, epidemic diseases were beginning to spread, and countless refugees were beginning to flood even those areas not directly involved in the fighting.

In the face of all this grim news, Henry Fairfield Osborn, President of the Museum, became convinced that mass starvation was likely to begin in Europe at any time. To bring his message to the public, Osborn and the trustees held a well-publicized luncheon at the Museum. The food they offered as a partial solution to impending starvation was whale meat.

Today, inviting the press to witness a black-tie affair featuring several different preparations of whale would be a form of suicide for any natural history museum. But as Ross MacPhee, a Curator in Mammalogy, points out, "Whaling was a fact of life in those days—and so was the fact that, aside from the oil, most of each whale was being thrown away."

Like most scientists, Osborn certainly didn't approve of the widespread whaling that was decimating so many species at the time. But he also knew that the Museum was powerless to halt or control the industry. "Given those realities, he thought of a use for the massive amounts of protein that would otherwise be wasted," MacPhee says. "It's not something we would do today—and as it turned out, the war ended in 1918 and starvation was averted without whale meat being used—but in the context of the time, Osborn made a thinking response to a human problem."

In seeking to influence the debate over conservation of endangered species today—for example, with the Hall of Biodiversity—the Museum's scientists must confront difficult issues with the degree of thoughtfulness that Osborn summoned, MacPhee says. "We can't be an enclave on New York's Upper West Side, telling the world to love and embrace what's left," he explains. "I feel that the only way we're going to succeed in conserving nature is by figuring out how to provide for human futures and animal futures at the same time. If we don't take human problems into account, how can we expect the people who have the final responsibility for protecting nature to listen to what we say?"

2

Evolution's Clay

BASHFORD DEAN AND THE LURE OF ARMOR

When members of any group of fishes become extinct, those appear to have been the first to perish which were the possessors of the greatest number of widely modified or *specialized* structures. . . . A generalized form is like potter's clay, plastic in the hands of nature, readily to be converted into a needed kind of cup or vase; but when thus specialized may never resume unaltered its ancestral condition: the clay survives; the cup perishes.

—*Bashford Dean, first Curator of the Department of Ichthyology, in* Fishes, Living and Fossil *(1895).*

In the early years of the Museum, no department drew more offbeat personalities, or encouraged more varied interests among its curators, than did Ichthyology. Preeminent among these personalities was Bashford Dean (1867–1928), perhaps history's only lifelong student of both armor and fish.

Dean was fascinated by armor in nearly all its natural and handcrafted forms. Giant fossil fish clad in massive armored shields or ornate armored breastplates worn into battle by the armies of the Japanese shogun—these were both compelling subjects worthy of long-term study. Remarkably, he was able to pursue his twin interests as both Curator of Arms and Armor at the Metropolitan Museum of Art and Curator of the American Museum's Department of Reptiles and Fishes.

Dean was born to an intellectual generation that prized varied knowledge. "He derived his early interest in natural history largely from association with his father, who himself was an enthusiastic collector and cataloguer of fossil invertebrates and a student of birds in the field," said William K. Gregory, Curator-in-Chief of Ichthyology, in a *Bashford Dean Memorial Volume* published in 1933. By the time he was seven or eight years old, Gregory added, Dean was already producing miniature "newspapers" on scientific subjects, including comets, meteors, and birds' nests.

Similarly, while Dean's interest in arms and armor was spurred by books about King Arthur and the Round Table, his enthusiasm was heightened by travels in Europe and visits to the homes of wealthy friends who owned pieces of antique armor. Clearly, young Bashford Dean always felt that he could pursue whatever caught his attention, or, as Gregory put it, "Thus his parentage, earliest training, and surroundings were essentially Victorian, in the best sense." The sense, that is, of being a participant in a wonderful world of limitless possibilities.

By the time Dean reached his early twenties, his parallel interests in armor and natural history had begun to converge. It was no surprise that he would be as interested in armored fish as he was in humans with armor, as he proved in his doctoral dissertation at Columbia University. He chose to focus on the anatomy and function of the pineal gland in ancient and recent fish, and especially in *Dinichthys* and other extinct fish that possessed their own great armored plates.

This first major effort was followed by many others that showed

Dean's ongoing interest in the origins and evolution of fish and their anatomical features. As he wrote in *Fishes, Living and Fossil* (1895), "Fishes hold an important place in the history of back boned animals: their group is the largest and most widely distributed; its fossil members are by far the earliest of known chordates; and among its living representatives are forms which are believed to closely resemble the ancestral vertebrate." In other words, if you want to learn about the roots of vertebrate evolution, look at fish.

By the early 1900s Dean began to express his views on evolution in a series of scientific papers and short articles in *Science* and other journals, focusing especially on comparing the development of eggs and embryos among different species of fish. Not all of his conclusions have been borne out by more recent findings, but Dean was laying the groundwork for important systematic studies that are continuing today.

Dean also conceived, worked on, and inspired the completion of one of the most influential projects ever on ichthyology: the monumental *Dean's Bibliography of Fishes* (published in three volumes between 1916 and 1923). This compilation of references to more than 40,000 books and articles on fishes is still recognized as one of the first large-scale efforts to transform ichthyology into an organized, efficient science, rather than merely one of the many enthusiasms of general naturalists.

Dean came to the Museum in 1903, first to oversee the collection of fossil fish in the Department of Vertebrate Paleontology, and then as Curator of the Department of Reptiles and Fishes. From the first, he was intent on displaying the specimens that fascinated him—a particularly difficult challenge when it came to fish. "In most museums they are exhibited preserved in fluid, sometimes delicately painted before they are placed in jars," he wrote in the *American Museum Journal* in 1912. "They are apt however to be shrunken, opaque, faded and generally unattractive, so that a visitor may pass them by and have but an imperfect idea of the *real* fishes, their graceful and curious forms and their beautiful colors."

While other museums relied on models made of plaster, wax, and wires, Dean was determined to present habitat groups displaying real fish. His main objection to such displays was that "the 'fish' is after all only a model, and we have sometimes the suspicion that it belongs in a museum not of natural history, but of art."

Under his guidance, museum preparators devised a technique similar to those used by Carl Akeley, the Museum's world famous collector of African mammals, when mounting elephants and other nearly hairless animals: a plaster mold would be covered with the fish's own skin and then painted to recapture the colors lost in preservation. This method passed muster with Dean, resulting in the creation of a Hall of Fishes that ranked with the most dramatic of any in the Museum (and, in redone form as the Hall of Ocean Life, still thrills museum visitors).

The original Hall of Fishes was also one of the first at the museum to attempt to explain important issues in evolution in terms the general public could understand. This, too, is a goal of the current hall, reflecting advances in systematics and evolutionary theory since Dean's time.

Until the early 1900s, Dean had sated his interest in European and Asian armor by amassing his own collection, and also by working to increase the holdings of the Metropolitan Museum. But while he remained associated with the American Museum until his death, Dean turned his attention increasingly to armor after about 1906. For a while he wrote on both ichthyological and artistic subjects (his 1912 output, for example, included both "Changes in the behavior of the eel during transformation" and "The gauntlets of the Earl of Sussex"), but armor and the Metropolitan's collection were clearly the true passion of his later life.

Not that Dean's two enthusiasms didn't continue to cross-pollinate. As W. K. Gregory pointed out in the *Memorial Volume*, Dean's "drawings of the evolution of various lines of helmets and pole arms in Europe strongly recall the phylogenetic tree of certain groups of fossil cephalopods, for in both cases a certain very primitive and ancient pattern gives rise to gradually diverging series which toward the end take on the 'phylogerontic' extremes that precede sudden extinction, through failure to meet new changes in the environment."

Or, as Museum President Henry Fairfield Osborn wrote after Dean's death in 1928, "With his consummate knowledge, taste, and authority, he combined a sense of evolution of design and of mechanism so that it may be said that in our great museum he laid the foundations of the evolution of fishes, and in the great sister museum across the Park the cognate evolution of armor."

J. T. NICHOLS AND THE ROMANCE OF NATURE

> Once more in from the deep sea, the same old sea, deep blue out there beyond the reefs, difficult and fascinating as ever, guarding its mysteries. Back into the world, but days, weeks, months must go by before this world would seem altogether real again. . . . No, it did not seem real, some day one must wake again to contend with a world of sails and winds and rolling sea.
>
> —*Ichthyologist J. T. Nichols, returning from a voyage around Cape Horn, in* Forest and Stream, *1908.*

When Bashford Dean began to turn his attention away from fish and toward armor, his investigations into the evolution and anatomy of fish were taken over and expanded by other Museum curators. Louis Hussakof, E. W. Gudger, and others continued to build the collection, describe and name new species, and study the evolutionary relationships among different groups of fish.

But while Hussakof, Gudger, and their colleagues were turning ichthyology into a truly scientific discipline, another curator in the department, a man who spent more than half a century associated with the Museum, hearkened back to the Victorian era that produced Bashford Dean. This was John Treadwell Nichols (1883–1958), a man who became an Ichthyology assistant in 1907 because (as he freely admitted) that was where an opening existed. As Curator Emeritus in Ichthyology James W. Atz, himself a veteran of nearly fifty years at the Museum, says, "J. T. Nichols was a self-taught ichthyologist of the old, old school. He was enthusiastic about many different aspects of natural history, not just fish."

Nichols was a prolific writer, describing many new species and producing at least one important reference work, *The Freshwater Fishes of China* (1943) based largely on collections made by herpetologist Clifford Pope during Roy Chapman Andrews's famed Central Asiatic Expedition. Nichols was also the founder of the American Society of Ichthyologists and Herpetologists and of *Copeia*, which was to become the premier journal on fishes, amphibians, and reptiles. But Nichols's life was aimed at a pair of horizons that embraced the entire natural world, with fish forming just one part of the mosaic.

His first horizon was sailing—or, rather, any form of ocean travel. Writing in the journal *Marine Life* in 1958 (the last year of his life), Nichols recalled his first true contact with the sea. It took place during a steamship voyage across the Atlantic when he was seven years old and was highlighted by the ship's passage near an iceberg.

After seeing the iceberg, Nichols recalled, he lay in bed, unable to sleep. "There was a first tangible, permanent picture etched in memory, to which others were to be added, and spell the beauty and romance of the vast, impersonal, omnipotent, ever-changing, but eternal sea."

Nichols's early sea voyages gave him an abiding interest in flying fish, those remarkable creatures that flee danger by launching themselves into the air and gliding on winglike fins for as much as two hundred yards. He wrote several scientific papers analyzing their vaulting and "flying" techniques and calculating the distances they traversed and the speeds they could attain.

Some of Nichols's conclusions could only have come from the countless hours he spent watching flying fish while sailing. For example, he saw that while on calm days a fish would simply glide briefly on its outstretched fins, "in a strong breeze, which is when it attains its maximum speed, elevation, and distance, its flight suggests that it utilizes wind power braced against the momentum of its heavy body, as soaring petrels and albatrosses presumably do." He also noted with some surprise that in the air flying fish can apparently see where they are going and alter course by banking left or right. "I have seen one flying parallel to the windward rail, being drifted over the ship by the wind, bank abruptly and go clear."

Oddly for someone so in love with the endless vistas of the open sea, the second horizon of Nichols's life was a purposely limited one, the borders of the six-hundred-acre estate in Mastic, Long Island, where his family had a summer home. Here Nichols undertook an intensive, half-century study of the birds and animals that shared the estate's grounds. From 1904 until his death, he entered his observations in dozens of journals, recording everything from bird nesting dates to unusual weather conditions.

Nichols was an inveterate bander of birds, capturing the same individuals repeatedly to learn about their migration and nesting habits. He studied the fish that inhabited the estate's wetlands. But his most elaborate long-term research involved box turtles, those endearing creatures that used to roam across much of Long Island but have largely disappeared in the face of encroaching highways and subdivisions.

For decades Nichols tried to catch every box turtle on the

Mastic estate; he even offered rewards to his children and grand-children for turning turtles in. He did not keep them captive, however. When one was captured for the first time, Nichols would "mark" it by carving "JN" and a number code into its bottom shell (a process that neither hurt nor damaged the turtle) and release it. Then, each time the turtle was recaptured, he would carefully record the event in his journal.

As the years passed, the turtles seemed to become old friends to J. T. Nichols. How could they not? One turtle, first captured and marked on July 4, 1918 (Turtle JN-18–13), subsequently turned up in 1919, 1920, 1923, 1924, 1925, 1926, 1933, 1946, and 1951. Other turtles were never found again and were pre-sumed dead, while still others were discovered suffering injuries and were nursed back to health before being released to be caught again another day. In the late 1980s, thirty years after Nichols's death, a survey of the Mastic estate, now a protected part of the Fire Island National Seashore, turned up many of the turtles bearing his inscription.

In a speech before the American Society of Ichthyologists and Herpetologists, the novelist John Nichols summed up his grand-father's unusual but productive career. "Grandpa was an eclectic man of science, to say the least. He wound up specializing in fishes in order to earn a living, but he was an avid and respected ornithologist, a fan of weasels, a good man with a bat, a turtle junkie, and intrigued by almost everything else."

The Search for the Fat Catfish

Sometime in the late 1930s a strong earthquake shook the Andes Mountains northeast of Bogota, Colombia. This alone wasn't unusual. Earthquakes are a common occurrence in that seismically active area. It was what happened after this earth-quake that surprised nearby villagers.

The earthquake sent silt cascading into a cold mountain lake named Lake Tota. In the days that followed, dead fish, appar-ently choked by the silt, started floating to the surface. But these weren't the familiar fish species caught by fishermen to feed local residents. They were bottom-dwelling catfish, normally only rarely seen floating dead on the surface. And though they were just a few inches long, they were fat. Incredibly fat. Each one was covered with rolls of blubber that resembled nothing so much as tiny rubber car tires ringing its body.

Thousands of these corpulent catfish eventually rose to the sur-face. Enterprising residents, loath to let this strange gift from the lake go to waste, soon found that the oily fish served very well as a candle. If you lit a fin, the body would burn for hours. For a time after the great die-off, local homes were brightly lit by burning cat-fish. Even so, masses of the dead fish merely rotted on the shores of the lake, the smell making it virtually unapproachable for a time.

Once these had finally rotted away, dead and dying fat catfish were again seen only occasionally in Lake Tota. Hoping to gather some specimens, a Colombian biologist named Cecil Miles vis-ited the area in 1942. In a local resident's home, Miles was lucky enough to spot a couple of the catfish being fried up in a pan for supper. He quickly retrieved the specimens from the frying pan, somewhat the worse for wear. Today, the fat catfish may be the only species in the world whose first specimen has scorch marks on it.

Miles described and named the catfish, giving it the name *Rizomichthys totae*. As it turned out, *R. totae* is closely related to several other catfish of Andean lakes and rivers, but with one important difference: All its relatives are slender, while the Lake Tota catfish is, of course, enormously fat.

What is strangest about the catfish's girth is that there is no reasonable explanation of why it looks the way it does. Mammals in cold climates often carry layers of fat or blubber, but catfish (unlike mammals) are cold blooded, and therefore would not need fat to maintain a warm core temperature. Similarly, while some animals use fat as a food reserve for times of food shortage, the mere fact that the catfish were so corpulent showed that food was plentiful in the cold lake bottom.

At around the same time that Miles was describing R. *totae*, local authorities were establishing a trout fishery in Lake Tota— a decision that some scientists believe pronounced a death sentence on the fat catfish. With the exception of a single specimen collected in 1957, the catfish hasn't been seen in decades, leading to the belief that the introduced trout have either eaten the catfish, or have outcompeted the smaller fish for food, sending *R. totae* into extinction.

Scientists at the Institute of Natural Sciences in Bogota, however, don't believe that the catfish is necessarily extinct. Nor does the museum's Ian Harrison, an ichthyologist who until recently was chairman of the Committee on Recently Extinct Organisms (CREO). (For more on CREO's efforts, see page 33). One of CREO's major goals is to determine whether creatures reported extinct really *have* vanished or just haven't been seen recently. The fat catfish provides a perfect example of an animal that has been declared extinct without any compelling supporting evidence.

"After all, before the earthquake, people almost never saw it," Harrison points out. "Just because they almost never see the fish today doesn't mean that it's not still down there."

Nor does Harrison believe that the introduced trout are likely to have sent the catfish into extinction. "The catfish live on the lake's bottom, up to sixty meters down," he says. "That's not preferred trout habitat. It just doesn't seem logical to put together the presence of trout and the absence of new catfish specimens and use that to declare the catfish extinct."

The only way to determine whether the fat catfish survives is to search for it in Lake Tota, and that's just what Museum and Colombian scientists did in late 1999. "We surveyed the lake, setting out deep-water traps and also trying to net the fish," Harrison explains. "We wanted to prove that it still exists, of course, but we also want to collect new specimens for study. With only ten specimens in collections now, we can't study any of them too closely."

Unfortunately, the initial search proved fruitless, although the scientists did encounter some local people who claimed to be familiar with the fish. (At least one resident said that he used the fish as a component in fireworks!) If future searches of Lake Tota do haul in some new specimens, Ian Harrison knows exactly what he'd like to do with them. "We need to establish its taxonomy, see where it stands in the group of similar (though skinny) catfish, which we can do by studying its DNA," he says. Experts in fat are also eager to study the fish to determine whether there's anything distinctive about its blubber.

Harrison has yet another goal. "I also really want to dissect some and examine their stomach contents. After all," he says, "they're just so *fat*. What on earth have they been eating?"

THE SWINGING PENDULUM

The investigations that gave him the greatest satisfaction, however, were the off-beat ones—unexpected productions of an ichthyologist that involved unusual observations and techniques and led to original, speculative conclusions.

—James W. Atz, in his obituary for former Ichthyology Chairman Charles M. Breder, Jr., in Copeia, 1986.

His unique contributions were important in the development of cladistic theory in systematics and vicariance theory in biogeography. In the process he had to reform his basic attitudes on many questions, and here again his means was through collaboration and discourse on a wide scale.

—*Gareth Nelson, James W. Atz, Klaus D. Kallman, and C. Lavett Smith, in their obituary for former Ichthyology Chairman Donn P. Rosen, in* Copeia, *1987.*

Every scientist has his or her own particular interests, enthusiasms, and preferred directions for research. Unlike Bashford Dean and many of those who followed him, long-time Ichthyology Chairman Charles Breder simply wasn't very interested in systematics. He considered the careful accumulation and assessment of characters a necessary evil at best. His true enthusiasm was for what he called the "ecology" of fish, centering on their social behavior, locomotion, hormonal changes, and other characteristics that could be studied only by using living specimens.

Breder's preference for the behavior and biology of living fish over the taxonomy of dead ones shouldn't be surprising, for he came to the Museum after twenty-three years as an aquarist and director of the New York Aquarium. His first association with the Museum, however—as a collector on a 1924 expedition to Panama, undertaken long before he officially joined the staff—was also almost his last.

Breder accompanied the explorer R. O. Marsh to the unexplored rain-forests of Darien Province, Panama, with the goal of collecting specimens of fishes, reptiles, and amphibians. He was spectacularly successful, bringing back nearly three thousand specimens, many of which were new to the Museum's collection.

But, as worried Museum officials found out midway through the expedition, the effort nearly cost Breder his life.

On June 4, 1924, George H. Sherwood, acting director of the Museum, received a cable from the Panama Canal Office in the Canal Zone: "Charles Breder sick Darien region three weeks admitted Colon Hospital May twenty-second. . . ." Breder almost died from what was probably yellow fever (two others in the party did perish); newspaper reports at the time claim he survived largely because his wife traveled to Panama and nursed him back to health.

Breder became an Ichthyology research associate in 1925, while continuing his position at the aquarium. A 1926 study of fish locomotion (a subject that would continue to interest him after he joined the full-time Museum staff) won an award from the New York Academy of Sciences, and was followed by many other articles on schooling, reproductive, and other behaviors of various fish.

Breder's tenure as Ichthyology chairman, which began in 1944, was notable for the number of women scientists either employed by or associated with the department. In an era when most Museum departments were exclusively male, Breder worked closely with Ichthyology staff members Priscilla Rasquin and Francesca LaMonte and ichthyologists Eugenie Clark and Evelyn Shaw, who were members of the closely allied Department of Animal Behavior. This gathering of women must have been unique in the scientific community at the time, and would be unusual even today.

Ichthyology's focus on behavior and other characteristics of living fish was strongly supported by Albert E. Parr, director of the Museum. Although Parr was an ichthyologist, he thought (as James Atz has written) "that the future of natural history museums lay more in their contributions to public education and scientific research than in their role as repositories of systematically maintained and studied collections."

Breder didn't share those radical ideas, and the fish collection continued to grow under his stewardship. But the department's true interests were reflected in published papers with titles like "Studies on the Structure of the Fish School," "Endocrine Imbalance and Tissue Hyperplasia in Teleosts Maintained in Darkness," and "Cancer Research in a Marine Laboratory."

Mexican cave characins—a group of remarkable, closely related fishes that lost their sight while adapting to life in pitch-dark caves—were a particular focus of Breder's research. To gather enough cave characins to make laboratory experiments possible, Breder had to organize expeditions far different from those designed merely to collect and preserve specimens. Visiting the complex series of Mexican caves where these fish were known to live, Museum collectors Ben Dontzin and Ed Ruda confronted the risks inherent in exploring the steep, craggy, and uncharted caves; the possibility of contracting histoplasmosis (a respiratory disease); and also the challenge of getting the fish home alive.

In a letter from base camp in Valles, Mexico, Dontzin revealed a secret of his success. "American tourists drive from Valles to Laredo [Texas] in cars. I have dinner with one that has a good car, looks prosperous, buy him a drink, then tell him my story. They usually offer to take the fish right to Laredo to the Broker's office." Remarkably, this technique worked, as most of the fish sent back by the broker (an agent hired to arrange transportation of the specimens within the United States) did arrive in good shape.

In a series of laboratory experiments, Breder and his colleagues demonstrated that there were actually a series of characin populations: Those that lived in caves far removed from the effects of daylight had no sensitivity to light, while those closer to surface waters could detect changes in brightness, despite being virtually blind. Further, when blind characins came into contact with their sighted relatives in above-ground streams, the two populations were able to hybridize—producing viable, fertile offspring.

If the Ichthyology department's focus had shifted dramatically away from systematic study of collections during Breder's reign as chairman, by the time he retired from the Museum in 1965 the pendulum was swinging back again. Much of the impetus for this change came from a young ichthyologist named Donn Rosen, a man at the center of the department's current reputation for pioneering research into the classification and evolution of fishes.

Rosen joined the department as a thirty-two-year-old assistant curator in 1961, becoming chairman in 1965. His early years coincided with those of James Oliver, who had become director of the Museum in 1960. Oliver was determined that the collection—neglected for too long—be dramatically improved, that the staff be enlarged, and that new exhibits be planned and installed. It was largely due to Rosen's unflagging energy (and skill at writing grant proposals) that so many of these dictates became reality, and that the Ichthyology staff and collections both moved into expanded new quarters during his tenure.

But Rosen's greatest accomplishment may have been to return the department's focus to collection-based research and to make clear that fish evolution was crucial to any broader understanding of vertebrate evolution as a whole. To him—and to all of the curators who followed him—the only way to achieve this understanding was through competent, thorough, systematic research. His own studies focused on a group of small fishes called the "poeciliids" (which include the common aquarium swordtail and platyfish species), but his dedication to systematics spanned all of ichthyology.

Rosen was also a participant in the greatest upheaval in the history of evolutionary theory since Darwin's time, the cladistics revolution. Originally called "phylogenetics," cladistics states that all relationships among species must be defined entirely through shared characters (physical, skeletal, or other traits), with the number of shared traits determining the closeness of two species' relationship. The cladistic tree that results from this system branches every time a new feature appears, providing a far more complex view of evolution than the linear, virtually straight pathway over time that characterizes more traditional, Darwinian evolutionary theories.

The man who first brought cladistics to North America was Gareth Nelson, one of the brilliant young ichthyologists who joined the department under Rosen. It was Nelson who returned from visits to Europe in 1966 and 1967 convinced that cladistics was the only way to approach questions of classification. And then (along with Entomology's Norman Platnick, Invertebrates' Niles Eldredge, and other pioneers) he stood up to the withering criticisms of those who held to traditional views of classification and evolution.

In the early years of the cladistics debate, there was frequently a generational dividing line between those who accepted and those who rejected the theory, with senior scientists in many museums and academics departments being the last to concede its merits. But Donn Rosen was different. Having offered Nelson a position at the Museum in 1967, Rosen not only willingly listened to (and argued with) the new curator's controversial ideas, but soon embraced them.

Working both apart and together, Rosen and Nelson also pioneered the use of cladistics to cast new light on questions of biogeography—the study of distribution of living and extinct organisms, and why species appear when and where they do. They were among the first to show that it was possible to correlate the distribution of animal and plant species with events in geographic history, studying geographic areas that underwent disruptive geologic, climatic, or geographic events (such as the inundation of a desert region by a sea or the rise of a new mountain range) and using cladistics to show the evolution of new species in those areas.

The revealing correlations that resulted from this method—which its proponents call "cladistic" or "vicariance" biogeography—remind us that the earth and its life, after all, share only one history. "It seems doubtful, at least to me, that the notion of congruence between geographical and biological patterns could ever be formulated in a testable way without cladistic information," Rosen wrote in his introduction to a 1981 book called *Vicariance Biogeography*, which he edited with Nelson. It is just as doubtful that the history of science in the United States would have taken the same course without the efforts of Gareth Nelson and Donn Rosen in support of this groundbreaking theory.

The Laboratory of the Sea

When he wasn't studying blind cave fish or other offbeat specimens in New York, Charles Breder likely could be found at the Lerner Marine Laboratory, a Museum research station located on North Bimini Island in the Bahamas. From 1948, when it opened, to 1957, Breder was administrative director of the laboratory, which provided a favorite base for research by dozens of scientists for nearly three decades.

The Lerner Marine Laboratory was founded by big-game fishing champion and long-time Museum benefactor Michael Lerner. The shoreside facility boasted arrays of aquariums (whose pristine seawater was pumped in directly from the nearby Caribbean) for the study of living fishes, crabs, and other creatures; extensive research facilities; and a variety of glass-bottomed boats, diving gear, and other equipment for use in pursuit of specimens.

For such Museum scientists as ichthyologists Vladimir Walters and Perry Gilbert and invertebrate specialist Dorothy Bliss, a stay at the Lerner Marine Laboratory in the 1950s was an exercise in the pure pleasure associated with productive research. "Yesterday was a good day," wrote Walters to Breder in a typical letter from the laboratory in 1957. "Perry Gilbert was elbow deep in the uteri of pregnant *Cacharhinus floridanus* all afternoon."

But it was probably Bliss, an expert in the biology and behavior of land crabs, who best expressed the joy of working in this setting. "I realize that I most appreciate the opportunities I had for quiet, uninterrupted work on living material always immediately at hand," she wrote to Breder after a 1952 stint at the laboratory. "I remember with deep pleasure the eagerness of all hands to fulfill my every wish. The atmosphere of the L. M. L. is truly unique and an inspiration to creative work."

Museum Parents, Museum Kids

Francesca LaMonte, Evelyn Shaw, Eugenie Clark, and the other women ichthyologists who came to Museum beginning in the 1940s were pioneers in many ways. Among the challenges some of them faced is one still being confronted today by professional women and men everywhere: How to be an involved, caring parent while simultaneously pursuing a fulfilling career.

The balancing act could be a difficult one. Before she had children, Eugenie Clark, a Museum research associate, could write in her 1951 book *Lady with a Spear*, "Women scientists have to buck some difficulties when it comes to field work but I had one decided advantage. A man in my position often has a family to support and is not free to travel. I was independent and free to go anywhere and do anything I liked, and there was only my own neck to risk."

By 1953, however, Clark had given birth to her first child, and a letter accompanying a grant proposal to the American Philosophical Society concluded with these poignant words: "I am applying for this grant to cover only the expenses necessary for a baby sitter for my nine-month-old daughter." (The form letter Clark received in reply from the society began, "Dear Sir"—but she did eventually receive the financial support she sought).

Evelyn Shaw, another Museum ichthyologist, took a different approach by bringing her new baby to work. "Of course you know that Evelyn Shaw is now a mommy, but a most unusual one," Curator Lester Aronson wrote to Eugenie Clark in 1951. "She is working away today like an eager beaver in her room, holding the bottle in one hand and working with the fish eggs and embryos with the other." Clark's response: "Hurray for Mama Shaw! I've got to hand it to her—there isn't any situation that can stump her."

Evelyn Shaw wasn't the only Museum scientist to choose this temporary solution to the childcare-work conundrum. Forty years later, husband-and-wife mammalogists Rob Voss and Nancy Simmons also brought their son, Nicky, to work each morning when he was an infant. When they traveled to French Guiana to undertake a survey of rain-forest mammals, they took eleven-month-old Nicky along. "In fact, he learned to walk while we were at the field station," Simmons recalls. "Once he could get around on his own, we had to wait until he reached a more rational age before we brought him back to the rain-forest."

For the children or grandchildren of curators, early memories of visits to their mother or father's workplace are indelible. "As I recall it through a small child's eyes, my grandfather's office at the Museum was a magical and chaotic place featuring stacks of books and papers, messy ashtrays full of burnt pipe tobacco, and countless bottles and jars of pickled fish," John Nichols (grandson of Museum ichthyologist J. T. Nichols) told the American Society of Ichthyologists and Herpetologists in 1991.

Gordon and Leslie Van Gelder, son and daughter of Richard Van Gelder, longtime chairman of Mammalogy, have equally vivid memories of visits in the 1970s. "To go to the Museum from our home in New Jersey meant we had to get up at 5:30 A.M., which made the whole experience seem dreamlike," says Gordon, whose father changed his schedule at the Museum so he could be home when his children returned from school each day.

Leslie Van Gelder adds, "The lights would just be coming on as we walked through the Museum's halls. We would have the run of the place—as long as no one saw us—and we felt somehow that the Museum was ours. As if we had some sort of special claim on this incredible place."

CICHLIDS: THE ENDANGERED MULTITUDES

In an ideal world we would, of course, argue to save everything, but the world we live in is far from ideal. The rachet of extinction clicks faster each day and our resources seem to diminish in inverse proportion. . . . There is an obvious need to know what's out there, how much there is of it, and how endangered it is, and as systematists we should have little problem in convincing the conservation community and the "public at large" of the central importance of our science.

—*Ichthyologist Melanie L. J. Stiassny, in* Systematics, Ecology, and the Biodiversity Crisis *(1992).*

Anyone with even a casual interest in the condition of the world's environment is aware of the threats facing individual species and entire ecosystems around the globe. The black rhinoceros, the Bengal tiger, the mountain gorilla, the rain-forests of the Amazon basin—all have received endless, and sorely needed, publicity.

But according to ichthyologist Melanie Stiassny, Curator-in-Charge and Axelrod Research Curator in Ichthyology, an even more serious crisis has thus far escaped much public notice. The plight of the planet's freshwater fish, by far the planet's most spectacular example of vertebrate biodiversity.

"While everyone knows that the earth is largely covered with water, few realize that only 2.5 percent of this is freshwater," Stiassny explains. "Yet even this percentage is misleading, as most freshwater is locked in polar icecaps, stored in underground aquifers, included as soil moisture, or found in other forms that cannot support fish populations. Remarkably, only one one-hundredth of a percent of the world's water is freshwater found in lakes, rivers, and other wetlands."

Even more amazingly, this tiny percentage of water is host to a spectacular number of fish species. Together, saltwater and freshwater fish make up by far the most diverse branch of vertebrate life, with about twenty-five thousand species identified so far. But even this total is certain to grow significantly. About two hundred new species of fish are described each year, and even more would be added to the list annually if more scientists were available to describe them. Stiassny estimates that the final total will probably exceed 28,500 species—more than the total number of bird, mammal, reptile, and amphibian species combined.

Most remarkable of all is the fact that about half of all living fish species are found in freshwater. "This means that freshwater biodiversity is about twenty-five times that of saltwater," Stiassny points out. "Or, to put it another way: more than one-quarter of the world's vertebrate biodiversity exists in the one one-hundredth of a percent of water that is freshwater. That's an incredible concentration."

For many years, Stiassny's research has focused on an extraordinary example of this concentration, the fishes known as "cichlids" (family Cichlidae). This fish family includes more than one hundred genera and, very conservatively, at least one thousand different species. In some African lakes cichlids demonstrate the most dramatic example we have of the ability of a single species to diversify into many new species in an isolated environment, a process called adaptive radiation and speciation.

Scientists believe, for example, that in Africa's Lake Victoria, one cichlid species evolved into more than three hundred species in perhaps as few as twelve thousand years (a stunningly short period in evolutionary time) allowing different species to occupy nearly every ecological niche in that enormous lake. Similar evolutionary explosions of cichlids have taken place in Africa's Lake Malawi and other lakes, while diverse groups of cichlid species are also found in South America, Asia, and elsewhere.

Clearly, studying the systematics of cichlids could occupy Stiassny's entire career. But while she remains deeply interested in the evolutionary history and adaptive radiation of cichlids and other fish, devoting herself solely to systematics for its own sake is a luxury she realizes she cannot afford. Instead, she believes that the insights gained by systematic study must be used as a tool for understanding and addressing the fast-advancing biodiversity crisis, whose devastating effects have begun to dramatically affect her field of interest.

"Between pollution, silting from habitat destruction on land, and human overuse, freshwater is the most vulnerable and most endangered of all habitats on earth," she points out. "Fish are true 'miners' canaries,' telling us about the state of the world's freshwater, and the situation is dire nearly everywhere on earth."

Nowhere is the vulnerability of freshwater and its fish more clearly evident than in Lake Victoria. In fact, Lake Victoria's cichlids, those fascinating examples of speciation and adaptive radiation, have in recent years been the victims of one of recent history's most horrifying (yet too little known) environmental cataclysms. Today, the plight of Lake Victoria's cichlids stands as a warning of what continued human interference will do to countless other groups of the world's freshwater fish.

Of the more than three hundred cichlid species that graced Lake Victoria a few decades ago, scientists believe that about two hundred are now extinct or threatened with extinction. While certain remaining species will undoubtedly survive, others will just as certainly disappear, continuing the reduction of cichlid diversity in this magnificent lake to a mere shadow of its former glory.

How could this have happened? According to Stiassny, the reasons are complex, but they all, either directly or indirectly, result from human actions. Though it is hard to believe, even this huge lake (about as big as Vermont, New Hampshire, and Massachusetts combined) is actually a fragile environment, vulnerable to almost any interference.

Some of the causes of the mass cichlid extinction are obvious. A growing human population has fished the lake more and more intensively, perhaps reducing population levels of certain species past the point of recovery. Degradation of lakeside environments has led to increased silting close to shore, reducing oxygen levels in these shallow-water areas to the point that fish there cannot survive.

But the chief cause of the extinction was something even more insidious and, once begun, impossible to reverse, the depredations wrought by an introduced fish, the large and voracious Nile perch. Reaching more than six feet in length and weighing six hundred pounds, this species was placed in the lake in the 1950s in hopes of increasing the fish harvest.

Studies have shown that, as the perch spread across the lake, populations of one cichlid species after another plummeted. The seemingly simple decision to introduce a nonnative fish to the carefully balanced ecosystems of the lake doomed scores of unique, irreplaceable cichlids (which had no time to evolve defenses against this powerful new predator) to extinction.

Ironically, the plan to boost the Lake Victoria fishery has worked . . . so far. Today, far more pounds of fish are caught every year than were brought in as recently as two decades ago, although where once eighty percent of all poundage came from cichlids, today eighty percent of the catch is Nile perch and only one percent consists of cichlids.

But the story is not yet complete. These radical changes in fish population balance have also drastically altered the lake's ecology. Specifically, while the lake used to be oxygenated at every depth, that is no longer true. Today, much of the lake for much of the year is unable to support any creature that relies on oxygen to survive.

Having rampaged through the cichlid population, the perch now appears to be depending on a single species of shrimp that can live in oxygen-starved waters to support its own ever-increasing numbers. If, as seems likely, the shrimp cannot handle this assault over the long term, the Nile perch will have extirpated their last abundant prey species, and the perch population too will plummet.

"What has happened in Lake Victoria is surely the most dramatic example of human-induced vertebrate extinction in recorded history," Stiassny has written. "The ultimate fate of Lake Victoria is still very much in the balance, as are the lives and fortunes of the millions of people in Kenya, Uganda and Tanzania who rely on its fisheries' yields for their very existence."

Lake Victoria is not the only place where cichlids are under threat, as Stiassny found when she visited Madagascar. She had traveled there to test a hypothesis that the island's few cichlid species lie at the very root of the cichlid family tree. "When I went to Madagascar and collected some specimens, I confirmed that they were, indeed, very primitive members of the family," she says. "I also found that several other of the island fish species—including catfish, mullets, and silversides—also represented the most primitive members of their respective families, a very interesting pattern that I didn't expect to see."

Finding these important species, however, was not easy, due to the condition of Madagascar's freshwater. "While I was there I saw so much deforestation, so much siltation in the rivers, so much introduction of non-native species—the situation was pretty bleak," Stiassny recalls. "Nearly everything that can be done to endanger freshwater habitats is taking place on Madagascar."

Partly in response to the threatened status of Madagascar's unique and irreplaceable fish, Stiassny has developed an innovative, even brave, new use for systematic analysis, which acknowledges that not every species of cichlid (and by extension, of fish) can be saved. It may be time, she says, for scientists, conservationists, and governments to practice some form of triage—to focus on saving those species deemed "most valuable," rather than making a hopeless attempt to save everything.

As Stiassny puts it, "Are all fish created equal? Systematic analysis has shown that some of those species found on Madagascar are the closest thing we have to ancestral species—they contain so much information about their families, and so much would be lost if they disappeared. You simply can't say the same about, for example, any one of the Lake Victoria cichlid species—it clearly isn't as important in what it has to tell us about cichlid evolution."

As she argues in scientific papers for incorporating conservation into systematic analysis, Stiassny is also reaching far beyond the scientific community in her efforts to speak out on biodiversity issues. Her efforts include articles for *Tropical Fish Hobbyist* and other popular magazines, lectures to the public, and—crucially—ongoing attempts to publicize the uniqueness of Madagascan fish to the island's own people. "For a long time, the national fish of Madagascar was the goldfish, which was introduced by a European for the amusement of the Madagascan Queen in the 1830s," she points out. "More recently, when Madagascar issued a set of stamps celebrating its wildlife, a cichlid was included—but it was a cichlid from Central America!"

Stiassny is hopeful that the message will get through, however, especially now that Madagascar has a growing scientific community of its own. "I believe that people have a great sense of pride in their natural resources, their patrimony," she says. "If you can tell them that a beautiful, rare species is known only from their own country, they *will* want to protect it if they can."

The Unchanging Coelacanth

While cichlids demonstrate the breathtaking speed with which adaptive radiation and speciation can take place, another fish provides an equally compelling example of evolutionary stasis. This is *Latimeria chalumnae*, better known as the "coelacanth." This famous fish is a member of a group that scientists confidently believed had been extinct for seventy million years—until 1938, when a living specimen was hauled up by fishermen near the coast of South Africa.

The living coelacanth, which can reach six feet in length and weigh 150 pounds, is remarkably similar to its relatives that lived in the late Cretaceous period and earlier. What insights it can provide us about the biology of ancient fish, however, continue to be debated, as was demonstrated by a fascinating discovery made at the museum in 1975.

That year, C. Lavett Smith, chairman and curator of Ichthyology, and Dr. Charles S. Rand, a professor at Long Island University in New York, dissected a coelacanth specimen at the Museum. They found that it was a pregnant female and that it contained five well-developed embryos, proving that, rather than laying eggs, *Latimeria chalumnae* gave birth to live young. Given the living species' other resemblances to its extinct relatives, it seems likely that they too were live-bearers.

Since 1938, perhaps four hundred coelacanths have been caught in the waters surrounding the Comoro Islands, and the numbers being brought in continue to rise. Scientists think that the death of this many individuals has substantially reduced the population of this slow-breeding species. It seems entirely possible that this magnificent fish, having survived unnoticed for millions of years, will not live out a century after its initial discovery.

3 Messengers from the World's Wild Places

MARY CYNTHIA DICKERSON: THE FORGOTTEN PIONEER

If we are to paint her truly . . . we must paint the diligent worker, drudging through details beautiful and ugly alike, never failing in the service of work, from the simplest task to the constructing of a marvelous replica of some little fragment of nature with every minute detail true to exact fact and set in an atmosphere of loveliness.

—*Maud Slye, in a eulogy for Mary Cynthia Dickerson,*
first curator of the Department of Herpetology,
in Natural History, *1923.*

History is fickle. It seems to pick and choose who shall remain famous for generations, and who—however well-known during his or her lifetime—will be lost to public awareness and confined to library catalogs, unpublished dissertations, and ancient volumes *of Who's Who.*

But sometimes history seems to be worse than fickle. Sometimes it seems plainly unfair. Today, even the most casual student of the Museum's history is familiar with the exploits of Carl Akeley, Roy Chapman Andrews, and Margaret Mead. Only a bit more digging will reveal abundant details of the accomplishments of dozens of other Museum scientists and explorers.

Yet today Mary Cynthia Dickerson is virtually unknown beyond the borders of the department she was the first to head. Her name doesn't even appear in many histories of American women in science. This is both a scandal and a shame, because she was in fact a shining example of the self-made naturalist, pursuing a career outside the lines of what society deemed normal for a woman at the dawn of the twentieth century and succeeding in everything she attempted.

Charles Myers, Curator Emeritus in Herpetology, pays tribute to her work in *A Collection with Expeditionary Flavor*, his manuscript history of herpetology at the Museum. "In addition to her varied contributions that included the establishment of a major herpetological collection, Mary Cynthia Dickerson also was responsible for establishing the American Museum as an influential force in herpetological research," he writes.

All we know about the struggles of Dickerson's early life must be intuited from a few sparse facts. Born in Hastings, Michigan in 1866, she spent her youth helping rear three younger brothers. She had to pay her own way through college, a challenge whose difficulty was reflected in the length of time it took her to graduate. Beginning in 1886 at the University of Michigan, she frequently took time off to work before finally graduating from the University of Chicago in 1897, when she was more than thirty years old.

She went on to teach natural history at the Rhode Island State Normal School and then Stanford University, undertaking her own studies of amphibians and other creatures during field trips with her classes. Before she joined the Museum, she wrote two popular books, *Moths and Butterflies* and *The Frog Book* (both illustrated with her own photographs), as well as a series of lovely articles published in the magazine *Country Life in America* under the heading "The Pageant of Nature."

It is a testament to both Dickerson's talents and the Museum administration's broad-mindedness that she was invited to join the scientific staff in 1908, despite lacking advanced degrees or an extensive record of scientific publication. Surprisingly, she came on board not as a herpetologist but as a staff member in the Department of Woods and Forestry.

In 1909, a mere eight months after her arrival, Dickerson was invited to join the newly organized Department of Ichthyology and Herpetology as the only herpetologist on staff, in addition to her Woods and Forestry duties. That same year, she joined the editorial staff of the *American Museum Journal* (later *Natural History*), becoming editor in 1910 and presiding over the magazine during a brilliant decade in which it published memorable works by Theodore Roosevelt, Robert Peary, Henry Fairfield Osborn, and many other scientists and explorers.

Between 1910 and 1920, the quiet, reserved Mary Cynthia Dickerson had to have been the hardest-working member of the Museum's staff. She was unfailingly willing to take on ever-greater responsibilities, no matter how busy she already was. She did want her efforts to be recognized, though, as she showed in a 1911 letter to President Osborn: "The men at the door will tell you that I seldom leave before seven P.M. and I work almost without exception evenings on Museum work," she wrote. "This is not a complaint—I wish to work—but simply that you may know the truth of the matter."

Somehow Dickerson managed to be efficient and productive in each of her three jobs, but her heart clearly belonged to herpetology. Her years as curator were marked by the exhibition of the Museum's first reptile and amphibian habitat groups, beginning with bullfrog models mounted in lifelike settings in 1911.

"An exhibit of any group of animals to interest other than technical students must be shown from the life standpoint and in relation to man, especially a group repellent because of mystery and myth man has inherited from a time of less knowledge," she wrote in an *American Museum Journal* article announcing the new display.

As important as exhibits for the public were to Dickerson, the growth of the study collection was just as crucial. During her curatorship, the collection expanded from just a few haphazard specimens to nearly fifty thousand, an accomplishment due largely to her skill at hiring talented herpetologists and sending them to collect in the United States, Central America, and elsewhere. "Such rapid building up of the collections is of vital importance, because all research—taxonomic, distributional, or morphological, as well as all exhibition, is based on the collections," she wrote in 1919. Ninety years later, these sentiments still serve as a guiding principle of the Museum's scientific departments.

Dickerson's countless responsibilities at the Museum meant she got to spend very little time in the field. Given her love of the natural world (which her friend Maud Slye described as "an intense love of beauty . . . an innate craving for the exquisite"), it must have been painful indeed for her to spend virtually all her time within the confines of New York City.

In her letters, the only surviving clues to her thoughts, there is never even a whisper of regret that the world she portrayed so vividly in her "Pageant of Nature" magazine articles was now largely forbidden to her. These letters, dozens of them, are always professional, respectful, and lacking deeply expressed feelings of any kind. They contain none of the joy and excitement that fill so many of the letters written by Roy Chapman Andrews, Carl Akeley, E. T. Gilliard, Margaret Mead, and other prominent members of the Museum staff.

According to Maud Slye, this same reserve characterized Mary Cynthia Dickerson in person. "The catalogued data of a human life are brief and quickly told; the living of them is slow, complex, and puzzling," Slye wrote. "Of Miss Dickerson it is not easy to paint a portrait that all shall recognize, for there is an urge upon the painter to portray the soul, and here was peculiarly a woman who all her life kept her soul remote from almost every contact."

On February 2, 1920, the Department of Herpetology was separated from Ichthyology, and Mary Cynthia Dickerson was named its first curator. Sadly, she did not have much of a chance to savor this honor. Late in 1920, she was stricken by a catastrophic and mysterious illness. She remained hospitalized until her death in 1923, at the age of fifty-seven.

After Dickerson's death, Maud Slye wrote: "What an inspiration of selection it was that gave her Mary Cynthia for a name—Mary, diligent, sweet, generous, ready in service, humble; Cynthia, the aspiring, the ardent seeker after the romance of the world and the romance of the cosmos! In her heart she was Mary; in her soul she was Cynthia; and always she tried to find her way."

Today, even as Mary Cynthia Dickerson's remarkable life has been forgotten, the accomplishments of the vibrant department she founded remain her lasting legacy.

M. C. Dickerson's Other Role

When Mary Cynthia Dickerson wasn't laboring to establish a strong, innovative Herpetology department or editing the *American Museum Journal*, she was overseeing the Department of Woods and Forestry. Today, all that remains of this department are a series of dioramas and other displays about

North American forests, but early in this century Woods and Forestry was considered one of the most important departments in the Museum, largely because President Morris K. Jesup wanted it to be.

Jesup is remembered nowadays for transforming the Museum into an ambitious, aggressive research institution by supervising the hiring of many of the world's most brilliant mammalogists, ornithologists, paleontologists, and other scientists, beginning in the 1880s. But his own main enthusiasm was for the Jesup Collection of North American Trees, into which he poured thousands of dollars of his own money, while prevailing on J. P. Morgan and other railroad moguls to ship tons of specimens to the Museum for free.

The collection was described in a 1910 Museum guide. "Each tree is represented by a section of trunk 5 feet high, cut lengthwise radially 2 1/4 feet, the cut surface showing the color and graining of the quartered lumber in its natural and polished state." Even with the addition of meticulously crafted models of leaves, flowers, and fruit, these do not sound like the most scintillating specimens to exhibit, and, other than Jesup, few staff members seemed to think so either. After Jesup's death in 1911, the department dwindled in prominence and both the exhibit and the department itself eventually disappeared.

Today, the centerpiece of the remaining forestry exhibits is the spectacular section of a giant sequoia tree, taken in 1891 from a 1,300-year-old, three-hundred-foot-tall tree felled by loggers in the Sierra Nevada Mountains in California. The tree, through its rings and scars, bears witness to such threats as unusually cold and dry years, burn marks repaired with new bark, and even a pair of bullet holes that injured the tree but did not kill it.

STALKING THE DRAGON

> If any man with sporting tastes and a real interest in natural history were told that true dragons were still living on a remote, little known island of the East Indies, what would he do?. . . . First of all, he would try to make sure that the reports were founded on fact, and then, having satisfied himself, he would begin, a little secretly, perhaps, to lay his plans.
>
> —*Museum trustee W. Douglas Burden,*
> *in* Dragon Lizards of Komodo *(1927).*

By the early 1920s, the Department of Herpetology had every reason to be proud. Its collection was now one of the finest in the United States, and among its staff and expert collectors were such eminent scientists as Gladwyn Kingsley Noble, Karl Schmidt, Charles Camp, and Emmett R. Dunn. Noble had succeeded Mary Cynthia Dickerson as chief curator, and under his leadership the collection continued to grow. Herpetological expeditions sent back specimens from Panama, the West Indies, and elsewhere, and more general collecting trips worldwide contributed specimens as well.

Still, it's impossible not to sense that some members of the staff felt that the department wasn't getting the attention it deserved. And who could argue? After all, the 1920s may have been the most exciting and adventurous decade in the history of the Museum—of any museum, in fact. This was the time that Roy Chapman Andrews and his intrepid fossil hunters were braving bandits and sandstorms in the Gobi Desert; when Carl Akeley was uncovering the secrets of the mountain gorilla in the rainforests of Central Africa; when the Whitney South Seas Expedition seemed to visit a different uncharted island every week. A reptile-collecting trip to Arizona could hardly hope to compete with these for publicity.

Fortunately, in the mid-1920s, Herpetology acquired what every department needed to raise its profile—a benefactor. This guardian angel was trustee W. Douglas Burden, who embodied many of the qualities most prized by the Museum's administration at the time: He was wealthy, he was enthusiastic about natural history, and he loved to hunt. By 1926, at the age of twenty-eight, he had already pursued bears, tigers, rhinos, and wild sheep across Asia and North America. Now he wanted to go after dragons.

For decades, local tales had told of enormous monitor lizards on Komodo, a volcanic island east of Java in Indonesia's Lesser Sunda Islands. The island's mythic qualities were only enhanced by its inaccessibility due to razor-sharp reefs, deadly currents, and fierce monsoon winds. The surrounding straits, explorer and evolutionary pioneer Alfred Russel Wallace wrote, "boil and foam and dance like the rapids below a cataract, so that vessels are sometimes swamped in the finest weather and under the brightest skies." No wonder that even the inhabitants of neighboring islands rarely visited Komodo, and no European scientist, Wallace included, had ever reached it.

In 1910, a Dutch colonial official finally made it to the island and collected the first specimens of the giant native lizards. But not until 1912 did P.A. Ouwens, director of a natural history museum on Java, get hold of a skin, thereby proving to the scientific community that these seemingly mythical creatures—lizards that could reach ten feet in length and could weight two hundred pounds—did exist. Ouwens sent collectors to the island for more specimens, and eventually named the new species *Varanus komodoensis*—or, as it has been known ever since, the "Komodo dragon." (The popular name still holds sway, even though the species is found also on three nearby islands.)

Douglas Burden, who had first learned of the komodo in a lecture by the Museum's G. K. Noble, realized that an expedition to the island for the Museum would be rife with adventure and publicity. He gathered a party that included herpetologist E. R. Dunn, hunter F. J. Defosse, Lee Fai (a Chinese cameraman), and Burden's wife, Katherine, and set off in early 1926.

The group first sighted the craggy mountains and misty forests of Komodo on June 9, making anchor late that afternoon. The Burdens went ashore, immediately seeing signs of abundant wildlife: deer, wild boar, and other creatures. They soon became enamored of the "lost world" they had reached. "Just as we went on board again, the sun was setting, and the rocky islets and purple sea were catching tints of gold from the sun and showers of color from the changing sky overhead," Douglas recalled in a *Natural History* article.

On June 11 the party began an in-depth exploration of the island. Before they found their first komodo, they noted the presence of the "carrabao," or water buffalo, a fascinating array of birds that included pheasants, fruit pigeons, and cockatoos, and a variety of arthropods, such as several-inch-long scorpions, millipedes, and centipedes.

After setting up camp, the group placed dead boars and other animals as bait, which soon began to attract komodos. "They are coming by the hundred to our baits, but mostly small ones," Katherine wrote to her family on June 14. "The cameraman got a picture of one sitting on his hind legs like a rabbit, with great lumps of pig passing down his body, like a frog in a snake."

The Burdens were fascinated by the eating habits of the larger individuals. Grabbing hold of the meat with sharp, serrated teeth, "the beast maneuvers this by seesawing back and forth on braced legs, giving a wrench at the bait with every backward move," Douglas noted. "Seen thus, with jaws buried in the meat, and neck curved forward and down, he bears a remarkable resemblance to *Tyrannosaurus* as restored in modern paintings."

Collecting and studying their first specimens, the group found that the komodos' appetites were prodigious even when they had to hunt for their own food. "I may add that we have not only found legs and hooves of buffalos in these animals' stomachs, but the heads of pig and deer, which are bigger than their heads," Katherine told her family.

The expedition had received permission to kill or capture only fifteen komodos, a total that was easy for them to reach, given the animals' abundance and unwariness. At first the hunting was left to Douglas Burden and F. J. Defosse, but soon Katherine—another in the long line of active, self-assured wives of Museum explorers—began to participate. In a headline whose melodramatic tone was characteristic of the time, the *New York Evening Post* reported on the development: "Woman Huntress Revolts Against Playing Safe—Kills Huge 'Malay Dragon.' "

Having collected twelve specimens (including those that are on display in lifelike poses in the museum's Hall of Reptiles and Amphibians), Douglas Burden was determined to bring a pair home alive. He succeeded in capturing and transporting two smaller individuals to the Bronx Zoo. Here they drew enormous crowds of onlookers, but unfortunately the animals languished in captivity and died. ("Monster Lizards Starve in Strike Against Cages; Scorn Chicken à la King," reported the *Evening Post*).

Today, the Komodo dragon survives, although its island habitat and small population (perhaps 3,500 total) put it under constant threat of extinction. In a meeting of nature and commerce of a kind that will only grow more frequent in the future, the Komodo Island lizards have survived partly by paying their own way. Today, using the same method employed seventy years ago by the Burdens, wardens put out slaughtered goats as bait, and crowds of paying tourists gather to watch as the dragons descend to tear apart their free food.

To help ensure the species' survival, captive-breeding programs have also been put into place. Specialists at the National Zoo in Washington have determined the best combination of food, temperature, and other variables, and have induced the great lizards to breed. Soon it may be possible to view this magnificent animal in the comfort of your local zoo.

But life in captivity diminishes the komodo, as it does tigers, crocodiles, and other large and threatened predators throughout the world. Fortunately, wild komodos ("truly a marvelous sight, a primeval monster in a primeval setting," as Katherine Burden put it) still exist, roaming free in the dense back-country forests of their island homes. May they do so forever.

The Pachyderm Diet

What did Komodo dragons eat?

We know that today these giant lizards hunt deer, wild pigs, horses, goats, and even huge water buffalo. Remarkably, though, research has shown that all these large mammals were introduced to the Flores Island group (the komodo's native islands) by humans after 3,000 B.C. The komodo itself evolved millions of years before that, of course, and would never have appeared if large mammals had been absent from its island homes. So what *did* it eat?

According to some respected researchers, the answer is obvious: The komodo ate elephants—in particular, now-extinct relatives of mastodons and mammoths called "stegodonts," whose fossil remains have been found wherever komodos (or their fossils) appear. Biologist Walter Auffenberg of the University of

Florida, whose years of fieldwork have provided the most complete descriptions we have of komodo habits and diet, first suggested the lizard-elephant link, and others, including physiologist Jared M. Diamond, a Museum ornithology research associate, have enlarged on Auffenberg's theory. As Diamond put it in a 1992 article for *Discover*, "One of the Flores elephant species was nearly full-size; the other was a half-size pygmy. Those pachyderms and their young would have been worthy prey, sufficient to explain the evolution of a big predator."

WHY THEY DO THE THINGS THEY DO

One of the most recent developments in museum work is the attention being given to living material. . . . The condition has arisen because the curator finds himself unable to answer many fundamental questions concerning his material without reference to live specimens.

—*G. Kingsley Noble, Curator of Herpetology and Experimental Biology, in* Natural History, *1930.*

Mary Cynthia Dickerson loved to write for the public about the habits of frogs and salamanders, loved to observe them in their roles as part of the "pageant of nature." But under her leadership, herpetology at the Museum focused on the systematic study of its ever-increasing collection of specimens. Not until Dickerson was followed as chief curator by Gladwyn Kingsley Noble in 1921 did the department begin to concentrate, as it would for decades, on the behavior of reptiles and amphibians.

Noble, who led the department for nearly twenty years, was an extraordinary biologist, well ahead of his time in his interest in systematics. While other herpetologists were still analyzing differences among species by comparing skeletal and other obvious characteristics, Noble also studied neurologic, endocrine, and even biochemical differences. In a remarkably prescient 1930 *Natural History* article, he even stated that "in considering the question of species origin, attention must be focused first upon the chromosomes," a conviction that would be supported by many of today's leading systematists.

Still, Noble believed that differences in behavior provided crucial clues to species' origin and variation. This conclusion led him to devise complex methods of studying behavior in the laboratory and even to change the department's name to Herpetology and Experimental Biology.

A typical series of experiments, beginning in the 1920s, saw Noble and his colleague L. B. Richards implant pieces of salamander pituitary glands under the tongues of female salamanders of the same species. They found that the implanted glands provoked egg laying in many different species of salamanders, sometimes months ahead of normal ovulation season. This gave the scientists the opportunity to compare differences in egg laying behavior and in the composition of the egg and embryo among species that might not otherwise breed at all in captivity.

"It has recently been emphasized that the mode of life history of an amphibian often furnishes a valuable clue as to the relationships of the species," the authors pointed out in a 1932 report in *American Museum Novitates*. "The pituitary technique, inducing a normal ovulation, should be of interest, therefore, not only to embryologists but to students of amphibian phylogeny who are able to secure the adults of the rarer species alive."

Such innovative techniques were typical of Noble's ambitions and accomplishments. Unfortunately, his fascination with such experiments grew to overwhelm his interest in the other tasks of

Herpetology, especially after Experimental Biology was split into a separate department in 1934. Noble headed both departments, but experimental biology was his passion, meaning that "the Department of Herpetology was allowed to drift. . . . There was no one (other than the preoccupied Noble) fully in charge or able to speak for, or to raise money for, Herpetology," says Charles Myers.

This era came to an end after Noble's death in 1940, when Charles M. Bogert was named curator of Herpetology, and Experimental Biology (later renamed "Animal Behavior") gained its own chairman. But Bogert's department was engaged in a nearly constant financial struggle throughout his stay; for most of the years between 1940 and 1954, he was the sole Herpetology curator.

Still, Bogert managed to continue to increase the department's all-important study collections, to about 184,000 specimens by 1969. Interestingly, his own research continued to meld experimental techniques that would have pleased Noble with more intensive descriptive work, a combination that has been dubbed a "new systematics."

Bogert's wide-ranging interests resulted in groundbreaking research into thermoregulation of reptiles, including a study undertaken with Museum paleontologist Edwin Colbert that attempted to determine if dinosaurs were cold blooded by performing temperature-tolerance experiments on alligators; analyses of communication among frogs (published in a fascinating 1960 book entitled *Animal Sounds and Communication*, edited by the Museum's W. E. Lanyon and W. N. Tavolga, and originally packaged with a twelve-inch, long-playing record); and a field study of homing instincts among toads.

Bogert also served as an inspiration to today's Herpetology curators, especially Curator Charles Cole, whose choice of a career was influenced by a meeting with the older herpetologist. "When I was thirteen my parents took me to the American Southwest, and I got a chance to visit Bogert, who was working at the Museum's Southwestern Research Center in Arizona," he recalls. "I just got hooked on the fieldwork, camping out and studying reptiles, and I saw this man who'd made a career out of doing that. And I thought—that's for me."

Today, more than forty years later, Charles Cole has revealed to us the surprising secrets of a group of lizards whose offbeat lifestyle would have appealed to Bogert's questing intelligence. For more than three decades, Cole has been among a handful of scientists studying lizard species that thrive, and successfully reproduce, despite being composed entirely of females.

THE LIFE OF A UNISEXUAL LIZARD

All of us who have been in this field a long time are working on subjects that contradict everything we learned in college. . . . It's in our training to be objective, but when something flies in the face of everything you thought you knew, you have to have the courage to look past your preconceptions.

—*Curator of Herpetology Charles Cole*

Since it takes both courage and vision to accept a scientific finding that contradicts the tenets you have been taught to believe, many scientists choose not to take the risk. For Ilya Darevsky, a zoologist at the Academy of Sciences in Leningrad, the test came in the 1950s when he discovered that certain populations of the lizard genus *Lacerta*, found in Armenia, appeared to be entirely female.

Darevsky could have assumed that this surprising finding was the result of chance. He could have refused to speculate on the cause, focusing instead on systematic and other studies. He could just have kept quiet. But he didn't. In 1958 he published a paper speculating that these female lizards didn't need males for the act of procreation. He also presented evidence that they could breed parthenogenetically, laying eggs that were viable despite the absence of any male sperm for fertilization.

Darevsky must have known that his claims would be greeted with derision by many scientists. After all, as Cole put it in a 1984 article in *Scientific American*, "at the time it was almost axiomatic that no vertebrate species could reproduce except through the union of the male's sperm with the female's egg."

While being without honor in his own and many other lands, Darevsky was indeed a prophet to some American scientists, especially Richard G. Zweifel (a curator in Herpetology) and Sherman A. Minton, a Herpetology research associate and professor at the Indiana University Medical Center. Both of these men had been studying a group called the "whiptail lizards" (genus *Cnemidophorus*) and had noted that certain populations in the southwestern United States seemed to lack males. Coming upon Darevsky's article, they allowed themselves to believe that perhaps their collections weren't skewed; perhaps they were finding only females because females alone existed.

By the standards of changes in the scientific conventional wisdom (which often happen with all the speed and agility of an ocean liner turning around), acceptance of the idea that all-female lizards species might exist came quickly, but not immediately. In 1962, William E. Duellman, a herpetologist at the University of Kansas Natural History Museum, and Richard Zweifel published a review of certain whiptail lizards that included a section titled "All-Female Populations of *Cnemidophorus*."

Having brought up the subject, however, the authors then left

its implications to future papers. "If it is established that parthenogenesis truly occurs in *Cnemidophorus*, this genus notorious
for its taxonomic difficulties will be subjected to additional com-
plications." This was all they would say about it.

Cole was a graduate student of William Duellman's at the
time this paper was written, and he recalls the caution expressed
by the eminent herpetologist when asked about this radical concept. "One of his other students asked Duellman whether he
thought the all-female populations truly represented unisexual
species, and he replied: 'Actually, I don't really think it's true
myself.' "

Richard Zweifel had fewer doubts. By the mid-1960s he,
T. Paul Maslin of the University of Colorado, and several other
herpetologists were convinced that as many as a half-dozen *Cnemidophorus* species contained only females. Zweifel went so far
as to call one species unisexual in a 1965 *Novitates* article, while
acknowledging that "parthenogenesis has yet to be demonstrated
unequivocally" in any whiptail-lizard species.

Proving parthenogenesis was an enormous stumbling block to
in-depth studies of these lizards, Cole says. "You can't demonstrate it in wild lizards," he points out. "How can you be
absolutely sure that you haven't missed collecting males, or that
individuals of an all-female species might be mating with males
of another, closely related species nearby?"

Even if members of apparently all-female species could be
induced to lay viable eggs in captivity, that wouldn't constitute
proof either, as females of some lizard species can store a male's
sperm internally for months before using it to fertilize their eggs.
No, unequivocal evidence was going to require the laying of
viable eggs by a female who was herself born in captivity and
kept isolated from males.

Cole and his associate Carol Townsend took on this difficult challenge. While the lizards seemed to adapt well to captivity at first, and even laid viable eggs, they gradually sickened and died for no clear reason, as did any hatchlings before they, too, could lay eggs.

"There are no set rules for overcoming these problems—you try this, you try that," Cole says. "After a lot of work, we found out that the lizards were suffering from a deficiency of vitamin D, which we could remedy with bulbs that radiate ultraviolet light." In the end, Cole and Townsend were able to achieve their goals and to prove parthenogenesis: Chihuahua whiptail lizards born in captivity were, in fact, able to lay eggs that hatched. This was a truly parthenogenetic lizard.

Today, scientists believe that about one percent of the three-thousand-or-so species of lizards are unisexual. "As we keep finding more lizard species, we also keep finding additional parthenogenetic species," Cole comments. "Unisexuality occurs in many different lizard families, in Asia, Africa, Pacific islands, wherever lizards occur. It's interesting that this adaptation has evolved so often independently."

Cole believes that unisexual lizards' ability to, in effect, clone themselves, may evolve because it provides reproductive advantages. "Many unisexual species occupy disturbed or 'edge' habitats, or areas whose plant communities have shifted in recent geologic times due to climatic changes," he explains. "A unisexual species may be able to colonize such an area rapidly, since only a single individual is necessary to begin colonization, and since every mature member of the species is able to reproduce."

Having proven that certain lizard species do, in fact, produce young parthenogenetically, scientists then turned to another crucial question: How?

The answer is elegant. Typically, in an individual of a bisexual species (one in which procreation requires both a female's egg and a male's sperm), all cells contain two complete sets of chromosomes. Cells throughout the body are constantly dividing, and prior to most cell divisions, both sets of chromosomes replicate themselves to ensure that the newly created cell also contains the same two sets.

But when specialized cells in the gonads produce sperm or egg cells, they pass on just one set of chromosomes (these single-chromosome cells are called "haploid" cells). Only during fertilization, when sperm and egg cells unite, is the usual complement of two chromosome sets restored.

Parthenogenetic species, it appears, differ from bisexual ones by producing egg cells that contain both of the mother's chromosome sets (these are called "diploid" cells because they have twice as many chromosomes as haploid egg or sperm cells). Since the egg already has the full complement of chromosomes, the set normally provided by the sperm is unnecessary, and it can begin to divide and differentiate on its own.

As if all this weren't mind-bending enough, researchers using precise and powerful DNA sequencing and other techniques have been able to figure out where these unisexual lizard species evolved from. "We know now that many unisexual species are hybrids of two separate bisexual species whose territory overlapped," Cole says. For example, scientists can tell that the unisexual C. *neomexicanus* of the American southwest is a hybrid of the bisexual C. *tigris* and C. *inornatus* because it contains a set of chromosomes from each parent species.

Typically, mating between different species produces sterile young (if any at all). But in this case, while any male offspring were sterile, at least one of the females had undergone a genetic mutation. It could produce diploid eggs, which allowed it to reproduce parthenogenetically. The result was an entirely new species, C. *neomexicanus*.

Scientists' ability to trace the lineage of unisexual lizards back to different parental species led to a remarkable conclusion, recounted in a pair of *Natural History* articles. In a 1989 article titled "A Lizard Foretold," Cole and three coauthors describe an interesting lizard species (genus *Gymnophthalmus*) that lives in the forests of northern South America. "It is small, with an average body length of about an inch and a half and a tail almost twice that long," they write. "The animal's dark brown color and the narrow, light stripe along its sides camouflage it in the ground litter where it lives." They then go on to discuss the hours that the lizard is active, its eating habits, and how it mates and produces young.

None of these facts are particularly unusual, except for one: The authors were describing a lizard that no scientist had ever seen. The evidence in the chromosomes of a known unisexual species made it possible for them to predict the existence of a new species in those tropical forests, and to know for a certainty that it must be out there somewhere.

This unknown lizard was first described in 1989. In 1994, *Natural History* printed the end of the story, "A Lizard Found." Here Cole describes the intensive field- and museum-work he, Carol Townsend, and others undertook in their search for the unknown lizard. Study of specimens in the Museum collection revealed the presence of a previously undescribed new species of *Gymnopthalmus* (now called *G. cryptus*), which could possibly have been the missing parent. But since the preserving fluid formalin destroys the chromosomes, fresh, unpreserved specimens would be necessary to be sure.

Those specimens came from Allan L. Markezich, a professor at Black Hawk College in Moline, Illinois. Markezich had read the 1989 article and knew that his own upcoming fieldwork in southern Venezuela would take him to areas where the predicted species should live.

During his third day of collecting in the rain-forest, Markezich was exploring along the edge of a flooded savanna when he heard a rustling sound at his feet. Crouching down and remaining still, he heard the rustling again, "and a small, snakelike, bronze-colored lizard cautiously appeared from under a clump of brown leaves. With a lunge and a quick grasp, I had the lizard in hand," he wrote in *Natural History*.

Eventually, Markezich collected six specimens from the dozens of quick and agile lizards he saw of this species. Through painstaking effort, four of them were kept alive and sent to the Museum. Intensive genetic analysis by Cole and biochemist Herbert Dessauer proved that Markezich's lizards were *G. cryptus*, and that this species was indeed the "lizard foretold."

POISON FROGS: TOXIC JEWELS

These frogs show remarkable variation, even within a single species, in behavior, habitat, and the toxins they carry around. By studying them, we're gaining insights into the evolutionary history of an extraordinary group of animals.

—*Charles Myers, Curator Emeritus in Herpetology,*
on the tropical poison frogs.

From the earliest days of colonial exploration of South America, European visitors were fascinated by the indigenous tribes' use of poisons as hunting aids. Poisons were particularly essential when hunting in the dense rain-forest, because even a wounded monkey, bird, or other creature might well disappear into the forest before dying. Many tribes, therefore, learned to daub plant poisons on arrow or dart tips to hasten the prey animal's death.

The most famous of these poisons, taken from the plant genus *Strychnos*, are strychnine and curare, muscle relaxants so potent that substances derived from curare are still used by anesthesiologists today. Among the first, and certainly the most vivid, written description of curare's effects appeared in the naturalist Charles Waterton's *Wanderings in South America* (1825), in which the author, visiting an Indian community in the Brazilian Amazon, undertook to test the potency of the poison (which he called "wourali") on a thousand-pound ox.

Three wourali-tipped arrows, each considered by the Indians to be sufficient to kill a large peccary (a wild relative of the pig), were shot into the ox. "The poison seemed to take effect in four minutes," Waterton reported, and immediately seemed to paralyze the ox. By the fourteenth minute, the animal "advanced a pace or two, staggered, and fell, and remained extended on his side with his head on the ground. . . . In five-and-twenty minutes from the time of his being wounded he quite dead."

But not all Indian peoples depend on plants for their poisons. At least one tribe, the Chocó of western Colombia, has long used the skin secretions of three species of colorful frogs. These frogs belong to one of the most remarkable amphibian families on earth, the Dendrobatidae (commonly called "dart-poison" or simply "poison" frogs), which encompass a few hundred species of widely varied, but often brilliantly colored, frogs found only in tropical regions of the New World.

For more than a quarter of a century, Charles Myers has been fascinated by the tangled systematics of this enormous family, by the extraordinary variability that exists even within a single species, and by the complex toxins that they carry in their skin. "I never intended to specialize in these frogs for so long," Myers says. "But the more I studied them, the more I realized how much I still had to learn."

The first report on the existence of poison frogs and their use in hunting appears to have come from an enterprising British seaman, Captain Charles Stuart Cochrane, in his *Journal of a Residence and Travels in Colombia* (1825). On leave from the navy, Cochrane explored the Andes Mountains, where he learned of a small frog, yellow on the back, with large, black eyes. This frog was kept in captivity by the local people until they needed its poison, at which time "they take one of the unfortunate reptiles and pass a pointed piece of wood down his throat, and out at one of his legs. This torture makes the poor frog perspire very much, especially on the back, which becomes covered with white froth: this is the most powerful poison that he yields, and in this they dip or roll the points of their arrows."

In an account published just a year or so later, a British colonel named J. P. Hamilton describes a similar scenario involving a different species of frog, adding a few details. Once spitted on the piece of wood, the frog is held close to a small fire, a process, Hamilton was told, that causes it to yield even more "perspiration."

Such accounts, according to Myers, are accurate descriptions of techniques still used by certain groups of Chocó Indians in Colombia, although the use of blowguns with poisoned darts is now declining. "We now know that the two frogs used by these Indians are the dendrobatids *Phyllobates aurotaenia* and *P. bicolor*," he explains. The toxins drawn from the frogs, Myers adds, are alkaloids, a group of complex chemicals once thought to exist only in plants.

For a long time these groups of Chocó were the only Indians known to utilize this remarkable hunting aid, and *P. aurotaenia* and *P. bicolor* were the only frogs whose toxins were used in this way. In 1978, however, Myers and his colleagues, John W. Daly (a chemist at the National Institutes of Health) and ethnozoologist Borys Malkin, reported on a new species of poison frog and a new method used by the Chocó to obtain the poison.

The inhabitants of some Emberá Chocó villages, isolated from those who use the frogs described above, rely on a species of frog that is so toxic they merely have to wipe a dart point across a living individual's back to obtain the poison they need. When Myers and Daly collected this frog in Colombia, Myers recalls, "we listened to the warnings of our Indian friends that it was more toxic than other poison frogs in the area, especially after a dog and a chicken died after eating our contaminated garbage."

The scientists named the new frog *Phyllobates terribilis*, and analyzed why it was so toxic that "a small fraction of the poison from one of the new frogs would be lethal to man if gotten into the bloodstream through an open wound." Myers and Daly discovered that the toxins in *P. terribilis* were the same as those found in the other two poison frogs, a particularly potent class of alkaloids called "batrachotoxins."

But *P. terribilis* possessed at least twenty times the amount of alkaloids found in the other species. It's no wonder the Emberá didn't have to bother with impaling the frogs or holding them close to a fire to obtain enough poison for use on their darts.

From the beginning of their research, Myers and Daly have been fascinated by the complexity and variety of alkaloids found in dendrobatid frogs. "When we first went to Colombia, we expected to find that each species of frog possessed a variation on one common set of toxins," Myers recalls. "Instead, we've identified several dozen new frogs and more than four hundred different alkaloids. A single individual frog may have two dozen different alkaloids in its skin, including new classes whose chemical composition has never been seen before in nature."

For many years Myers kept colonies of poison frogs in his laboratory at the Museum, which led to a remarkable discovery:

The first generation of frogs born in captivity was no longer poisonous. Nor were any subsequent captive-born generations. "We weren't sure whether this sudden lack of toxicity was due to laboratory conditions (such as an absence of enough ultraviolet light) or another cause," Myers said. "But owing to John Daly's work, we now suspect that most poison frogs are actually getting their alkaloids from food sources."

In other words, frogs are born nonpoisonous. They gradually build up their toxicity by "sequestering" in special skin glands the alkaloids carried by the tiny insects that make up their food. "It's a mind-boggling thing, to realize that there's an almost microscopic world in the tropical forest in which mites, ants, and other tiny insects—which we haven't yet identified—are carrying these remarkably strong, toxic poisons around," Myers says. "We don't know where the insects get the toxins, but it's conceivable that the alkaloids do originate in plant sources."

Perhaps the most remarkable aspect of Myers's research involves his long-term study of a single species of dendrobatid frog, *Dendrobates pumilio*. This frog is native to Nicaragua, Costa Rica, and western Panama, but it was his discovery of a complex of Panamanian populations that particularly interest the herpetologist. In this small geographic area, the single species of frog has evolved to boast nearly all the colors of the visible spectrum from red to blue. Some populations are pure orange, navy blue, or green, while others are black with white stripes or yellow, emerald green, or orange with black spots.

In addition, different populations of this one species are different sizes. Some populations are arboreal while others prefer to live on the ground. Some are secretive while others don't seem to care who sees them. Nor do all populations secrete the same alkaloids. In fact, scientists have identified more than eighty different toxins, and one population of frogs may harbor twenty-four alkaloids.

"We suspect that part of the extraordinary diversity of this species may reflect the repeated rise and fall of sea levels, which created and then reconnected islands to the mainland over the course of thousands of years," Myers explains. "But not all the variation can be so simply explained, as we find different-colored populations on the adjacent mainland and even on a single island."

Clearly, the study of dendrobatid frogs could consume the rest of Charles Myers's career, but he doesn't intend for this to happen. "I'm actually quite interested in the relationships between tropical American snakes," he says. "I also hope to finish a project in Panama, where I lived for three years and did my first tropical fieldwork." In addition, for many years he has been leading collecting trips to the tepuis, the isolated and little-studied "table mountains" of Venezuela and neighboring countries.

A visit to Myers's office in the Museum bears out his desire to study a broader range of reptile and amphibian life. One afternoon he is poring over an illustration of a newly discovered lizard's tail—not the entire lizard, just the tail. "This is a specimen we brought back from the tepuis," he explains. "We found this tail in the stomach of a new species of snake. Presumably, the snake struck and the lizard, as lizards do, dropped its tail and escaped." He shakes his head. "This is the first time I've ever written a species account based on just a tail—with the rest of the type specimen possibly running around alive somewhere."

The interest and amusement that lights up his face as he considers this odd possibility prove that for Charles Myers the world of reptiles and amphibians remains a trove whose treasures he has just begun to examine.

A Worldwide Web of Concern

Museum scientists have always depended on the knowledge and skills of local naturalists to aid in collecting and studying rare animals. Until recently, however, these naturalists were invariably self-trained. In most developing countries, no money or will existed to offer university or graduate training programs in biology or environmental science. Today, though, that has changed. Museum researchers are working with local scientists from dozens of countries, creating a worldwide network of study, collection, and conservation.

"What we try to do is establish a relationship with skilled scientists, even if we can't hire them as full-time staff," Charles Myers explains. "By naming them research or field associates, we allow their association with the Museum to help them with their careers at home, while also providing some financial support and time in our laboratories when possible. Meanwhile, they provide us with specimens and other data that we might not be able to get any other way."

Dr. Lily Rodríguez is a perfect example of this encouraging trend. A Museum field associate, she primarily works for APECO (a conservation organization) and the Museo de Historia Natural de la Universidad Mayor de San Marcos in her native Peru. She shares specimens with the Museum, and is the discoverer and co-describer, with Charles Myers, of a new dendrobatid frog native to Peru's Manu National Park. But she can also take on responsibilities at home that could not be attempted by the Museum's full-time curators.

For Rodríguez, these responsibilities include intensive work with little-contacted Indian tribes in the spectacular, and still largely undisturbed, tropical forests of southeastern Peru. "Right now I'm working on teaching the indigenous people about conservation," she explains during a visit to the Museum.

"The government wants every region in the country to be 'productive,' to make money, but in this area it is very difficult to accomplish," she continues. Ecotourism, already a major source of income at Manu, might be one solution, but, as she points out, employing the skills of indigenous people in the service of tourism (without diminishing their dignity or disrupting their societal structure) is a great challenge.

At the Museum, Rodríguez is using Herpetology's sound equipment to study recordings of frog calls. "My work with indigenous people prevents me from doing as much research as I'd like, but it is worth it," she says. "Because if we can't make this region productive without destroying the lives of the indigenous people, here will come the roads, the settlers, the oil companies—and no research will be possible in the future."

4   The Original Creation Tale

GEMS AND MINERALS: ROMANCE AND REVELATION

In looking over the gem cases, it is quite possible to linger a long time over each group of gems in recounting the interesting facts of their nature, associations, and origins. This superb tourmaline, darkly green, with the hue of a sun-sprayed spruce, tells of Mt. Mica in Maine, where so many glorious specimens have been discovered. . . . These rich "pigeon-blood" garnets recall the ant-hills in New Mexico, where either the ants or scorpions have carried them to the surface to afford free room for the erection of their chambers and galleries. These pale turquoises carry us back to prehistoric excavations in New Mexico. . . .

—*L. P. Gratacap, curator in the Department of Geology, in* The American Museum Journal, *December 1900.*

The lure of minerals and gems has captivated both scientists and the public at the American Museum since its earliest days. Visitors flocked to the first modest gem showcases, and today the rows of glowing amethysts, emeralds, sapphires, azurites, and many others in the Morgan Memorial Hall of Gems and Guggenheim Hall of Minerals continue to inspire wonder. Even now, when we more fully understand the geologic processes that produce these treasures, it's hard not to marvel at how such magnificent objects can be created deep within the earth.

In its earliest years, the Museum was little more than a repository for scattered groups of fossils, insects, and other specimens, but by early in the twentieth century it could boast one of the finest collections of any natural history museum on earth—a transformation largely due to the enthusiasm and generosity of the Museum's friends and benefactors. Earth and Planetary Sciences (currently part of the Division of Physical Sciences and formerly called, among other titles, Geology, Mineralogy, and Mineral Sciences) was particularly fortunate, for it had two extraordinary guardian angels, George F. Kunz and J. P. Morgan.

Many of the Museum's most spectacular and important gems are the product of Kunz's unceasing efforts. A prominent member of New York's social circles, the elegant and learned Kunz (1856–1932) was fascinated by the beauty, history, and properties of gems. As gem expert for Tiffany & Co. and honorary curator of precious stones for the Museum (a position created for him), he was able to pursue his interests, acquire countless gems for Tiffany, and build spectacular collections for eventual acquisition by the Museum.

The first of these collections was spurred by the great Paris Exposition of 1889. Kunz convinced Charles L. Tiffany, founder of the famous store, of the importance of impressing European jewelers with both the quality and quantity of North American precious stones. Tiffany then dispatched Kunz on a continent-wide search that resulted in a collection of stones, crystals, and other specimens so magnificent that it won a gold medal at the Paris Exposition.

Bringing the collection back to New York, Kunz was loath to break it up. Instead, Tiffany offered it to the Museum for $15,000, which the Museum's trustees thought too high a price. But it was actually a bargain, as an outside expert soon appraised the collection at $20,000. The gorgeous stones might have been dispersed if the famous financier J. P. Morgan hadn't stepped in. Contributing $15,000 (Tiffany & Co. donated the rest), Morgan made sure that the Museum acquired its first important gem collection.

This was neither the first nor last time that Morgan or his son, J. P. Morgan, Jr., helped the Museum develop into a world-class institution, able (as its founders had profoundly hoped) to hold its head up proudly with the great museums of Europe. Most famous for its financial backing of many great fossil-hunting expeditions of the late 1800s through the 1920s, the Morgan family lent equally crucial support to the gem and mineral collections, but rarely with greater impact than followed the installation of the first Morgan-Tiffany Collection.

Placed on display, the collection was an immediate popular success, as Kunz recalled in a 1913 article in the *American Museum Journal.* "The specimens were displayed in two long cases on the upper floor," he wrote, "and some five years later the fact that the tile pavement on both sides had been worn to a considerable depth along the line where the cases stood, gave testimony to the interest excited in the general public."

A second Paris Exposition, this one in 1900, produced an even more eye-opening display of philanthropy by Morgan. Again he sent Kunz on a treasure hunt, this time across the world, spending an estimated one million of his own dollars in the effort. The resulting display at the Exposition won a grand prize before proceeding to the Museum. Together, the two Morgan-Tiffany collections contained 2,176 gems and minerals and 2,442 pearls, including many rare and scientifically valuable specimens.

Throughout the first decades of this century, the Museum's trove of gems and minerals continued to grow, with Kunz himself donating many fine specimens. With the opening of the current halls in 1976, the fruit of Kunz's labors—and those of many others—can be seen in all their glory.

Strolling through the halls, or even looking at a photograph of one of the gem or mineral treasures, it's hard not to think that the limpid green of an emerald, the sparkle of a star sapphire, or the red fire of a ruby is the product of magic, not science. Magic has in fact been associated with gems and crystals for many centuries. According to current Earth and Planetary Sciences Curator George Harlow, "Magic isn't necessary for these gems and crystals to be wonderful, even transcendental—but we still do have a medieval desire to have magic in our lives, and our fascination with these stones reflects that."

George Kunz, Curator Herbert P. Whitlock, and Harlow himself have written about the magical qualities attributed to gems. Kunz seemed to take a special pleasure in detailing the myths and legends surrounding them, returning to the subject again and again in his voluminous writings.

One example: In *Shakespeare and Precious Stones* (1916), a book typical of his wide-ranging literary interests, Kunz discusses every reference to gems in the Bard's work and traces Shakespeare's allusions as far back as recorded history will allow. Following a quote from the poem "Lover's Complaint" ("The deep-green emerald, in whose fresh regard/Weak sights their sickly radiance do amend"), Kunz adds, "This proves the poet's familiarity with the idea that gazing on an emerald benefited weak sight, an idea expressed as far back as 300 B.C. by Theophrastus, a pupil of Aristotle, and repeated by the Roman Pliny in 75 A.D."

The "magical" qualities of emeralds were of particular fascination to Kunz, who went into greater detail in *The Curious Lore of Precious Stones* (1913), perhaps his best-known book. Referring often to his own library of centuries-old manuscripts, Kunz spins tales of the emerald's ability to reveal truth. This ability was, he pointed out, a definite threat to magicians, "who found all their arts of no avail if an emerald were in their vicinity when they began to weave their spells."

Nor was the emerald alone in supposedly having magical powers. Writing in *The Curious Lore of Precious Stones*, Kunz points out that the sapphire had long been considered a regal gem, and that kings wore it about their necks as a defense against harm. "The sapphire was like the pure sky, and mighty Nature had endowed it with so great a power that it might be called sacred and the gem of gems," Kunz writes. "Fraud was banished from its presence and necromancers honored it more than any other stone, for it enabled them to hear and to understand the obscurest oracles."

Legend says that the star sapphire is particularly powerful. Kunz tells of how the great adventurer Sir Richard Burton owned a large star sapphire (also called an "asteria") which he carried with him as a talisman on his travels, "for it always brought him good horses and prompt attention wherever he went."

The origins of the Museum's 563-carat Star of India, the largest star sapphire ever found, have a mysterious quality that befit a gem of such magnificence. Presented by J. P. Morgan in 1900, the Star (originally mined in Sri Lanka) has "a more or less indefinite historic record of some three centuries," according to Kunz, but he never deigned to tell what that record was or where the gem went during its "many wanderings." "If only we knew the sights this stone may have seen!" write Museum geologists George Harlow and Anna S. Sofianides in *Gems & Crystals from the American Museum of Natural History*, adding, undeniably: "No matter, the Star of India is magnificent."

For many decades, the Museum's main focus on gems and minerals involved collecting and displaying them. In-depth study of the collection rarely took place, largely—according to today's staff—because between 1869 and 1976 the department could never claim more than a single full-time curator. "For two years in the 1970s there was actually no curator at all," says Martin Prinz, curator of the meteorite collection, who came to the Museum in 1976. "Finally, a committee was formed to decide: Do we abandon more than one hundred years of history, or do we build a new department?"

The ultimate decision was to rebuild. Today, Earth and Planetary Sciences includes four curators (Prinz, Edmond Mathez, George Harlow, and Associate Curator James Webster, who is also Physical Sciences division chair) and numerous other staff members.

George Harlow, curator of the mineral and gem collections, is showing in his work that these treasures are far more than merely beautiful, magical objects. "Gems and crystals are fascinating and beautiful—they have immediacy," he says. "That's a great hook: Once you have someone's attention, you've overcome the greatest challenge, and you can begin to show them things about mineralogy in general that are stunning and revealing."

Rocks and minerals, for example, can provide insights into some of the central questions of earth science, including the most basic: How was our planet created? "This is our ultimate origin myth, the ultimate question: Where did we come from?" Harlow says. "The chemistry of crystals that are found deep in the earth can give us clues to our origins."

Harlow is particularly interested in the processes taking place in the earth's mantle, the vast region that lies between the earth's solid crust and metallic core and comprises about eighty-four percent of the planet's volume. Yet, since no one has ever directly observed even its uppermost boundaries, studying the mantle involves painstaking analyses of the composition and chemistry of rocks created there and then brought to the surface by natural processes (such as volcanic eruptions) or by researchers.

These analyses, by casting new light on how rocks are created in the mantle, can provide important insights into the creation of the earth itself. But, as in every scientific discipline, the first steps to gaining such insights involve basic research—that is, determining the composition of the mantle and learning how it differs from our conceptions.

Harlow, for example, has long studied the crystal chemistry of pyroxenes and amphiboles, mineral groups formed at high pressures in the mantle. He is particularly interested in how pressures enable these minerals to accept elements that are not found in samples formed at low pressures.

In one surprising finding, he and his colleagues discovered that pyroxenes found in diamonds were rich in potassium. This showed that these pyroxenes must have been formed in a region far richer in potassium than was previously thought possible in the earth's mantle, as well as demonstrating their potential for incorporating potassium at high pressure.

To study the composition of minerals, Harlow uses a variety of technologies and devices, including the electron microprobe, which focuses a beam of electrons on a piece of mineral, exciting the electrons within the mineral, and causing them to release X rays of specific energies. The electron probe then determines the intensity of these X rays, allowing precise and detailed analysis of the different elements within the mineral. Without this and other devices, Harlow and his colleagues would never be able to gain such important clues to the creation of these minerals; with such technologies, they can begin to draw a more complete, more accurate picture of geologic processes than ever before.

While the Earth's unseen mantle provides a rich source of information, other fascinating processes are taking place right on the surface. According to Harlow, one of the most exciting new directions in mineralogy concentrates not on the rocks themselves, but on how they interact biologically with the environment. "In essence, we're focusing on the fact that rocks are out there, exposed to air and water," he explains. "The rocks weather, and as they weather they release certain substances and absorb others from the air and water. But we have very little idea of how the process occurs on a molecular level—and we need to answer those questions before we truly understand what's happening, for example, when air, water, and minerals interact at toxic waste sites."

Another new frontier involves study of interactions between minerals and the human body. "After all, our bodies produce stones, and our limbs are essentially minerals," Harlow points out. "Medical researchers have developed a technique in which they take a particular kind of coral with the right porosity, heat it, sterilize it, and use it as a bone implant. Because of the coral's structure, the surrounding real bone will grow over and replace it, creating new bone where otherwise there wouldn't have been any."

Such discoveries are frequently based solely on empirical evidence, Harlow says. "But now we've begun looking at the mechanics of how these processes work. Mineralogy is a mature science—most of the minerals have been named, most of the big questions answered—and now we've been waiting for the science's next big paradigm shift. I think we're seeing it in surface interactions, bio-mineralogy, and medicine."

The Soul of an Emerald

The twelve-sided, 632-carat Patricia emerald isn't only one of the Museum's treasures—it's one of the largest and most spectacular emeralds ever found. Discovered in the Chivor Mine in the Colombian Andes in 1920 and donated to the Museum in the 1950s, it also recalls a fascinating story of age-old tradition and brutal conquest.

Historians believe that Chivor was first worked by the Chibcha Indians in the thirteenth century. The emeralds excavated from this rich mine were used as spiritual offerings by Chibcha chiefs and priests, and the fame surrounding the gems spread so far that other pre-Colombian civilizations—including the Maya, Aztecs, and Inka—sent emissaries to trade for the most beautiful stones.

When the Spanish *conquistadores* arrived in Colombia in the sixteenth century, they too became enamored of the emeralds' beauty. Crushing all resistance among the Chibcha, torturing those who refused to reveal the source of the gems, the Spanish soldiers soon located Chivor (then called "Somondoco"). The soldiers immediately took over the mine, conscripting local Indians as slave labor to continue the mining process.

The mistreatment of the enslaved miners continued for more than a century, ending only when mismanagement caused the haul of emeralds to dwindle, resulting in the mine's closing in 1675. The surrounding jungle encroached and, remarkably, soon the site of this great mine was lost to history.

It might have been lost forever had not a Colombian mining engineer named Don Francisco Restrepo discovered a three-hundred-dred-year-old manuscript in a Dominican convent in Quito,

Ecuador in the late nineteenth century. The manuscript described the mine's location and gave some pertinent geographical details of the surrounding mountains and plains. After eight years' search, Restrepo rediscovered Chivor and began to redevelop it— a process which took an additional fifteen years.

Finally, beginning in 1911, full work at the mine resumed. Again Chivor began to produce glorious emeralds, with the hope that someday another as spectacular as the Patricia emerald will appear.

MYSTERIES OF THE LIVING EARTH

> I find high-risk research fascinating. I know we're pursuing something that is on the very edges of respectability, but I don't care. I think you have to follow interesting ideas, even if there's a good chance that they're wrong—because otherwise, how will you ever know if they might be right?
>
> —*Curator Edmond Mathez, on his studies of the possible interrelationship among electrical phenomena, fractured rocks, and earthquakes.*

How does someone decide to study earth science?

For Edmond Mathez, at least part of the answer is simple. "Many, many geology students get interested because they simply love to be outdoors," he says. "They're rock climbers, they camp in the mountains under the stars, and at some point they begin to wonder: How did those rocks get there? They want answers, so they begin to study geology."

At first, Mathez continues, "you're out in the mountains and the fields because it's fun. Eventually that sense of play evolves into a deeper enjoyment of your work, but the fundamental sense of play remains, even when the work requires enormous financial and family sacrifices."

Earth science is so enjoyable to Mathez and others because they don't see the planet as just a mass of dead, static rock. To them, the earth is constantly evolving, constantly changing. Merely asking the question, "How did those rocks get there?" (and then discovering that they had been created in the Earth's mantle, and were somehow uplifted to a 12,000-foot mountainside) demonstrates the vitality of both the planet and the scientific discipline that studies it.

It's no surprise that geologists find themselves drawn to two of the most dramatic, unpredictable events that characterize the living earth, earthquakes and erupting volcanoes. Over the years, Museum scientists have been no exception, and on at least two occasions curators have risked their lives to get close to volcanic eruptions, to glimpse a portal to the fiery processes that are always taking place deep beneath the earth's crust.

The more famous of the two occasions took place in May 1902, when Museum President Morris K. Jesup sent geologist Edmund Otis Hovey to Martinique. Just a few days before Hovey set out, a catastrophic eruption of Mt. Pelée had destroyed the city of St. Pierre, causing the death of all but one of the city's 30,000 inhabitants (the one survivor: a prisoner saved because his cell was below ground).

Hovey spent several days charting the topography of the eruption of Pelée and another volcano, Soufrière, which had erupted at the same time on the nearby island of St. Vincent. He risked his life to get within yards of Pelée's still violently active crater (which he described as "a scene of wild and terrifying grandeur"), collected specimens of lava and other volcanic rock, and resolutely refused to describe the horrors that he had seen in the ruined city.

Forty years later, Frederick Pough, chairman of the department, had the opportunity to witness a far less catastrophic but even more significant event, the birth of a volcano near the town of Paricutín, in Michoacán State, Mexico, in early 1943.

According to Pough, the most reliable story describing the volcano's earliest days came from a local farmer, who stumbled upon a smoking fissure in one of his fields. By the time he returned with other witnesses, a small cinder cone was already emitting loud rumblings and ejecting dust and small rocks.

At first, the cone grew larger only gradually. "Visitors commenced coming as soon as the news reached the larger communities, and the early comers had the pleasure of being able to drive their cars almost to the foot of the rapidly growing cone," Pough wrote in *Natural History* later in 1943. "Easy-chair sight-seeing with considerable traffic congestion on a road never intended for such wear, continued for some weeks, while the volcano piled its hot blocks ever higher."

The volcano (christened Paricutín) soon began to grow more active. A lava flow created a semicircular twenty-foot-tall plateau topped by jagged fifty-foot peaks around the cone, which itself grew more and more rapidly. "By the fourth month since its formation the cone had risen to about 1000 feet," Pough reported. "Above this towered a tremendous column of black dust, rising over six miles in the air and shedding a shower of coarse and fine particles over an area of many square miles."

Arriving on the scene, Pough explored the ashfall (in some places nine feet deep); watched the volcano send out huge "volcanic bombs," molten rocks that cooled in fantastic shapes as they flew through the air, often shattering explosively upon hitting the ground; and recorded the fact that lightning not associated with any storm (Pough believed it to be caused by static electricity) did in fact crackle about the cone—a phenomenon long suspected to be the product of the vivid imaginations of those who had witnessed earlier eruptions.

In Hovey's time, and even in Pough's, the study of volcanoes largely involved observing an eruption and its effects and attempting to devise an accurate portrait of a volcano's "behavior." Museum scientists, including Edmond Mathez and Division Chair and Associate Curator James Webster, choose to study the Earth's magma (what lava is called before it reaches the surface through a volcanic eruption) from a far more research-oriented perspective. These scientists are working on the frontiers of Earth science, analyzing little-understood phenomena and pushing the limits of both the technology needed for analysis and their own ability to interpret the implications of any results.

Webster studies what are called "volatiles," found within magmas: water, carbon dioxide, chlorine, fluorine, and other compounds that remain dissolved in the magma as long as it is confined underground, but turn into gas when reaching the surface during a volcanic eruption.

These volatiles play an important role in driving eruptions, Webster says, using the image of a bottle of seltzer to illustrate his point. "When closed, the bottle has carbon dioxide gas at some pressure above the seltzer and below the cap, as well as carbon dioxide dissolved in the liquid," he explains. "Pop the cap, and bubbles appear—the carbon dioxide in the liquid, released from the confining pressure, turns into gas and escapes."

An erupting volcano follows a similar progression. "The eruption of Mount St. Helens is a great example," Webster says. "The magma near the surface had a lot of water and carbon dioxide dissolved in it. Then there was a sudden faulting at the surface that removed the confining pressure of the rock—identical to popping the top off a bottle of seltzer—and the result was an eruption driven by these released volatiles."

Webster also probes the behavior of another volatile, chlorine, in certain types of magma, lava, and volcanic gases. This research may provide important clues to understanding the atmosphere's chemistry, as certain chlorine compounds, present in the atmosphere in gaseous form, have been implicated as possible causes of acid rain, depletion of the earth's ozone layer, and global warming.

On another tack, also involving chlorine, Webster is studying deposits of lead, tin, copper, zinc, and other ore metals that are found near magmas. It turns out that dissolved chlorine tends to bond to metals in magma; then, when underground streams of hot water run through the magma, the water carries both the chlorine and concentrated amounts of ore to a new location.

"We're interested in the relationship between chlorine concentrations and what metals come out of the magma," Webster says. "Ideally, if we can measure the volatiles that remain in a piece of volcanic rock—inclusions of glass inside a volcanic crystal, for example, often contain trapped volatiles—we can predict whether the magma that produced the rock would have created an ore deposit."

This possibility remains unfulfilled so far, Webster acknowledges. "At least we may be able to eliminate some of the trial-and-error involved in locating ore deposits, by ruling out the possibility that a certain magma would have created a deposit," he says. "That advance alone would provide a tremendous commercial benefit to economic geologists."

Ed Mathez's study of magma involves precise analysis of trace elements (minute quantities of certain elements) found in different minerals. Analyzing rocks found in the Bushveld Complex, South Africa, which formed from cooling magma, he has determined that the rocks' formation was influenced by the reaction of the partially crystalline rocks with magma and fluids flowing through them. In studying the geochemical changes which these fluids exert on rocks—changes that he believes are fundamental to the evolution of rocks in the Earth's crust and mantle and of platinum and other ore deposits—Mathez is focusing on yet one more of geology's surprising frontiers.

Mathez has also turned his attention to another of the Earth's mysterious—and cataclysmic—events, earthquakes. Typically, however, he has approached this interest from an unexpected direction. He was studying submarine basalts, which are lavas that erupt on the ocean floor under great pressure, and was particularly interested in inclusions of the melted rock that were trapped by growing crystals in the basalts.

Using an electron microprobe to study the inclusions, Mathez discovered that each one was bisected by a minuscule microcrack. Unexpectedly, he found that every microcrack had carbon on its surface. "It turns out that at the moment a rock cracks, carbon bonds to the newly exposed surfaces."

Scientific research typically progresses in completely unanticipated ways, Mathez points out, and this surprising discovery led him to ask a new question: Does carbon on newly cracked rocks have any effect on the rocks' electrical conductivity? "Specifically, I'm interested in what happens when rocks break during earthquakes," he says. "I'm studying whether carbon has some influence on the processes that take place prior to earthquakes, such as the bizarre electrical disturbances that are well-known earthquake precursor phenomena, but whose causes are not known."

Mathez describes the study methods he and his colleagues are using: "Currently, we're taking little cylinders of rock and crushing them at high temperature and pressure—400–450 degrees Celsius and 1,000 atmospheres. We're creating fractures as

slowly as we can, and then monitoring changes in electrical conductivity of the rock."

The problem, of course, is that laboratory conditions can only
simulate the conditions that exist in nature, not precisely dupli-
cate them. Before an earthquake, rocks may in fact begin to form
microcracks very slowly. Science must attempt to reproduce in a
few hours a process that may actually take place over days, even
years.

"If I had to venture an opinion, I'd say that these experiments
to test our theory will probably fail, either because we can't do
the experiments correctly or because we can't demonstrate what
we hope to," Mathez acknowledges. "That's the risk of high-risk
research, but I think the possibility of failure is less important
than the importance of bringing our imaginations to bear on
these unanswered questions."

Our Dynamic Planet

Listen to the scientists in the Division of Physical Sciences,
and you'll hear them return again and again to the same
theme: the earth isn't just a hunk of dead rock that we happen to
live on. It's a volatile, ever-changing, sometimes dangerous place,
as alive as any inanimate object can possibly be.

In 1999, the Museum unveiled its new Hall of Planet Earth, a
spectacular new exhibit that portrays the living Earth in all its
glory. Videos, computers, and an abundance of creative displays
demonstrate the relationship between the Earth and everything
that inhabits it. Perhaps the most stunning of the displays focus
on volcanoes, long a particular interest of the Museum's scientists and currently the chief research interest of Curators James
Webster and Ed Mathez.

Video screens show scientists perched on the rim of active volcanoes, sampling the gases emitted from the smoking cones. Photos, more videos, and text detail the process leading to explosive eruptions, such as the catastrophic eruptions of Mt. Vesuvius, St. Helens, and Pinatubo, all characterized by the spewing of lava, hot rocks, and ash over a wide area.

Scientists are equally interested in effusive eruptions, where volcanoes expel basalt from the Earth's mantle. Basalt is a fluid lava that doesn't erupt explosively, but forms extremely hot flows that often resemble glowing rivers.

The best-known example of effusive eruptions can be found on the island of Hawaii, where such flows are a common sight in Hawaii Volcanoes National Park. But effusive eruptions most often happen deep undersea, where they build into great mountain ranges known as mid-ocean ridge systems. Researchers are particularly interested in effusive eruptions that bring magma (molten rock) up from deep in the earth to penetrate moving tectonic plates at the surface.

Such undersea effusive eruptions, enormous enough to create the entire chain of Hawaiian Islands, are among the most vivid examples of the earth's remarkable dynamism. No visitor to the Hall of Planet Earth will ever mistake our planet for a hunk of old rock again.

METEORITES: INTERPLANETARY WANDERERS

People will always be fascinated by meteorites. Every year I get many, many requests to examine some piece of rock that someone thinks might be a meteorite. I'm sorry when I have to say that it's not of extraterrestrial origin, that it's just a rock or piece of industrial slag—people are so disappointed that I think they usually don't believe me.

—*Martin Prinz, Curator of the Museum's*
meteorite collection.

Usually, we depend on scientists to interpret the mysteries of the natural world for us. How a caterpillar metamorphoses into a butterfly, how salmon can migrate hundreds of miles to breed in the exact spot where they were born, even why some species go extinct while others thrive—these phenomena would seem like magic if not for the concrete explanations science can provide.

But in one important instance, the public has been way ahead of the experts. Since ancient times, people have reported seeing stones falling from the sky. One stone, which fell in Phrygia, had been widely known for centuries when it was moved to Rome in 204 B.C., a move considered so significant that the ceremonies attending it were recorded in contemporary histories. A shower of stones was reported to have fallen near Rome as early as 652 B.C., and yet another stone, which fell in the fifth century B.C., was so famous that the Roman scholar Pliny the Elder (who, incidentally, died during an eruption of the volcano Vesuvius in A.D. 79) wrote of it five hundred years later.

Nor were European civilizations the only ones to have recorded the fall of glowing stones from the sky. Societies on every inhabited continent have seen, noted, and often venerated these visitors from above. In some cases, meteorites were considered sacred or magical objects. One such stone, proclaimed an image of the goddess Diana, was said to have "fallen down from Jupiter," while others were considered miracles of God and placed in churches to be worshiped.

Today, it is common knowledge that chunks of rock float through space, are occasionally pulled into the earth's atmosphere, and either burn up as meteors ("shooting stars") or reach the ground, at which point they are called "meteorites." But until just two centuries ago, western scientists flatly refused to believe that the events witnessed by so many people throughout history were actually occurring. The scientists seemed to be saying, "Who are you going to believe? Me or your own eyes?"

The experts' strenuous denials make for remarkable reading today. Even the founder of modern chemistry, the brilliant eighteenth-century French chemist Antoine-Laurent Lavoisier— whose own research was so visionary and controversial that he eventually paid for it at the guillotine—refused to believe reports of stones falling from the heavens. As part of a three-man committee in 1772, Lavoisier opined that one such stone was actually just an ordinary rock that had been sent flying after being struck by lightning.

In 1794, the German physicist E. F. F. Chladni took the time to gather reports of objects falling from the sky, and came to the inescapable conclusion that chunks of iron and stone, born somewhere outside earth, did on occasion descend to our planet. Yet what was inescapable to Chladni remained heresy to others, especially the powerful opinion makers in the French Académie Royale des Sciences.

But even the obstinate French scientists found their beliefs tested by a series of meteorite falls in the years that followed Chladni's bold announcement. A shower of stones fell at Siena, Italy, in June 1794 (the scientists said this was the product of an eruption of Mt. Vesuvius, 250 miles away); a fifty-six-pound rock crashed to earth in December 1795, in Yorkshire, England (it was created by dust particles condensing within a cloud, according to the experts); and a myriad of stones fell from a cloudless sky in India in December 1798 (the scientists couldn't explain this one, but still refused to accept Chladni's theory).

Then, in April 1803—as if finally, irrefutably, to put an end to all debate—a meteorite fall of three thousand stones took place near Paris, in L'Aigle, France. To add extra emphasis, the fall, which again took place under a clear sky, followed the appearance of a giant fireball and a huge explosion. Noted physicist and astronomer Jean-Baptiste Biot hurried to the scene, and soon the French experts made an important proclamation: Stones did, in fact, descend from the sky down to earth.

Not that this final 1803 announcement entirely convinced all the skeptics. Following the arrival of a meteorite in Connecticut in 1807, President Thomas Jefferson was said to have remarked that it was easier to believe that Yankee professors would lie than to believe that stones would fall from heaven.

Once convinced, however, scientists worldwide began to search for meteorites and to record the tales associated with dramatic falls. In a typical 1887 book, *A Chapter in the History of Meteorites*, for example, a British scientist with the apposite name of Walter Flight tells dozens of such stories. One fireball, witnessed in Iowa and Missouri in 1876, "was a very brilliant meteor, and a very noisy one also," Flight recounts. "A series of reports, twenty-two in number, were heard during its transit. . . . The rumbling thunder of its artillery, together with its flashes of brilliant light, brought people from their beds with an apprehension that the great Civil War had broken out afresh."

An 1882 fall in Indiana was even more dramatic. "Some men who were riding home through a very heavy snowstorm suddenly became aware of a large meteor moving near them with inconceivable rapidity and a rushing roaring noise," Flight writes. "The light was so brilliant that it blinded them, and, notwithstanding the storm, lighted the entire neighbourhood as clearly as the brightest day at noon. When nearly overhead it exploded with a tremendous report. The entire party was prostrated, horses and men, and some of them did not recover their sight until some twenty-four hours later."

Dramatic meteorite falls still take place, of course. Perhaps the most famous recent one occurred on October 9, 1992, when a fireball was witnessed by thousands of observers as it traveled from western Pennsylvania to New York before crashing into a car in the New York City suburb of Peekskill. The portion of this meteorite now in the Museum's collection still has the car's red paint on its surface.

According to Curator Martin Prinz, the fact that the meteor was so widely observed had important scientific implications. "We were lucky. The meteorite fell on a Friday night in October, which is prime high-school football night," he says. "So there were many parents outside with their video cameras already on, and they taped the meteor as it went past."

As a result of this fortuity, scientists were able for only the fourth time to trace a meteor's trajectory accurately. By following the fireball's course across the sky, the videotapes allowed scientists to calculate the meteor's path back to its origin, the asteroid belt that lies between Mars and Jupiter. "As it happens, all four meteors whose trajectory we know come from the asteroid belt," Prinz says.

Throughout the 1800s and until early in this century, the public seemed endlessly fascinated by meteors and meteorites. Henry A. Ward, whose famous Ward's Natural Science Establishment supplied museums and collectors with dinosaur skeletons, precious gems, ancient corals, skins, mounted specimens, and countless other objects, was so enamored of these extraterrestrial visitors that he nearly abandoned his interest in anything else.

"I am given over—mind and heart—to my Meteorites," he wrote to the Museum in 1899. In a letter to Ward four years later, Museum geologist L. P. Gratacap wrote in wonderment, "The mysteries of the Celestials claim all your attention. It is curious to speculate what may become of you in another world. Unless supplied with meteorites I suspect you will be quite unhappy."

Ward was not alone in his determination to uncover and collect meteorites, as is shown by the stories behind several magnificent specimens in the Museum's collection. The famous Cape York meteorite (including the masses called "Ahnighito," "the Woman," and "the Dog") were first shown to the explorer Robert E. Peary by Greenland Eskimos in 1894, and Peary made several attempts to retrieve the meteorites from their harsh, icy home before finally succeeding in 1897. Another famous meteorite, Willamette, was so hotly desired following its discovery in Oregon in 1902 that the state supreme court had to decide ownership.

Yet, according to Martin Prinz, by the early 1900s scientific interest in meteorites had dwindled. Scientists had learned that most belong to one of three broad categories: irons, composed mainly of metallic iron and nickel; stony meteorites, composed of a variety of minerals mainly made up of silicon and magnesium oxides; and stony irons, rarer types that are composed of a mix of metals and stones. "Having undertaken comparatively crude analyses of meteorite compositions, they'd discovered everything that their technology allowed them to," Prinz comments. "There was very little left to learn at that time, and the study of meteorites entered some barren years."

This fallow period actually lasted until 1957, when the Russian launch of Sputnik brought a new, cold-war focus to planetary science. "At about the same time, the development of the electron microprobe gave us a far more powerful and sensitive tool for analyzing the composition of meteorites," Prinz says. "Using the microprobe, I could take a piece of dust, do about a hundred analyses of its content, and then hand you the dust back. And the electron microprobe is just one of an array of new devices for analyzing meteorites."

Before coming to the Museum, Prinz studied moon rocks

brought back by the Apollo missions in the early 1970s. When moon landings were abandoned, and no new samples were forthcoming, he broadened his focus, joining the Museum staff in 1976 as curator of the meteorite collection, and also to study the increasing number of unusual meteorites that have turned up in recent years.

"In the two hundred years that science has recognized the existence of meteorites, about three thousand have been found outside of Antarctica," Prinz says. "Of course, one meteorite might include thousands of different pieces—as is the case with Canyon Diablo, the meteorite that caused the giant crater in Arizona—or just a single chip."

Three thousand meteorites seems like a surprisingly small number, but this total only paints a fraction of the true picture. Since 1969, when a team of Japanese geologists stumbled across some meteorites while studying Antarctic mountain ranges, scientists have retrieved an astounding 15,000 meteorites from Antarctica. One American geologist, a man named Bill Cassidy, led expeditions that collected between seven and eight thousand Antarctic meteorites—or more than twice as many as have been found on the rest of the earth combined. Japanese scientists have collected a similar number during their expeditions to Antarctica.

It turns out that Antarctica's "frozen desert" conditions—the driest of continents, it receives virtually no precipitation—are nearly perfect for the preservation of meteorites, which weather away very quickly in most earth environments. This means that, prior to the first scientific exploration, nearly every meteorite that has ever fallen on Antarctica was still sitting there, waiting to be discovered.

Far more important than the quantity of Antarctica's meteorites are their quality, Prinz says. "Of course, most of what's been found there is similar to what we already have," he says. "But Antarctica also has given us some extremely rare specimens, and even twelve moon rocks that were ejected from the moon's surface during a violent meteorite impact and ended up here."

One Antarctic specimen that Prinz recently analyzed reveals the chemical complexity of the environments in which some meteorites have formed—as well as what they have to teach us. This meteorite belongs to a rare group known as ureilites, but differs from other ureilites by containing abundant chromite and carbon minerals, including graphite. Previously unknown interactions between the chromite, carbon, and other minerals in the meteorite resulted in the production of the rare minerals brezinaite and eskolaite, and even one mineral that is yet unnamed.

Prinz believes that this specimen originated deep within a planetary body, and must have been thrown into space when the planet collided with a very large comet, asteroid, or other object, and broke apart. As an editorial comment in the Museum's 1993–94 *Annual Report* says of this surprising meteorite, "It is a stark reminder that our present sampling of the solar system is far from complete."

Prinz takes an even broader view, pointing out that meteorites are composed of material created billions of years ago, and thus provide an invaluable window to the distant past and its geologic processes. "I see meteorites as history books that can tell us about the creation of the solar system and of the earth itself," he says. "Right now all we have are 'dead bodies,' but if we study them carefully enough, they can help us reconstruct the crime."

Is It a Meteorite?

Meteors are the most public of scientific phenomena. You don't have to be a scientist to watch a shooting star or to witness the fall of a meteorite. Anyone lucky enough to be in the right place at the right time can boast of the next great meteorite find.

Of course, not every chunk of rock that looks like a meteorite actually is one, but this doesn't stop the public from being eternally, even incorrigibly, hopeful. Writing in the Museum newsletter the *Grapevine* in 1937, Curator Herbert Whitlock told a typical story, of a veterinarian who arrived at the Museum one day carrying a roundish object that he claimed was a meteorite.

According to Whitlock, the veterinarian's story went like this: "He was standing just inside his barn door when he heard a distinct rap upon the roof, and stepping out found the messenger from the stars lying on the ground at his feet. What else could it be but a meteorite?"

Whitlock was skeptical. He believed the object to be a calculus, a stony mass that forms around a foreign object inside the stomach of a cow and is then ejected. But the curator offered to cut the object in two to study it further. When the two halves were returned, "it was found that the band saw had exactly divided the wire nail in the middle of the supposed meteorite," Whitlock wrote. "As I subsequently pointed out to my friend, the veterinary, if the thing was not a stomach calculus, but a meteorite, why then the gates of Heaven must be put together with wire nails."

5   Tiny Glories of Biodiversity

EARLY INSIGHTS

> Lest donors may hesitate to give collections which cannot be generally exhibited, it may be well to say that the collections now hid away in drawers and apparently useless are of great value for study purposes. Many of them show transitions in pattern and color between species and species and between species and varieties which have a direct bearing on important problems of evolution.
>
> —*Unsigned editorial note on the Museum's largely undisplayed butterfly collection, published in the* American Museum Journal, *1900.*

Entomologist David Grimaldi, curator in the Division of Invertebrate Zoology, wants visitors to know that little has changed in a century at the Museum. "We have half of all the described diversity on earth in one room here at the Museum—in many ways, we are biodiversity," he points out. "Without the work done on insects and spiders here, science would never have developed the theories of evolution that allow us, for example, to create a cladistic design for our new dinosaur halls."

The connection between entomology, taxonomy, and evolution at the Museum dates back for as long as its scientists have been studying insects. Learn a little about the department's immense (almost incomprehensibly large) collection, and it's easy to see why.

"Currently, we have at least eighteen million specimens of at least three hundred thousand insect and spider species—and the true number may actually be closer to five hundred thousand," Grimaldi explains. What is even more remarkable is that this collection comprises only a fraction of the species that exist on earth today. The true number of species of arthropods (the group that contains insects, spiders, and crustaceans) is so large, and so unstudied, that reputable scientists have estimated the number as ranging anywhere from 5 million to 30 million species.

That compares to about nine thousand bird species and fewer than thirty thousand fish species—and fish boast the greatest diversity of all vertebrates. As Curator and former Entomology Chairman Norman Platnick has written: "Let me be blunt: speaking of biodiversity is essentially equivalent to speaking about arthropods. In terms of numbers of species, other animal and plant groups are just a gloss on the arthropod theme."

From its earliest days, the Museum has been engaged in a never-ending effort to expand the collection. The first accession came in 1870, before the first Museum building had been erected. As a result, this gift of 3,800 beetles from Baron von Osten-Sacken, Russian consul-general in New York, had to be stored downtown in the offices of a Wall Street banking firm.

By the time Curator William Beutenmüller (1864–1934) came to the Museum in 1888, the collection was still tiny, but at least there were storage rooms to keep it in. As the department's sole full-time curator, Beutenmüller was forced "to be in turn lepidopterist, coleopterist, orthopterist, dipterist, hymenopterist, and a number of other 'ists,' " as a Museum biography put it, describing an individual who studies, respectively, moths and butterflies; beetles; roaches, mantids, and grasshoppers; flies, and wasps, ants, and bees. Given this almost overwhelming challenge, he succeeded in publishing a steady series of papers on different insect groups, including his specialty, moths.

Beutenmüller and the Museum administration were also concerned with displaying important specimens to the public, especially those insects found in the New York City region. The *Journal* described a 1900 exhibit containing nearly ten thousand specimens: "The long ellipse of cases in the centre of the hall, containing phalanx after phalanx of shield-backed beetles, little and big, of grasshoppers, crickets, moths, butterflies, are suggestive of the far-off ages of coal formation when multitudes of rustling insects must have everywhere crowded the sultry air."

Beutenmüller's efforts to expand the collection included a half-dozen expeditions between 1895 and 1911 to the Black Mountains of North Carolina. This region's isolated mountain ranges and valleys contain many insect species found nowhere else, enabling the curator to collect more than thirty thousand specimens of more than a thousand insect and spider species.

Beutenmüller's successor as curator, Frank E. Lutz, took the department's collecting efforts to new horizons. As early as 1914 he was organizing trips to Cuba. "We beat the insects and spiders off the trees into umbrellas; swept the vegetation with nets; chased the creatures flying in the blazing sun; chopped into logs and dug into the white, hot sand," Lutz wrote of the Cuba expedition in a 1914 *Journal* article. The result was an accumulation of more than ten thousand specimens, many of which were new to science.

After his Cuba forays, Lutz focused on collecting insects closer to home, describing new species sent in by other collectors, and essaying innovative experiments on insect behavior. In one series of studies, he measured the amount of ultraviolet light (invisible to us, but not to many arthropods) reflected by different flowers, insects, and spiders, with a goal of understanding how the world looks to what he called "its principal inhabitants."

In one conclusion, reported in a 1933 *Natural History* article, he pointed out that most yellow flowers reflect a substantial amount of ultraviolet light. "In this connection a yellow spider much given to hiding in yellow flowers is interesting," he wrote. "According to theory, the yellow color of the spider prevents flower-visiting insects from seeing it against the background of a yellow flower in time to avoid being caught. However, the spider is only slightly ultraviolet and, so, to an insect that can see ultraviolet the yellow spider must be rather conspicuous as it sits on a yellow-ultraviolet flower."

Lutz was also an early proponent of allowing nature, rather than blanket spraying of insecticides, to combat insect pests such as the tent caterpillar, blamed for destroying groves of ornamental and fruit-bearing trees. "The tent caterpillar has been bound by a 'Balance of Nature' between it and its environment, including its diseases and insect enemies, in such a way that in any given district the years of caterpillar abundance have been followed by years of scarcity with astounding regularity," he pointed out in an ahead-of-its-time 1936 article in *Natural History*. "On the other hand, if the balance has been disturbed— well, the result will be interesting scientifically but possibly not pleasing to the wayside committees of garden clubs. When Man interferes with Nature's biological set-up, he is very apt to make a mess of it."

Victims of an Ongoing War

The Museum's giant model of an *Anopheles*, the malaria mosquito, never fails to draw a crowd. At seventy-five times life size, this insect is a real eye-catcher for even a casual visitor. For anyone familiar with the Museum's history, however, this display has a haunting resonance. Since the first paleontologists, entomologists, and other researchers ventured into the field a century ago, malaria and the Museum staff have known each other all too well.

Some of these encounters have been fatal. Mammalogist and anatomist Harry C. Raven, one of the most prominent curators at the Museum during the first half of the century, died at age 55 in 1944 after a long, painful struggle with the disease. In 1965, ornithologist E. T. Gilliard died (at only 53) of a heart attack, contributed to by decades of recurrent malarial fevers and years of increasingly toxic treatments for the disease.

Even as recently as 1978, decades after prophylactic treatment with chloroquine and other drugs had supposedly eliminated the risk of contracting malaria, another leading Museum curator found out differently. Mammalogist Richard Van Gelder was traveling in Kenya when, as he reported in *Natural History*, "a mosquito bit me. Since I am seldom bitten by mosquitoes, I remember it clearly. As that mosquito bit, its saliva carried into my blood some tiny organisms that had been waiting in its salivary gland for this moment."

These organisms were microscopic protozoans called *"Plasmodium falciparum."* Since Van Gelder had been taking his chloroquine, most of the protozoans were killed by the drug circulating in his bloodstream. But not all. "It is those few that did not succumb that have made medical history," he wrote.

When Van Gelder finished his course of chloroquine, the *P. falciparum* population in his bloodstream exploded. "By April 30, some six weeks after the mosquito had bitten me, there were as many as 200 parasites in every drop of my blood, perhaps a billion in my whole body." He had become the first reported individual to be infected with chloroquine-resistant malaria by a mosquito in Africa.

Van Gelder's report of the travails that followed make for frightening reading. For months, he suffered recurrent fevers (as high as 104.5 degrees Fahrenheit), chills, anemia, an enlarged liver, and other symptoms. And though drugs eventually cured him of the disease, his bout with malaria left marks that lasted the rest of his life. "He wasn't yet fifty years old when he contracted malaria," says his daughter Leslie, "but he came out of the experience an old man. He never again had the energy and strength he'd always had before."

What is the cost of malaria? "For me, it meant ninety-two days out of work, twenty of which I spent in hospitals," said Van Gelder, as well as the less quantifiable long-term effects. For the world as a whole, the costs are incalculable. In 1996, the Centers for Disease Control and Prevention placed the number of people affected by malaria each year at a staggering 300 million. Although new prophylactic medications can now prevent chloroquine-resistant strains of the disease, no expert believes that the protozoans have "lost" and that modern medicine has "won." Quite the reverse: the struggle against malaria is clearly an ongoing war whose final battle is at best years away—and whose ultimate fate remains frighteningly in doubt.

STORIES OF INFINITE COMPLEXITY

How important are insects and other arthropods? Important enough that scientists from other departments study them, along with those of us in Entomology. I think that at any given time, a third of the biologists in this Museum are studying various arthropod species.

—Entomologist David Grimaldi.

Almost since the birth of science at the American Museum, curators in the departments of invertebrates, animal behavior, and others have chosen to focus on insects and spiders. While William Beutenmüller was the sole member of the entomology department, another prominent entomologist was also working at the Museum: William Morton Wheeler, curator of the Department of Invertebrate Zoology from 1903 to 1908 and a specialist in ants.

Even decades later, the intensity and excitement that Wheeler brought to his research on ants are still vivid. He wrote close to two hundred papers on the subject. A glance at the contents of just the 1905 and 1906 *Bulletin*s reveals that he contributed fourteen of the fifty-five articles published in those years. Thirteen were about ants, on subjects ranging from descriptions of new species to interpretations of ant behavior. In 1922, long after he'd moved on to Harvard University (becoming a Museum research associate), he wrote a monumental, eleven-hundred-page *Bulletin* on the "Ants of the American Museum Congo Expedition." Seventy-five years later, it remains one of the longest and most comprehensive *Bulletin* articles ever published.

Wheeler was particularly fascinated by the life history and evolution of the parasitic and slave-making ants. Queens of parasitic species invade the nests of other ant species, are "adopted," and then enlist the help of the workers to raise their offspring.

Slave-making species invade alien nests en masse, killing or driving away the queen and workers, and carrying off the larvae and pupae. When the captured pupae hatch and grow into adulthood, they are used to gather food, to rear their captors' young, and to perform other tasks—in other words, as slaves.

Wheeler was not the last Museum scientist to be fascinated by parasitic and slave-making ants. Forty years later, entomologist T. C. Schneirla, curator of the now-defunct Department of Animal Behavior, intensively studied the behavior of army ants, those extraordinary species whose enormous colonies sweep across the rain-forest floor, overwhelming and consuming all insects and other small creatures in their path.

Schneirla was especially interested in the patterns of army-ant behavior. He found that the onward march of the army was based not on the commands of a leader but on a complicated set of stimuli (including the character of the terrain and presence or absence of prey) that "approximate the principles of hydraulics even more closely than those of military tactics," he and Gerard Piel wrote in a 1948 *Scientific American* article. "[R]aiding activity as such is only incidental to the process. Its essential character is determined by the stereotypical behavior of the individual ant with its limited repertory of responses to external stimuli."

These limitations occasionally lead to an unexpected result, as Schneirla found when he came upon a group of army ants on a sidewalk of the research station on Panama's Barro Colorado Island. The group, containing about one thousand Eciton ants, had apparently been caught in a rainstorm that had washed away the scent trails left by the rest of the colony. Most of the ants were gathered in a cluster, but a few were marching in a circle around the periphery of the larger group.

"By noon all of the ants had joined the mill, which had now attained the diameter of a phonograph record and was rotating somewhat eccentrically at fair speed," the scientist reported. "At dawn the next day the scene of action was strewn with dead and dying Ecitons [in the absence of food, they were starving to death]. . . . By 7:30, 24 hours after the mill was first observed, the various small myremicine and dolichoderine ants of the neighborhood were busy carting away the corpses."

Schneirla found this behavior intriguing enough to study it further in his laboratory in the Museum. His explanation for why it occurs, given in the *Scientific American* article, was elegant and convincing. "The circular track represents the vector of the individual ant's centrifugal impulse to resume the march and the centripetal force of trophallaxis [a complex set of food-exchanging behaviors] that binds it to its group. Where no obstructions disturb the geometry of these forces, as in the artificial environment of the laboratory nest or of a sidewalk, the organization of a suicide mill is almost inevitable."

Fortunately, as he pointed out, nearly every natural environment has an abundance of obstructions. "The jungle terrain, with its random layout of roots and vines, leaves and stones, liberates the ant from its propensity to destroy itself and diverts it into highly adaptive patterns of behavior."

The lure of studying the natural history of insects appeals to today's entomologists, much as it did to Schneirla, because of its nearly infinite variety and complexity. "Insects teach us things that vertebrates can't," says David Grimaldi. "The intricacy of ecological relationships among insects, and between insects and plants, is unparalleled—so complicated and closely co-evolved. There's nothing like it elsewhere in the animal kingdom."

But for Grimaldi and other Museum entomologists, insect behavior, however enticing, must usually take a back seat to a far greater task: Developing a system of relationships among the species belonging to different insect families—families that may include tens of thousands of described species and countless more that are yet to be identified. This is the job that has challenged entomologists since the earliest years of the department, and that continues to fill most of their waking hours today.

EVERYTHING IN ITS PROPER PLACE

Returning from our long African journey, we were naturally keen to know the scientific results. As we got more than sixteen thousand insects, it will be readily understood that complete returns will not be available for a very long time, if ever. . . . The insects are so numerous that the entomologists, working as hard as they may, cannot classify them all. Many centuries must pass, I suppose, before we know the insects of the world as well as we now know the birds.

—*T. D. A. Cockerell, Entomology research associate
and professor at the University of Colorado,
in* Natural History, *1933.*

Call it classification, systematics, or taxonomy, the process of understanding life on earth begins with giving each species a name. On a planet that may harbor five million or more insect and spider species the completion of that job seems as distant today as it did to T. D. A. Cockerell sixty-five years ago. But that doesn't mean it isn't worth doing everything possible to identify new species and to make sure that those previously named have been placed in the correct groups.

At times the task can seem overwhelming. Grimaldi points out that even areas whose fauna has been studied remain a virtual mystery when it comes to insects. "I could send an undergrad with a net to some of the most intensively studied field stations in the neotropics—such as Barro Colorado Island in Panama—and ask him or her to swing the net several times. I guarantee that in that net will be many new species. In fact, I believe that it's most likely that only about twenty percent of the species in that net will have been previously described."

Grimaldi, although best known for his work on insects preserved in amber (see page 139 for more on this fascinating research), also studies living species of flies of the family Drosophilidae, more commonly known as fruit flies. As in any group of insects, a huge number of species remain to be discovered and described. "I'm studying one genus of South American fruit flies, which contained thirteen species when I started," he explains. "In my monograph, I'm describing 130 new species—and I believe that if you scoured South America, you might end up with a total of three hundred new species."

While the job can seem daunting, it's also inspiring, Grimaldi says, since it so often involves a sense of exploration and discovery, of visiting new frontiers. Adds Curator Norman Platnick: "That's what makes it interesting to get up and come to work in the morning—you're looking at stuff no one's ever seen before."

Fortunately, given the magnitude of the task, today's entomologists are not the first to attempt to bring order to the chaos of arthropod classification. "Ours is a very historical science," Grimaldi says. "Taxonomy is elegant because it is classical. We're depending on research that can be two hundred years old to validate names or give us a basis for revisions."

Building upon the department's early research, later curators such as Charles Michener, Mont Cazier, Willis Gertsch, and many others continued the slow, frustrating job of refining systematic techniques and devising classifications for a wide variety of insects and spiders. Beginning in the 1970s, however, perhaps invigorated by the controversial arrival (and eventual acceptance) of cladistic theory, the Department of Entomology began to produce an extraordinary number and variety of papers, with Curators Frederick Rindge, Pedro Wygodzinsky, Norman Platnick, and others studying everything from assassin bugs to moths to spiders.

Today, this vibrancy continues to be in evidence, as does a remarkable diversity of research goals and techniques. "One way that we make an overwhelming job more manageable, of course, is to specialize," Grimaldi says. As a result, he focuses on fruit flies, Division Chair and Curator Randall T. Schuh on plantbugs, Curator James Carpenter on wasps, Curator Jerome G. Rozen on parasitic bees, and Curator Emeritus Frederick Rindge on inchworm moths.

Much as Willis Gertsch was before him, Curator Norman Platnick is the Museum's resident expert on spiders. Currently, scientists recognize about 106 families containing some 3,050 genera and 36,000 species, but no one considers that an accurate world total. "Some estimates range as high as 180,000 species, but I believe we've described about half of what's out there," Platnick says. (Only in entomology would a revision upward from 36,000 to 75,000 species be considered "conservative.")

Platnick's own greatest enthusiasm is for "hunting spiders"— a group whose members do not build webs to catch prey, but his wide-ranging interests and the chaotic state of spider classification has led him to focus on many other spider groups over the years. Until 1995 his research had for years focused on the spiders of Chile, especially the extraordinarily diverse ground spiders of that country's little-studied temperate forests.

"I first got interested because I was working on a genus of ground spiders, and saw from museum specimens that different species within the genus seemed to occur cheek-by-jowl in Chile," he explains. "I'd never seen anything quite that dramatic before, so I went down there to see if I could actually find the species I'd seen in collections. Sure enough, they were there, and more as well."

Platnick's prodigious output on Chilean and other South American ground spiders is reflected in Museum publications, as is his sense of the magnitude of the task he faces in untangling spider relationships. In a typical example, a 1995 *Novitates* article titled "A Revision of the Tracheline Spiders (Araneae, Corinnidae) of Southern South America," cowritten with Entomology volunteer Curtis Ewing, the authors begin with this curt statement: "The current generic classification of the New World tracheline species is thoroughly unsatisfactory." They go on to describe thirteen new species, transfer twenty-two species to a new genus, and describe new ranges for several species.

In 1995 Platnick began a new long-term study in Australia, which he describes as "probably the least-known place on the planet." The collections of Australian arthropods in museums are extensive, but virtually unstudied. "There's enough material in collections to keep twenty taxonomists busy for the rest of their lives," he says. "Pick a specimen at random, and chances are it will be undescribed—although it may take you a year of research to find out."

Platnick is focusing on the ground spiders of the superfamily Gnaphosoidea and, within that, the family Gnaphosidae, members of which occur throughout Australia. The superfamily is known to contain at least 150 Australian species, but of course the total when Platnick's research is complete is sure to be far higher, probably at least 650.

How much work needs to be done before the extent of Australia's spider fauna can be estimated? One hint can be gained from the first focus of Platnick's current fieldwork, a well-known group of species commonly called "white-tailed spiders." "When we began, there were nine species known within a single genus," he comments. "As of now, we've identified seventy-three species and nine genera."

But these findings, however important, are just a first tiny step toward the entomologist's ultimate goal. "I'm interested in finding everything that's there," he says of Australia. "To do that, you have to work in country for a long time—and that's what I intend to do."

All entomologists take on an enormous task when they choose to study arthropods. But the scientist who specializes in the order Coleoptera may be grappling with the greatest challenge of all.

Coleoptera are beetles, which comprise by far the greatest number of species of any arthropod order. Thus far, scientists have described about 400,000 beetle species, representing perhaps one out of every three living species of any animal found on earth. It hardly needs to be said that this estimate is significantly—perhaps spectacularly—low. The truth is that no one has the slightest idea how many beetle species there are on the planet; reputable scientists have come up with estimates ranging from about 1 million to 10 million or more.

Even trying to comprehend classifying every beetle species is an invitation to madness. So Curator Lee H. Herman, the Museum's beetle specialist, doesn't even try. "I do everything one piece at a time, not looking at the forest, but at each tree," he says. "Sometimes I do feel a little overwhelmed, but the feeling passes, and I'm back doing what I do."

What Herman does is bring order to the classification of the beetles belonging to the family Staphylinidae, more commonly called "rove beetles." Lest anyone think he is taking an easy way out by focusing on a single family, Staphylinidae contains perhaps 40,000 species, making it one of the largest families of animals in the world. "The key is organization—I break off pieces that make sense," Herman says. "Of course, to do this requires a deep familiarity with your subject, which involves looking and looking. That's why I may spend ten years on a project."

Throughout the 1990s, Herman has been involved in two ambitious projects that reflect his familiarity with Staphylinidae. The first is a world catalog of references to every species in the family (except for one subfamily), compiled on a year-by-year basis since the first mention of the family in 1758. "I'm tracing taxonomic changes, new discoveries, the addition of morphologic characters, and biological and geographic information over time," he explains. "When I'm done, I hope we can publish it online, so it can be constantly updated as new information comes in."

Herman's second project centers on a single subfamily of Staphylinidae, called "Paederinae." "Previously, every time I would go to do a smaller project within the subfamily, I'd have to look at *all* these genera to see where the species went," he says. "Now, I'm sorting out about 6,500 species in about 220 genera, figuring out where they go."

The painstaking quality of this work is apparent when Herman describes how the study began with the Museum's own extensive collections and an additional group of 55,000 specimens borrowed from the Field Museum in Chicago. Herman must look at every specimen, dissect beetles belonging to every genus, and undertake frequent trips to Argentina, Ecuador, Guiana, and other sites to collect specimens that do not appear in the collections.

"What I'm interested in doing is building a platform that shows: this is what we know," Herman says. This platform, he adds, will allow him and others to seek the answers to questions regarding behavior, phylogeny, or distribution, far more effectively than ever before.

When asked why he has chosen such a daunting task, Herman smiles. "I like the beauty of these beetles," he says. "And organizing data out of chaos brings a sense of beauty as well."

THE ROOTS OF DIVERSITY

My interest in amber started with studying fruit flies in amber. I was absolutely mesmerized, enamored with the exquisite preservation of these tiny flies. I started by working just with amber from the Dominican Republic, but this quickly led into an obsession with amber all over the world—and particularly what amber can tell us about critical times in the evolution of both insects and flowering plants.

—*David Grimaldi*

No entomologist can avoid a sense of curiosity about the evolution of the insects. Such extraordinary diversity, such a vast network of speciation, must be the result of a story of unparalleled complexity—if science could only figure out a way to unlock the past. In recent years, David Grimaldi and other scientists have uncovered the closest thing yet to a key, spectacular assemblages of ancient insects perfectly preserved in amber.

Scientists have known for centuries that millions of years ago living things—insects, plants, even lizards and frogs—sometimes got trapped in amber (the sticky resin produced by trees), which then fossilized. The exact process isn't yet understood, but it appears that chemicals called terpenes within the amber "fix" the insect or other trapped organism, replacing the water within the tissues and preventing any bacterial decomposition—a process Grimaldi calls "ambalming." The results are perfectly preserved specimens that seem as if they'd been alive yesterday.

The best known and most thoroughly studied amber deposits are found in the Baltic region and the Dominican Republic on the island of Hispaniola. In the Dominican Republic, Grimaldi and other scientists have uncovered enough insects to gain a compelling view of the life and ecological associations of arthropods as they occurred 25 to 30 million years ago.

In a book called *Dino Fest: Proceedings of a Conference for the General Public* (1994), Grimaldi and Invertebrate Zoology Curator Rob DeSalle reported on some of these associations, including their favorite from Dominican amber: "[Seven] small white cocoons hang from a twisted spider web; tiny holes show where the tiny adult wasps emerged from their pupal cases (as larvae they must have dined on the spider that spun the web)."

Yet this remarkable specimen does more than provide a fascinating glimpse of an ancient melodrama, as the authors point out: "Of course, there are myriad adult parasitic wasps in Dominican amber. Based on the life histories of their living relatives, we can infer which kinds of insects, also preserved in Dominican amber, they had parasitized."

Sometimes the specimens' preservation reveals associations of breathtaking subtlety. For example, only one type of bee (the stingless *Proplebeia dominicana*) is very common in Dominican amber. "Like stingless honeybees do today, *P. dominicana* harvested resin to construct intricate nests inside tree cavities, and it must have routinely harvested (and often got caught in) resin from the Dominican amber tree. Some bees still have balls of resin attached to their hind legs," Grimaldi and DeSalle write. "We can even tell what kinds of flowers the extinct bee foraged, by examining the microscopic sculpturing on pollen clinging to the hairs of some bees."

Amber also provides the clearest picture yet of Dominican vertebrate life, whose fossils in rock are extremely rare. Thus far, the

Dominican deposits have given up specimens of small *Anolis* and gecko lizards, frogs, and even bird feathers and strands of hair from mammals.

Again, extrapolation from indirect evidence and comparison to similar living species allows scientists to create an intriguing and convincing picture of the island's ancient ecology. Among arthropods found commonly in Dominican amber are a variety of parasites that lived by sucking vertebrates' blood, including mosquitoes, horseflies, fleas, and, of special interest, ticks.

"The few ticks that have been found are *Amblyomma*. Since this genus feeds on birds and mammals, there was little way to infer on which it fed, until one specimen surfaced containing two hairs with the tick: these ticks fed on mammals," the authors write. "Mammals, birds, and reptiles lived in the Dominican amber forests: we just have not yet found their fossilized bones."

While Grimaldi retains an intense interest in Dominican amber, in recent years he has been consumed by amber that is both far closer to home and far older. In New Jersey are amber deposits dating from the Cretaceous (ranging from 65 to 95 million years old). As of 1996, these deposits had already produced more than forty pounds of amber containing one hundred new species of insects belonging to fifteen new orders. "*Everything* is new," Grimaldi says.

The presence of insects in New Jersey amber has been known for decades, but possible sites had been little explored. In a 1988 article for *Natural History*, Grimaldi described how he went about searching for new deposits. "An amber hunter in New Jersey begins by scouting out abandoned clay-mining pits with a thin, but dense, dark gray layer that bears lignite (wood in the process of fossilization). The rest of the work is done on hands and knees at a patch of rain-washed exposed clay. Even before they are cleaned, the unearthed bits sparkle ruby red and clear yellow, the characteristic colors of the two predominant kinds of amber in this area."

The amber uncovered in this way, however, is likely to consist of tiny fragments containing few if any insects. Not every clay mine or other promising site contains enough amber to make excavation worthwhile. "But if you look hard enough, you may find concentrated sources, which we were fortunate enough to find in New Jersey," Grimaldi says.

The New Jersey deposits have thus far provided an abundance of remarkable specimens, including the world's oldest known bee, mosquito, black fly, and mushroom, as well as flowers from a 90-million-year old oak tree and a feather that is the oldest terrestrial record of a bird in North America. Amazingly, the same sites that have yielded much of the amber have also provided an array of 90-million-year-old flowers preserved in clay. These tiny flowers are composed of charcoal (they were probably transformed by a forest fire that swept through the forest leaf litter), and are so stunningly preserved that even the most delicate stamens, anthers, pollens, and other structures are still visible.

As with the Dominican specimens, such finds may allow Grimaldi to start constructing a fascinating ancient story of ecology and evolution. The New Jersey discoveries are particularly compelling because of the insights they may provide into the interaction between flowering plants and insects during the Cretaceous period.

"There is no question that certain groups, like termites, bees, and higher flies, were intimately wedded to the great explosive radiations of flowering plants during the Cretaceous," Grimaldi says. "These New Jersey sites, which contain one of the most exceptional biological communities ever found in the Cretaceous, lie right at the cusp of that great explosion."

The Molecular Systematics Laboratory

The Museum's molecular systematics laboratory (actually two separate 5,000-square-foot labs) is the location for some of the most important taxonomic work undertaken at the Museum. Under the direction of Invertebrate Zoology Curators Ward Wheeler and Rob DeSalle, the labs, by extracting and then analyzing DNA sequences, provide crucial genetic information to a variety of curators in nearly every scientific department.

Here, for example, Ornithology Curator George Barrowclough studies juncoes and other birds, while Curator Joel Cracraft seeks to untangle the knotty classification of birds of paradise. Mammalogy Associate Curator Nancy Simmons undertakes ambitious phylogenetic work on bats. Invertebrates Curator Ward Wheeler seeks insights into changes in insect morphology through study of genetic mutations. And other scientists both within and outside the Museum study a variety of equally complex and important issues, adding the information gained from DNA to the morphological data that is the bedrock of modern systematic research.

The laboratory's most famous study thus far came in the early 1990s, when it undertook an analysis of DNA from a termite trapped in Dominican amber 25 to 30 million years ago. In the era of *Jurassic Park* and its sequel and spin-offs, the possibility that ancient DNA might still be retrievable (and clonable) has undeniable public appeal.

The study, first reported in a *Science* article by Rob DeSalle, postdoctoral fellow John Gatesy, David Grimaldi, and Ward Wheeler, was a success. The group extracted and sequenced (admittedly fragmentary) DNA from the termite *Mastotermes*

James Shackelford riding with a local resident on the high-spirited, adventurous, and still-renowned Central Asiatic Expeditions of the 1920s.

Central Asiatic Expedition leader Roy Chapman Andrews (right) with the dinosaur eggs identified as belonging to *Protoceratops*, but revealed by Museum scientists in the 1990s to have been laid by *Oviraptor*.

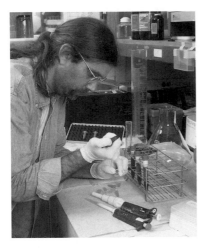

In the Molecular Biology Laboratory, scientists perform delicate experiments using advanced technology—such as retrieving DNA from a termite that was trapped in amber millions of years ago.

Named for early gem expert George Kunz, the Kunz Axe is a stunning reminder of Mexico's mysterious and long-vanished Olmec peoples.

One of the first important Museum dinosaur finds, *Ornitholestes* was an agile, intelligent, fast-moving predator. This made it controversial in the early 1900s, when scientists were determined to believe that all dinosaurs were slow-moving, dull-witted creatures.

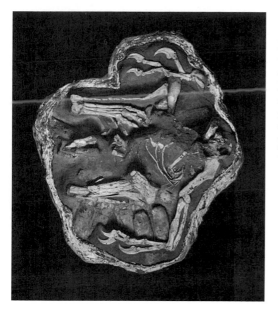

From the Museum's 1990s Gobi Desert expeditions, one of the most spectacular dinosaur discoveries of all time: a fossil *Oviraptor* perched on its nest in exactly the same brooding posture used by modern birds.

The awe-inspiring Komodo dragon. The expedition that sent Museum trustee Douglas Burden and his wife, Katherine, to the remote Indonesian island of Komodo was just one of many adventures sponsored by the Museum in the 1920s.

A typical day for Museum ichthyologists J. T. Nichols and Francesca LaMonte.

The ammonites, some of the dominant animals in the Earth's oceans for tens of millions of years, disappeared during the same mass extinction event that doomed the dinosaurs sixty-five million years ago.

Though the tale of its discovery and three-century history has been forgotten, the great Star of India (the largest star sapphire ever found) remains one of the Museum's most bewitching gems.

The Yakut shaman diorama, like so many of the Museum's anthropological exhibits, allows visitors a glimpse of a vitally important ritual.

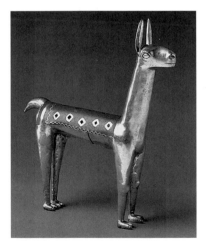

Though it looks like any other finely crafted spear point, the Folsom Point proved that humans had settled in North America far earlier than most anthropologists believed.

Tragically, many of the exquisite silver and gold statues created by Inka artists were melted down by the Spanish following the conquest of the Inka Empire. Only a few, like the Royal Llama, escaped destruction.

Two towering figures in the early history of paleontology: Henry Fairfield Osborn (right) and fossil-hunter extraordinaire Barnum Brown, at the 1897 dig that unearthed *Diplodocus*, the first dinosaur collected for the Museum.

This rare 1860 photograph shows how ships came from all over the world to collect guano from Peru's famous Chincha Islands—nearly destroying a valuable industry and local way of life in the process.

Secretive Museum patron Childs Frick and ace collector Peter Kaisen, with a few of the thousands of fossil mammals they unearthed across the United States.

Ropes, pulleys, electric drills, paintbrushes, and great patience: the massive task of recreating a tropical coral reef in a Museum exhibit.

Magnificent trackways of both plant-eating and meat-eating dinosaurs were discovered in Glen Rose, Texas, by Roland T. Bird, and then excavated and brought back to the Museum.

Curator, writer, photographer, editor: Mary Cynthia Dickerson, one of the most important figures at the Museum in the early 1900s.

Morris Jesup, the visionary Museum president who brought many of the world's most brilliant scientists to New York's Upper West Side.

Bashford Dean, a true Victorian generalist and expert in both ancient armored fish and medieval armored humans.

Margaret Mead, whose years-long studies of developing cultures revolutionized the field of anthropology.

Carl Akeley, an early environmental hero, dedicated his life to protecting Africa's rare mountain gorillas.

Libbie Hyman spent years producing the massive six-volume *The Invertebrates*, which remains a classic in its field.

Curator F. W. Putnam hired brilliant anthropologists, including ethnologists Franz Boas and Clark Wissler, and then gave them the resources to undertake some of the most ambitious expeditions in history.

Frank M. Chapman's unrelenting efforts helped save North America's herons and egrets from extinction.

Niles Eldredge's research on trilobites developed into the revolutionary and controversial evolutionary theory known as "punctuated equilibrium."

Melanie Stiassny, who juggles collection, research, and environmental concerns in her role as curator-in-charge of Ichthyology.

Neil Landman, surrounded by the ammonites that teach us so much about ancient oceans and the phenomenon of mass extinction.

E. T. Gilliard, who braved ill health and oft-wretched conditions to study the transcendently beautiful birds of paradise and bowerbirds of New Guinea.

Monsters at our feet: the building of the forest floor diorama and its greatly enlarged invertebrate creatures.

electrodominicus, and used the information to add to their knowledge about the classification of living termite species.

But both Grimaldi and DeSalle caution against any rush to extract DNA from more than a select group of amber specimens. "Every time you extract DNA, you partially destroy a specimen," Grimaldi says. "When you use a rare or unique species, you may be destroying morphological information whose importance you don't even recognize. And for what? Genetic information that may be so fragmented that it is virtually worthless."

DeSalle is equally vehement in urging caution before attempting future extractions of ancient DNA. "We're just not at the point where the information we get from DNA matches what we get from morphology," he says. "I don't think there's any reason to do it unless you've got a really important question you need to answer—and no other way to answer it."

6   Stories of Stasis and Change

THE SIGNIFICANCE OF LITTLE THINGS

We seem important to ourselves because of our intimate knowledge of mankind, derived from the evidence of our senses. Niagara and the Grand Canyon seem huge to us. Yet the telescope reveals among the stars wonders of such magnitude that, in comparison, our earth dwindles to an insignificant speck and the human beings upon it shrink to the dimensions of microscopic germs. . . . Therefore, size is relatively unimportant. The most significant factor is life, which is of the same nature in microscopic organisms as in ourselves.

—*Curator of Living Invertebrates Roy W. Miner, as quoted by D. R. Barton in "A Modern Gulliver,"* in Natural History, *November 1941.*

From the earliest days of the Museum's history, its scientists have been entranced by some of the most fascinating yet little-understood members of the great panoply of life on earth: Invertebrates, creatures with no backbones ranging from protozoa to beetles to snails. Invertebrates can teach us perhaps the most important lessons of all about evolution and biodiversity.

Why evolution? Because such extinct invertebrates as ammonites and trilobites lived and evolved for such a long time—scores of millions of years—and left such an extraordinary fossil record. "It's impossible to study ancient invertebrates," says Niles Eldredge, a curator in the Division of Paleontology and an expert in trilobites and evolution, "and not be interested in the ways species evolve."

Why biodiversity? Because there are hundreds of times more invertebrate species—including insects and spiders—living today than the combined total of all vertebrate species. Because every entomologist on earth could spend the rest of his or her life describing new invertebrate species, barely take time to eat and sleep, and have no chance to keep up with the flood of new species to discover. (For more on past and current research on insects and spiders, see Chapter 5, "Tiny Glories of Biodiversity.")

You can learn a lot about evolution by studying ancient mammals. You can study biodiversity by cataloging the birds of the tropical rain forest. But for insights into these fascinating, critically important subjects that you simply can't find elsewhere, you must understand the significance of little things.

Invertebrate specimens were among the first to join the collection at the nascent American Museum. In fact, it was an important collection of fossil invertebrates that helped bring the Museum to the brink of bankruptcy during its shaky first years—while simultaneously leading to the hiring of its first high-profile curator.

In 1874, before the first building was even open, the museum spent $65,000 for a huge trove of fossil invertebrates owned by Professor James Hall, official New York State geologist. This collection was one of the finest in the world, comprising more than seven thousand species, and the Museum trustees who had okayed the purchase thought it was exactly the kind of acquisition to help bring the new Museum the respect it needed.

The Museum did gain respect in the scientific community, but made an almost fatal miscalculation in expecting any great enthusiasm among nonscientists. As Douglas Preston puts it in *Dinosaurs in the Attic*, his 1986 history of the Museum, "The Museum hoped to pay for the Hall Collection with a public subscription. Unfortunately, the public proved to be quite uninterested in an aggregation of gray invertebrate fossils. Very little money came forth."

As a result, the Museum's trustees had to pay for the collection out of their own pockets—an onerous commitment that led them to forbid most other expensive purchases. As a result, when the Museum's first building opened in 1877, the few visitors who ventured to this northwest frontier of Manhattan found the exhibition halls to be virtually empty. "By 1880, the Museum was on the brink of extinction," Preston writes. "Museum President Robert L. Stuart had said that when he retired, he would recommend closing the Museum if no one could be found to take his place."

The man the trustees found to replace Stuart in 1881 was Morris K. Jesup, who transformed the Museum exhibition areas, its collections, and its mission. Jesup realized immediately that the public was far more likely to be interested in large, spectacular creatures like lions than in fossil invertebrates. As far as fossils went, it was fine for the curators to collect these small specimens, but couldn't they bring in some dinosaur fossils as well? Perhaps even some entire dinosaur skeletons to fill the empty exhibition halls?

By the time Jesup arrived and changed the Museum's course, the administration (led by Theodore Roosevelt) had already hired a specialist to oversee the benighted Hall Collection: Robert Parr Whitfield (1828–1910), an associate of Professor Hall's and a vitally important participant in the building of a successful museum.

Whitfield, nearing fifty by the time he came to the Museum, grew up in Oneida County, New York, a region then famous for its abundant fossils. Like Barnum Brown, George Gaylord Simpson, and many other budding paleontologists, he spent his youth collecting and studying fossils, but unlike these men, Whitfield never had the benefit of university training in his field. "At the age of nine, the boy [Whitfield] began work in a cotton mill, later entering the shop of his father, who was a spindle maker," wrote geologist E. O. Hovey. "School education did not fall to his lot; in fact . . . his entire school training amounted to less than three months of time in all, and he never saw the inside of a school house as a student after he was twelve years old."

Whitfield played an important role in the development of research at the Museum. He also had strong ideas about departmental organization, as he showed in an 1890 letter to President Jesup objecting to the naming of a separate curator to lead each department. "The result of such a course is most generally that each head of a department will have their own views in regard to arrangements," he complained. "The fewer heads there are, the better the results."

At least during his lifetime, Whitfield's views held sway, as can be seen in this litany of staff positions he occupied during his three decades at the Museum:

1877–1884	Curator of Geology
1885–1886	Curator of Geological and Mineralogical Department
1887–1890	Curator of Geological, Mineralogical, and Conchological Departments
1891–1900	Curator of the Departments of Geology, Mineralogy, Conchology and Marine Invertebrate Zoology

1901–1909   Curator of Department of Geology and
             Invertebrate Paleontology

The fluid nature of departmental categories reveals much about the youth of both the Museum and the natural sciences it was studying. Research into invertebrates, in particular, seemed to have trouble finding a home, and through the years both the objects on display and the scientists studying the important collection have been moved frequently.

Once the Museum's finances were restored to order and more popular displays were installed in the new building's vast showcases, R. P. Whitfield was able to study and display the vast Hall Collection without worrying whether it would support the entire Museum. "The Hall Collection of fossils was his idol," wrote Hovey, "and its care and interests were constantly on his mind." This intense focus on the Museum's fossil invertebrate collections as a whole allowed Whitfield to produce many important scientific works, including an enormous catalogue of the Museum's more than eight thousand type specimens, published in 1898. (Type specimens are those from which a new, previously unknown, species is identified.)

One of Whitfield's greatest accomplishments was to establish a regular forum for the Museum's scientists to publish their research findings. At Whitfield's urging, President Jesup funded a new journal, the *Bulletin of the American Museum of Natural History*, beginning in 1881. Whitfield wrote the first five articles for the new journal and contributed many other articles until 1910, the last year of his life. Today, the *Bulletin* continues to be one of the leading journals of scientific research in the world, regularly publishing the findings of Museum invertebrate biologists Neil Landman, Niles Eldredge, Norman Newell, Judith Winston, and others—as well as the findings of scientists from every other biological department in the Museum.

Showing the Invisible

For decades during the first half of this century, Museum scientists and preparators engaged in an ambitious effort to spur public interest in some of the smallest of all invertebrate animals: the microscopic, single-celled organisms known as protozoa, which include amoebas, paramecia, and countless others known only to scientists.

As early as 1909, Roy W. Miner was employing his colorful writing style to describe these minute organisms in a lead *Journal* article. "Swarming in countless millions in both fresh and salt water, and at times even in the bodies of other animals, they are the most abundant and widely distributed of all life," Miner wrote. "Though this vast world of creatures is so important and surrounds us on every side, penetrating, as it were, all the interspaces between the larger forms of life, yet it is invisible to our eyes, and were it not for the compound microscope, we should be absolutely ignorant of it, except in its effects."

In his writing, Miner could have made laundry interesting— but he would never have succeeded in capturing Museum visitors' attention if not for the brilliant artistry of preparator Herman O. Mueller, descendant of a long line of German glassblowers and the man responsible for some of the most beautiful objects on display in the Museum.

Along with making the glass coral polyps for the coral reef group, Mueller labored for years to create a series of glass models of protozoa. Working with almost incomprehensible delicacy, utilizing tiny particles of various types of glass to produce subtle changes in color and texture, he was able to reproduce the most delicate cell walls, filaments, and other structures that make protozoa as diverse and mysterious as snowflakes. Today, the results of Mueller's decades of labor still provide an unparalleled look at these little-known microorganisms.

THE COMPLICATED LIFE OF SMALL ANIMALS

> Have you ever met a crab walking along a path and wondered how the crab has managed to survive so far from the sea, since crabs always live in sea water—or do they? . . . For all that shrimps, lobsters and crabs are familiar animals, how much do you know about them as moving, feeding, breathing, reproducing organisms—*living* organisms?
>
> —*Invertebrates Curator Dorothy Bliss,*
> *in* Shrimps, Lobsters and Crabs *(1982).*

Invertebrate animals occupy nearly every environment on earth. They thrive in temperate and tropical forests, inhabit frigid mountaintops, make up the vast preponderance of undersea life, even survive on the Arctic tundra and Antarctic ice cap. Where life is found on the planet, invertebrates are certain to be there.

So it should be no surprise that invertebrates can be found in many of the Museum's halls. Mollusks and their long relationship with human cultures are featured in the Mollusks and Our World hall. Ammonites occupy their own showcase, as do a giant millipede and other magnified invertebrate dwellers of the forest floor. But one fascinating exhibit—showing a Caribbean coral reef and its inhabitants—can easily be overlooked, as it resides in the dramatic Hall of Ocean Life, and tends to be overshadowed by the gigantic blue-whale model hanging overhead and the dioramas featuring leaping dolphins, hulking walruses, and other more spectacular creatures.

The Caribbean exhibit shouldn't be missed, because it involves one of the world's most ancient, complex, and fascinating ecosystems. Coral polyps are tiny invertebrate animals, each of which secretes a rocklike skeleton around itself. In uncountable numbers, colonies of polyps form coral reefs, extraordinarily rich ecosystems that can harbor dozens of species of fish and many other marine animals.

The diorama is also notable because so much effort took place in constructing an accurate replica of a living reef. Only a few times in Museum history has a curator striven as hard and for as long as did Curator of Living Invertebrates Roy Waldo Miner in seeking to transplant a coral reef into a New York City building.

Miner and a covey of assistants, including several preparators, modelmakers, and artists, made five separate trips to the Caribbean over a span of twelve years, beginning in 1923. During the initial expedition to the reefs of Andros Island in the Bahamas, the explorers had access to an amazing "submarine tube," which was exactly what it sounds like: A long tube extending down thirty feet from a specially designed barge and culminating in a spherical viewing chamber much like a bathysphere.

In these days of scuba, research submersibles, and robot subs that can explore the undersea world thousands of feet beneath the surface, it's hard to remember a time when glimpses of even the shallow-water reef environment were a rare and precious gift. But in 1923 the diving tube, which allowed a comfortable descent to about thirty feet, granted almost unprecedented access, as Miner pointed out in an enthusiastic article he penned in 1924 for a newspaper called *Mid-Week Pictorial*.

"Our first glimpse through the window of the submarine tube revealed a sight so marvelous as to be almost startling in its strange beauty," Miner wrote. "A dense forest of palmate corals, like stone trees with interlacing branches, of which the uppermost pierced the water surface, rose from the reef platform and melted into the pearly blue of the watery fog, while beams from the afternoon sun penetrated between their fronds and illuminated numerous schools of fish which passed in solemn review before us, lighting up their brilliant color patterns like gleaming jewels."

After recovering from their first view of a "fantastic world belonging to a strange planet," Miner and his assistants spent hours every day sketching, photographing, and filming the reef and its inhabitants. Then, on this and succeeding trips, they utilized early diving helmets to descend and collect among the coral heads. Remarkably, a Museum artist named Chris Olsen actually painted reef scenes while seated twenty feet beneath the ocean surface, equipped with waterproof paints and canvas, weighted brushes, and, of course, a diving helmet.

But the hardest job was yet to come: reconstructing the beauty, complexity, and fragility of the reef ecosystem in a habitat group. Merely cleaning the forty tons of delicate, often branching coral required six months of hard work, and mending broken branches and fans took weeks more. Each specimen was then coated with beeswax "to simulate the animal layer, which in life invests the coral," as Miner put it, and artists carefully painted the faded specimens with oil paints to recapture their natural colors. Before the great coral heads could be placed in the diorama, ironworkers designed and erected a frame capable of supporting the massive specimens while remaining invisible.

The background and smaller reef inhabitants also received careful attention. Modeler Chris Olsen created a great limestone cavern backdrop; glassblower Herman Mueller modeled glass replicas of living coral polyps; preparators made wax models of hundreds of reef fish; and artist Francis Lee Jaques painted the glowing background.

The resulting habitat group, which finally went on display in 1935, portrays a dimly lit scene that comes close to capturing the beauty and mystery of a real reef—close enough, at least, that it should inspire generations of young Museum visitors to visit the real thing. As Miner wrote in a statement of philosophy shared by the Museum's scientists and preparators today, "The ideal museum group is not merely a work of art. It is a record of living beings in their natural state and environment, depicted in their proper relations to their surroundings, and emphasizing the truth that the real unit in nature is the association rather than the individual."

Miner wasn't the only Museum specialist in invertebrates to study coral reefs. But Curator Emeritus Norman Newell, who has been associated with the Museum for more than fifty years, has chosen a far more rigorous route. He has tackled a variety of fascinating questions surrounding ancient and modern reefs, the use of the fossil record to study evolution, and—pivotally—the mass extinction of much of the world's marine life that occurred during a period around the time of the end of the Permian and beginning of the Triassic period, about 248 million years ago.

In 1995, Newell and Museum research associate William Boyd (emeritus professor at the University of Wyoming) published a *Bulletin* article, "Pectinoid Bivalves of the Permian-Triassic Crisis," the last in an important series of ten papers on the extinct members of a group of bivalves known as pectinoids. (Bivalves are animals with two-valved shells, such as clams.) By studying populations of these bivalves on either side of the line separating the Permian from the Triassic periods, the authors were seeking further insights into what might have caused the mass extinction of that time.

Newell and Boyd's research, while not firmly supporting a single hypothesis, shows that diversity of pectinoid bivalves declined from about twenty-three genera in the middle Permian to just five in the late Triassic, and didn't begin to recover until millions of years later. "So they shared the great mass extinction with most other groups of marine invertebrates," the authors conclude. "The crisis extended some tens of millions of years and was slow, rather than catastrophic."

The authors don't subscribe to a single theory as to what caused the mass extinction. As they say at the conclusion of the article, "The search for some general explanation of the Permo-Triassic mass extinction is still in full swing, with many, by no means mutually exclusive, viable hypotheses." These hypotheses, they go on to explain, include lowering of sea levels, flooding of continents with oxygen-poor water from the deep sea, changes in salinity, strong volcanic eruptions, sudden climatic changes, gamma-ray bursts from super novas, and a collision between the earth and a large comet or asteroid.

Scientists may never learn exactly why the earth's oceans went through a period of such dramatically depressed productivity during the Permian-Triassic crisis. It is likely that a combination of the factors listed above contributed to the extinction—and also quite possible that other factors, as yet undiscovered, also played a major role.

Newell and Boyd feel that their most important discovery—detecting a downward trend in the ratio of certain carbon isotopes that parallels the progressive extinction of bivalve species to the Permian-Triassic boundary—may provide important new directions for research. Rather than depending on fossil evidence alone, they say, scientists should combine geochemical and fossil evidence to learn what happened to the pectinoid bivalves and so many other marine invertebrates at this time.

Like Norman Newell, other department curators have studied both living and extinct invertebrate species. Curator Emeritus William K. Emerson, for example, has written prolifically on fossil mollusks from Baja California and other locations, while also researching the distribution of living mollusks in the tropical eastern Pacific Ocean. This important work, focusing on Clipperton, Cocos, and the Revillagigedo and Galapagos Islands, is providing insights into both the evolutionary history of the region's mollusks and the islands' biogeography as isolated outposts of land within the eastern Pacific's major oceanic current systems.

Newell's research on living mollusks builds off one of the most extensive collections in the Museum. In 1874, just five years after its founding, Catherine Wolfe (daughter of John David Wolfe, the Museum's first president) purchased the Jay Collection and gave it to the Museum. This collection included fifty thousand specimens of fourteen thousand mollusk species, and was just the first of many large collections that came to the Museum in the years that followed. Today, the Museum harbors a stunning 275,000 catalogued lots of living and fossil invertebrates, an irreplaceable resource for scientists worldwide.

Not all invertebrate specialists studying living species have focused on mollusks. Libbie Hyman and Dorothy Bliss both turned their attention elsewhere, but could not have been more different in the approaches they took to research.

Libbie Hyman (1888–1969) never wanted to study a single species or even group of invertebrates. Instead she chose to look to broader horizons. Her chief enthusiasm, she wrote, was for nature in general. "This first took the form of a love of flowers," she said, adding, "I believe my interest in nature is primarily aesthetic."

She also always claimed to have little interest in basic research. "I do not regard any of this work as of outstanding importance," she said of some of her early studies at the University of Chicago. "I am not a research type." According to former Museum invertebrates curator Judith Winston, however, Hyman was being too modest. As Winston pointed out in a newsletter published by The

American Society of Zoologists, Hyman "published more experimental papers than many scientists ever do."

Still, since Hyman didn't see herself as being cut out for research or (as she also claimed) for teaching, what was her role to be after her arrival at the Museum in 1937? Her decision was to take on the immense task of producing *The Invertebrates*, the first work to compile and organize all known information about the vast number of creatures without backbones.

Hyman worked on the treatise for more than thirty years, and eventually produced six large volumes. For this accomplishment above all she was awarded the Daniel Giraud Elliot Medal of the National Academy of Sciences and the Linnean Gold Medal of the Linnean Society of London—in both cases, she was the first woman zoologist ever to receive the medal.

"Her books provided a synthesis of phylogeny that clearly influenced teaching and opinion about the groups she covered," Judith Winston wrote in 1991. "While discoveries of the last 30 years have resulted in many changes in our thinking about invertebrate phylogeny, her work still provides a framework against which new ideas can be tested and sets a standard of excellence that can still inspire us."

While Libbie Hyman's love was for nature in general, Dorothy Bliss chose a far more intense focus for her research. Bliss (1916–1988) was a neuroendocrinologist who studied the effects of hormones on the nervous system. As a curator and eventual chairwoman of what was then called the Department of Living Invertebrates, she focused almost all of her life's work on hormones in crustaceans, particularly in a single species of tropical land crab named *Gecarcinus lateralis*.

Between 1956 and her death, Bliss studied how hormones influence the crab's ability to molt, to maintain a water balance in its body (a particularly important factor for a land crab), and to move. Among her findings were that captive crabs molted only when temperature, moisture, and illumination matched those found at the end of the crab's burrow. In improper conditions, molting was delayed by release of previously unknown "molt-inhibiting factors" from cells located in the crab's eyestalks.

The lifelong intensity of Bliss's desire to learn about the innermost workings of crabs remains striking today. In *Shrimp, Lobsters and Crabs*, an in-depth popular book she wrote in 1982, she gave a hint as to why she pursued the path she did, writing that "there is a fascination about shrimps, lobsters, and crabs, their structure, their behavior, the lives that they live." Throughout her life and through her work, Dorothy Bliss helped us share her enthusiasm for these often little-noticed creatures.

AMMONITES AND MASS EXTINCTION

> I enjoy studying ammonites because they can tell us so much about evolution in the Mesozoic Era. Why? Because there were so many of them and they were so widespread. You can call the Mesozoic the Age of Dinosaurs—but to me it was just as much the Age of Ammonites. And that means you can track their history through both time and space.
>
> —*Neil Landman, Curator in the Division of Paleontology.*

The study of ammonites—shelled extinct relatives of the modern-day nautilus, octopus, and squid has a long but sporadic history at the American Museum. After R. P. Whitfield's death in 1910, responsibility for the collection was assumed by the Department of Geology, under the leadership of curators more interested in earth science than paleontology. Similarly, when most Museum fossil hunters went into the field, they were looking to make the next great dinosaur or mammal find—rarely taking the time to excavate small, seemingly unspectacular invertebrate specimens.

Luckily for the Museum's collection, there were exceptions to this pattern. During a 1918–1919 expedition to Cuba, Vertebrate Paleontology's Barnum Brown collected a large number of ammonites from the Jurassic period, excavating in seven different sites that covered 15 million years of Jurassic exposures. Soon after his return, invertebrate paleontologist Marjorie O'Connell undertook the first truly systematic and paleogeographic analysis of ammonites ever made at the Museum.

As reported in a 1921 issue of the in-house Museum newsletter, *Museologist*, O'Connell's goals were similar to those of scientists studying extinct animals today. "Biologically the specimens are interesting because they throw new light on the broader problems of organic evolution and the laws which control it," the newsletter explained. "Geologically the collection is valuable because it marks the only occurrence of rocks of Jurassic age in the West Indies and makes possible the establishment of a geological column of rock formations which can be compared with those of Mexico and Europe."

When O'Connell and Brown combined the paleontological and geological data, they found that they were able to draw a far more accurate map than any before of the extent of the Jurassic oceans. The widespread ammonites allowed them to conclude that the oceans of the time stretched from Mexico to cover much of what is now Europe, inundating most Mediterranean countries and parts of Russia, Germany, France, and England.

The Museum's next important ammonite collection was excavated by mammalogist Herbert Lang during the Museum's Vernay Angola Expedition of 1925. Perhaps because he was no paleontologist and the chief goal of this expedition was the collecting of mammals and birds, Lang got the material to the

Museum in good shape but with little supporting information. Then it had to wait until 1940 for a qualified invertebrate paleontologist, Curator Otto Haas, to study it. Haas produced a two-hundred-page *Bulletin* article that still stands as a model of careful description and analysis.

If ammonites received only occasional attention during the Museum's first century, that is clearly no longer the case. Pay a visit to the large, sunlit office of Curator Neil Landman, and you'll step into a room that fulfills the dream of any child who's ever wondered what a fossil-hunter's office looks like. Every surface seems to be covered in ammonites: Tiny specimens whose delicately whorled shells seem as fragile as flowers; larger ones burnished red, brown, even golden, depending on the color of the sediment in which they were preserved; ammonites lining the tops of tables, arranged so every few inches represent a million years of evolution.

Landman himself takes evident pleasure in being surrounded by these fascinating remnants of ancient times. During a conversation, he wanders around the room, stopping frequently to pick up one or another ammonite to demonstrate a point he is making. "One of the things that makes studying ammonites so satisfying is how much information is packed into their shells," he says, cradling a specimen whose shell has been laid open to reveal its spiral chambers. "Since every ammonite adds new chambers as it grows, each one contains a complete record of its life history."

Remarkably, this record includes the ammonite's embryonic growth, the first delicate chambers created while it was still in the egg. "Every so often we find an exceptional specimen with no matrix—no rock—adhering to the shell, and we can use a scanning electron microscope to study the smallest details of the chambers," Landman says. "To have such a complete record means that we have many characters to compare systematically, including shell shape, the design of the septa [the partitions between chambers], and other features that allow us to put together ammonite genealogies."

Though his office seems to contain enough specimens to occupy a scientist for years, Landman has long realized that productive systematic work depends on a steady influx of new specimens. Therefore, each year he collects specimens in Montana, South Dakota, and Wyoming, which were all part of a vast Cretaceous seaway that stretched from the Arctic to the Gulf of Mexico and from the Rocky Mountains at least to Kansas. Since some of this sea's ammonite species have also been found in Greenland and Poland, it seems that this seaway must have connected in some way with oceans covering what are today parts of Europe and Greenland.

Just as Barnum Brown's Cuban ammonites allowed him and Marjorie O'Connell to delineate the borders of a Jurassic ocean, Landman's specimens enable him to practice the science of paleobiogeography in the Cretaceous. "Since ammonites were active swimmers, and many species were widely distributed, they give us an opportunity to understand where the seas were," he explains. "These intercontinental correlations, as we call them, give us crucial data about life in ancient times."

While careful, rewarding systematic work and paleobiogeography are both central aspects of Landman's research, he (along with other ammonite specialists) finds himself drawn to one of the most fascinating questions surrounding these cephalopods: Why did every last ammonite become extinct at the end of the Cretaceous period?

The mass extinction at the end of the Cretaceous is by far the most famous cataclysm in earth's history. This was the extinction event, apparently spurred in part by some enormous collision between the earth and a giant comet or asteroid, that claimed the great dinosaurs, all pterosaurs, ichthyosaurs, and plesiosaurs, and countless smaller creatures. So it shouldn't be surprising that ammonites disappeared as well.

But what bothers scientists is another question: Why did ammonites become extinct while their relatives, the nautilids, survived? (Today, 65 million years after the last ammonite, nautilids still live in the South Pacific and Indian Oceans.) A glance at the Late Cretaceous data makes it seem as if the situation should have been reversed.

After all, as Landman points out, in the last part of the Cretaceous (called the "Maastrichtian"), ammonites were far more diverse than the nautilids, with about twenty-one genera compared to a mere seven nautilid genera. In sheer abundance they were equally dominant: At least one estimate put the number of individual ammonites in South Dakota rock strata in the hundreds of millions, compared to fewer than ten thousand nautilids.

So what happened? "We'll never know for sure, so any hypotheses are speculation," Landman warns. "But I believe that their ultimate extinction—and the nautilids' survival—may have been due to differences in their early development."

When living nautilids hatch, they are already quite large and able to swim actively. Almost immediately after hatching, they descend to just above the sea bottom at depths of about one thousand feet (their preferred habitat). Once there, they act as scavengers, showing little preference for specific foods. Analysis of fossil nautilids indicate they may well have followed a similar lifestyle.

"Ammonites, on the other hand, were tiny—about half a millimeter—at hatching," Landman says. "It seems that they spent the early portion of their life as plankton, swimming near the surface of the ocean."

Surface waters are far more sensitive to environmental changes than are deeper waters. Changes in ocean currents, oxygen levels, or chemistry would therefore leave the inhabitants of surface water—such as the ammonites and other planktonic animals—uniquely vulnerable to extinction. And, in fact, a large portion of planktonic animals died out at the end of the Cretaceous. The free-swimming adult ammonites might have been able to survive the drastic environmental changes of the time, but their young could not.

"It's strange," Landman says, gazing down at the fossils that are all that remain of this once-dominant group of marine animals. "Looking at ammonites during the late Cretaceous, you would have thought that they'd go on forever. It just goes to show how unpredictable the history of life is."

A Squid's Journey

The most dramatic exhibit in the Museum's Hall of Ocean Life features the great blue whale, the largest animal ever to live on earth. But the spookiest display in the same hall features a different kind of whale, the sperm whale, grappling with another giant creature. This creature, the giant squid, remains one of the most mysterious and elusive of all large animals.

The giant squid is a monster-sized, deep-sea version of the familiar squids that populate shallower waters. Scientists know that giant squids can reach sixty feet in length and weigh in at a thousand pounds. Large individuals can have eyes as big as soccer balls, although no one knows what purpose these eyes serve in the squid's pitch-dark haunts nearly a half mile below the ocean's surface.

In a way, it's remarkable that scientists know so much about the giant squid, because no one has ever seen one of these magnificent animals alive. Everything we know comes from dead specimens caught in the fishermen's nets—and even from sucker marks left by squids' tentacles on sperm whales, which scientists think hunt and eat the squids.

Now, for the first time, visitors to the Museum will have the chance to get an up close look at an actual giant squid, though not a living one. Late in 1997, a New Zealand fishing boat pulled up a dead but intact twenty-five-foot-long squid in its nets. The squid was promptly placed in the boat's freezer, where it remained until the boat returned to shore. There it was turned over to local scientists, who eventually decided to donate it to the Museum.

The squid cleared customs at New York's Kennedy Airport by being stamped "seafood." Once at the Museum, though, it wasn't destined to become calamari but rather to be studied by Neil Landman and other invertebrate specialists. From there it traveled one last short hop to its final destination, a huge tank in the Hall of Biodiversity. Here it provides Museum visitors with a striking example of the diversity of the Earth's living creatures, and of how much we still have to learn about the animals that inhabit the last frontiers of our planet.

PUNCTUATED EQUILIBRIUM: BURSTS OF EVOLUTION

The norm for a species or by extension, a community is stability. Speciation is a rare and difficult event that punctuates a system in homeostatic equilibrium. That so uncommon an event should have produced such a wondrous array of living and fossil forms can only give strength to an old idea: paleontology deals with a phenomenon that belongs to it alone among the evolutionary sciences and that enlightens all its conclusions—time.

—*Stephen Jay Gould and Niles Eldredge, announcing their theory of punctuated equilibrium in* Models in Paleobiology *(T. J. M. Schopf, editor), 1972.*

Paleontology curator Niles Eldredge studies the long-extinct arthropods called trilobites (those ancient relatives of crabs, lobsters, and pill bugs), but a few minutes of conversation or a glance at his list of published works makes it clear that he has another passion: sharing the fascinating "inside story" of modern science with the world outside the scientific establishment. Among the stories he has to tell is one that turns on its head everything most of us thought we knew about evolution.

In 1972, Eldredge and Stephen Jay Gould, professor of geology at Harvard University and Frederick P. Rose Honorary Curator in Invertebrates at the Museum, developed the theory they called "punctuated equilibrium"—or, as Eldredge casually refers to it, "punc eq" (pronounced "punk eek"). This theory states that Charles Darwin was wrong in some of the crucial details of his revolutionary theories of evolution.

Darwin believed that constant environmental pressures—the endless battles of natural selection, resulting in the survival of the fittest—caused steady, gradual, and virtually constant evolution in every species. Punc eq states that this is not true; instead, evolution of species into new forms takes place in dramatic bursts separated by huge time spans in which virtually no evolution takes place at all.

"As a neonate in 1972, punctuated equilibrium entered the world in unusual guise," wrote Eldredge and Gould in a 1993 article in *Nature*. "We claimed no new discovery, but only a novel interpretation for the oldest and most robust of palaeontological observations: the geologically instantaneous origination and subsequent stability (often for millions of years) of palaeontological 'morphospecies.' " That is, among extinct animals, the fossil record has always demonstrated long periods of stasis punctuated by evolutionary bursts that "instantly" (in geologic time) creates new species.

"Rather than accept the fossil evidence showing that one of Darwin's central tenets needed adjusting, paleontologists claimed that the record itself was flawed," Eldredge explains. "No one can argue that there are notorious holes in the fossil record, but all of the evidence points to punctuated equilibrium as the mode of evolution."

In a *Natural History* article cowritten by Niles and Michelle J. Eldredge in 1972 (the year the theory was announced), the authors used a trilobite (*Phacops rana*) that inhabited the Devonian seas of North America to demonstrate how the fossil record supports the idea of evolutionary bursts. "*P. rana* had a very large compound eye on each side of the swollen, rounded middle region of the head, prompting the name rana, which means frog," the Eldredges wrote. "Each eye is covered with many lenses arranged in vertical rows around the eye. Twice in the long evolutionary history of this trilobite, the number of vertical rows of lenses was reduced, giving rise to a new variety of *P. rana* each time."

Extensive research, which involved hunting for *P. rana* specimens from New York to Michigan, showed that the transition from eighteen rows of lenses to seventeen and then to fifteen took place in two brief bursts. In both instances, the transition occurred in nearshore environments of the eastern Devonian sea, at times when the sea shrank in size on its western edge. Each time, the more primitive form of *P. rana* (the one with greater numbers of lenses) disappeared, replaced when the seas returned by the new variety that had evolved in the east. Except for these dramatic events, the trilobite existed unchanged (once with eighteen rows, once with seventeen) for as long as 8 million years.

"Perhaps the most amazing feature of the entire *Phacops rana* story is its stasis—a persistence against change—through vast amounts of time," the authors concluded. "Contrary to popular belief, evolutionary change seems to occur infrequently, and usually in small, isolated populations in a short span of time. The bulk of species' history is stasis, and there is no inexorable, progressive evolutionary march through time."

As might be expected, such pronouncements raised a storm of controversy. Amid what Gould and Eldredge call "an astonishing lack of evidence" for Darwin's gradualistic theories, other paleontologists severely criticized punc eq's reading of the fossil record. So did evolutionary biologists studying living species, despite the fact that evidence seemed to indicate a punctuated course of evolution and speciation among living creatures as well.

As the authors point out, the theories developed by the brilliant evolutionist Ernst Mayr (an ornithologist at the Museum for many years) show that speciation tends to occur in small populations isolated from the parental stock, *not* in a steady course in large, central populations. This mode of speciation, they add, "would yield stasis and punctuation when properly scaled into the vastness of geologic time," much as it did with *P. rana*, in which the new form, having evolved in isolation, swept across the Devonian sea after a period of environmental upheaval.

Gould, Eldredge, and many other scientists (notably Steven M. Stanley and Elisabeth S. Vrba) have refined the theory of punctuated equilibrium since 1972. Early on, Gould and Eldredge focused on the tempo of the evolutionary bursts, seeking to delineate patterns over time. Today, more research focuses on the causes of stasis and evolution, as well as on creating a new definition of "macroevolution," an overview of evolutionary trends among all species over time.

In the quarter of a century since the theory was unveiled, it has gradually become more widely accepted in the scientific establishment. Ernst Mayr, who had criticized the theory, relented somewhat in the face of overwhelming evidence. "I agree with Gould that the frequency of stasis in fossil species revealed by the recent analysis was unexpected by most evolutionary biologists," he acknowledged in his 1992 book *The Dynamics of Evolution.* "It's not that everyone agrees with us, but at least they are willing to discuss it," Eldredge comments.

Recently, researchers have discovered evidence of punctuated equilibrium in the evolution of mollusks, mammals, and other groups. And, in a fascinating series of laboratory experiments reported in 1996, a team of Michigan State University scientists found that bacteria tended to evolve to greater size over time, but that this evolution took place in sudden bursts after thousands of generations with no observed change. In other words, punctuated equilibrium.

Despite such encouraging support for their theory, Gould and Eldredge are taking the long view as to whether they've uncovered the true design of the evolution of life. This is how they conclude their 1993 update in *Nature:* "Thus, in developing punctuated equilibrium, we have either been toadies and panderers to fashion, and therefore destined for history's ashheap, or we had a spark of insight about nature's constitution. Only the punctuational and unpredictable future can tell."

7   The Life and Times of the
Ancient World

BIRTH OF A QUEST

> Please pardon my seeming negligence in writing for Cope
> quarry is a veritable gold mine and I have been in bones up
> to my eyes. . . . Wish you were here to enjoy the pleasure of
> taking out these beautiful black, perfect bones.
>
> —*Paleontologist Barnum Brown, in an 1897 letter to Curator*
> *of Fossil Vertebrates Henry Fairfield Osborn, upon discovering*
> *the first dinosaur ever collected by the museum.*

The place where pure science and public enthusiasm meet is a
junction that all great fossil hunters know well. No one understood the essential relationship between research and publicity
better than Henry Fairfield Osborn, founder of the Museum's
Department of Vertebrate Paleontology (DVP) and relentless
promoter of every department's scientists and their findings.

When Museum President Morris Jesup lured Osborn away
from Princeton University in 1891 and gave him full freedom to
create the new department, the Museum's patchwork collections
included virtually no vertebrate fossils of any kind—and not a

single dinosaur bone. Elsewhere in the United States, Othniel Charles Marsh, Edward Drinker Cope, and other famous collectors were garnering front-page newspaper headlines for their remarkable fossil finds, many of which were ending up in other natural history museums. For the ambitious and self-confident Osborn, this was an intolerable situation, and one that could not be permitted to last.

One of Osborn's first successes was arranging for the Museum to buy Cope's enormous collection of fossil mammals and reptiles, including dinosaurs. But he realized as well that he had to send collectors into the field to explore the many as-yet-untouched fossil beds that others would reach if the Museum didn't. To that end, Osborn hired a group of paleontologists as determined and talented as any ever associated with a single museum at one time, including Barnum Brown, Walter Granger, W. D. Matthew, Albert Thomson, Jacob Wortman, J. W. Gidley, and many others. Together, these collectors were responsible for the discovery of countless dinosaurs, fossil mammals, and other important ancient animals.

While Osborn was planning the Museum's first major paleontological expedition—an 1897 exploration of the Como Bluff region in Wyoming—museum paleontologists were already undertaking less ambitious fossil hunts. One of the earliest was W. D. Matthew's prospecting trip to a coal mine in Egypt, North Carolina, in 1895.

Mines have long been attractive sites for paleontologists, as they provide unparalleled access to rich fossil beds that might otherwise remain unreachable. On the other hand, attempting to remove fossils from a coal mine in the 1890s carried serious risks, which Matthew—in the spirit of fossil hunters then and now—both acknowledged and ignored. During an 1894 scouting trip to the mine, Matthew had worked closely with a supervisor named Williams. Upon returning in 1895, he found that the supervisor had been killed in a mine explosion. Matthew noted the tragedy in a letter to Osborn and then went to work.

Osborn, whose specialty was fossil mammals, had hoped Matthew would be able to collect some in the mine. In a June 13, 1895 letter, though, the collector reported that he had failed, but not really. "Have not succeeded in getting any mammal bones," he reported. "Of the saurian remains I have made some very good hauls. The best so far is what appears to be a head, with jaws over two feet long."

Having painstakingly collected the head and hundreds of associated bones, Matthew brought his find back to the Museum. Restored, it turned out to be a superb specimen of a ten-foot-long reptile called *Rutiodon*, a member of a superficially crocodilelike group known as phytosaurs that lived in the late Triassic period, at the same time as the earliest dinosaurs.

Scientifically important, Matthew's *Rutiodon* has historical resonance as well: It is the first specimen in the Museum's world-famous catalogue of fossil reptiles, the very first entry in a list that, within a decade, would include *Tyrannosaurus*, *Apatosaurus*, *Ornitholestes*, and other famous dinosaurs.

The Museum's great dig at Como Bluff and adjacent sites near the Wyoming town of Medicine Bow, which began in 1897 and lasted until 1904, allowed such young paleontologists as Barnum Brown and Walter Granger to gain essential collecting experience in the field. As importantly, the expedition proved that rich sites for dinosaur fossils still existed in the American West.

As with Matthew's journey to the Egypt coal mine, the Museum's first expedition to Como Bluff, whose fossil beds dated from the Jurassic period, was not designed to collect dinosaurs. Cope and Marsh's excavations in previous years had removed most of the important dinosaur specimens, but Osborn hoped the Museum's team might be able to find some overlooked remains of Jurassic mammals.

When this goal proved elusive, the fossil hunters started excavating some promising nearby exposures, where their luck soon changed. Brown immediately found masses of dinosaur bones, soon identified as belonging to the gigantic sauropod *Diplodocus*. It was "the finest specimen that has ever been found in the Jurassic," Brown wrote to Osborn with understandable excitement.

This specimen was the first dinosaur ever excavated by the Museum, leading Osborn to proclaim in the 1897 Annual Report: "Thus has been inaugurated the second great division of the [department's] work, namely the history of the reptiles of North America."

THE SEARCH FOR THE LIVING DINOSAUR

> We should like very much to have your account of the new and remarkable animal called *Tyrannosaurus rex*, which you are confident you can describe in two or three pages. We hope this reptile is a handsome bird and not an ugly fish like some of the quadrupeds in your previous articles, for we do not want to scare mothers and children.
>
> —*Letter to Henry Fairfield Osborn from R. U. Johnson, associate editor of the* Century Magazine, *June 7, 1906.*

When paleontologists study a dinosaur specimen, their methods are quite similar to those an ornithologist, for example, uses when studying modern birds. The dinosaur skeleton, or whatever was found of it, is analyzed for distinctive characteristics, allowing the researchers to determine which previously known dinosaurs the new specimen is most closely related to. The goal, as always, is to devise as complete a cladistic tree of relationships as possible, with an eye to greater understanding of the course of evolution.

When it comes to dinosaurs, this can be a frustrating job. As the Museum's Mark Norell, division chair and Curator of the division of paleontology, points out, "The fossil record is so poor that we'll never be able to chart dinosaur evolution in any complete way." The best that can be done is to learn where the new dinosaur fits in, and whether it changes in any significant way what scientists thought they knew about dinosaur relationships.

Yet most paleontologists want even more from a dinosaur skeleton. They want to envision the living animal, to gain insights into its feeding, breeding, and other habits. But trying to deduce dinosaur behavior can be doubly frustrating, and for a simple reason: There are few living creatures whose habits permit us to come up with believable correlations with dinosaur behavior. (By contrast, a paleontologist studying, say, mammoths, would at least be able to use the behavior of living elephants for comparison.)

Birds, the only surviving dinosaurs, do provide some clues. Ostriches and other large, flightless birds allow us to imagine how extinct theropods (those bipedal carnivores that included *Velociraptor*, *Tyrannosaurus*, and others) might have moved. Similarly, analysis of dinosaur nesting sites discovered in Montana and, more recently, by Mark Norell and other Museum scientists in the Gobi Desert of Mongolia can include comparison with the techniques used by different groups of modern birds. (For more on the Museum's extraordinary Gobi finds, see pages 198-207).

Skeletons do grant some insights into general dinosaur behavior. The knifelike teeth of many theropods evince a diet of meat, while *Edmontosaurus* and *Iguanodon*, with their thousands of ridged cheek teeth designed for grinding, were obviously plant eaters. Similarly, bone structure shows us that *Allosaurus* and *Tyrannosaurus* walked on two legs, *Triceratops* and *Ankylosaurus* on four.

But again, paleontologists want to learn—or intuit—more, and they always have. A glance through the history of dinosaur discovery at the Museum reveals an extraordinary network of guesses, theories, suppositions, and retractions over the whys and wherefores of dinosaur behavior. These struggles show how generations of brilliant scientists have wrestled with the lessons that can be learned from the scantest of traces left behind by long-extinct animals.

A dramatic example of the start-and-stop nature of dinosaur behavioral studies can be seen in Henry Fairfield Osborn's discussion of a small Jurassic theropod called *Ornitholestes*, first discovered during a Museum expedition to Wyoming in 1901. As Osborn recalled in a 1917 *American Museum Journal* article, he first studied the skeleton soon after its discovery and "reached the conclusion that this little dinosaur was a carnivore and preyed upon the primitive contemporary birds. . . ."

Following his initial analysis, Osborn named the specimen *Ornitholestes* ("Bird Robber") and went on to say, "The theory was that by great speed and very alert movements *Ornitholestes* was able to overtake and capture its prey."

While there is absolutely no evidence that *Ornitholestes* ate birds, the rest of this description fits perfectly with most current theories (based on careful analysis of skeletal structure) on the speed and agility of such small carnivorous dinosaurs. The Charles Knight illustration that accompanies Osborn's *Journal* article, which shows *Ornitholestes* having just grabbed *Archaeopteryx* (the famous ancient bird), is again unprovable in detail but ahead of its time in spirit; it was a direct blow against the then-prevailing belief that dinosaurs were sluggish, slow-moving creatures.

Yet Osborn renounces his own earlier conclusions in his 1917 article. "It is an interesting instance of how one discovery in science affects another that this theory of the habits of the ancient 'bird robber' has become untenable through the subsequent dis-covery of another dinosaur. . . ." he writes. The discovery that supposedly disproved his theory was of *Struthiomimus*, a small theropod that, unlike the sharp-toothed *Ornitholestes*, had no teeth at all, only a horny bill. Osborn concluded that toothless *Struthiomimus* must have eaten plants or fruit, and therefore that an active, predatory life for its "ancestor," *Ornitholestes*, must have been out of the question. And so a clear-eyed view of dinosaur behavior, almost achieved in the early 1900s, had to wait for future generations of scientists to prevail.

Tyrannosaurus rex, the most famous dinosaur of all, provides another object lesson in the frustrations of interpreting behavior from bones. From almost the instant that Barnum Brown discov-ered the first *Tyrannosaurus* skeleton near Hell Creek, Montana, in 1902, the public was enraptured by the concept that such a massive carnivore had once inhabited western North America. (Despite the amusingly squeamish tone of the *Century Magazine* editor quoted at the start of this section, the public has always loved dinosaurs that seemed designed to "scare mothers and children.")

By the time Brown discovered a second, even more beautifully preserved, *Tyrannosaurus* skeleton in 1908 (the one now on dis-play in the Museum), the public was hungry for descriptions of what the enormous dinosaur was like when it was alive, and Brown was more than willing to assuage that hunger. "A huge herbivorous dinosaur *Trachodon*, coming ashore for some favorite food has been seized and partly eaten by a giant *Tyran-nosaurus*," he wrote in a 1915 *Journal* article, describing a pro-posed Museum display. "Whilst this monster is ravenously consuming the carcass another *Tyrannosaurus* draws near deter-mined to dispute the prey. . . . With colossal bodies poised on massive hind legs and steadied by long tails, ponderous heads armed with sharp dagger-like teeth three to five inches long, front limbs exceedingly small but set for a powerful clutch, they are the very embodiment of dynamic animal force."

Interestingly, the posture of the 1915 skeletal restoration of the 1908 specimen—probably the single most recognizable dinosaur skeleton in history—seems to undercut Brown's claims. Head held high, tail dragging on the ground, this *Tyrannosaurus* seemed capable of an energetic shuffle at best, not a dynamism that would enable it to overtake speedy prey.

In recent years, experts in skeletal anatomy have determined that *Tyrannosaurus* (and other theropod dinosaurs) was capable of a "stalking" pose: head low, back horizontal to ground, tail held high as a counterweight. Now *this* is a dynamic design. A visitor stepping into the Hall of Saurischian Dinosaurs and confronting this enormous, low-slung predator has no trouble believing that *Tyrannosaurus* could pound along at great speeds, certainly fast enough to overtake slower dinosaur prey.

Typically, however, the vision of *Tyrannosaurus* as a sleek, agile hunter is not the only view held by modern paleontologists. A vocal group insists that the dinosaur was simply too large and unwieldy to chase living prey, and may in fact have been an eater of carrion, a vulture, locating and feasting on dead meat. Gazing at the breathtaking stance of the Museum's skeleton, a visitor may find this hypothesis hard to accept, but it is the fate of behavioral theories that they are always controversial and often unprovable.

Sometimes a single important find can pique the interest of everyone from the most experienced paleontologist to the youngest dinosaur enthusiast. Nearly ninety years after it was found, the "mummy" dinosaur *Edmontosaurus* (a member of a group of plant-eating dinosaurs called hadrosaurs, or duck-billed dinosaurs) remains one of the most thought-provoking dinosaur specimens of all time.

The mummy dinosaur was found and excavated by Charles Hazelius Sternberg and his three sons, a team of freelance fossil hunters. Sternberg was a remarkable man, devoting his life to collecting fossils, despite the fact that no museum would employ him full time. He frequently spent more money prospecting than he received in payment for specimens, and seemed at times to live a frighteningly hand-to-mouth existence. "He is penniless and completely worn out," commented a Museum curator after visiting the seventy-three-year-old Sternberg's spartan camp.

Perhaps driven by the omnipresent threat of failure, Sternberg used his great fossil-hunting skills to discover some of the finest dinosaur skeletons ever. He excavated the type specimen of *Pentaceratops* and supplied the Museum with *Albertosaurus* and many other exceptional specimens. But perhaps his greatest glory was the mummy *Edmontosaurus*, found by his son George and excavated by the four Sternbergs in Converse County, Wyoming, in 1908.

While the vast majority of dinosaur skeletons are found disarticulated (with most of the bones separated and, frequently, scattered), this specimen was preserved exactly where and as it fell. When the Sternbergs found it, the skeleton was lying on its back, its hind legs (partly weathered away) drawn up, its forelimbs pointing outward, and its head pulled backward and to the right. It looked remarkably like some large animal that had died recently, not 65 million years ago.

Sternberg and Osborn would have been excited enough to find a dinosaur skeleton in such fine condition, but the *Edmontosaurus* was even more spectacular: It had been preserved in such pristine condition that its bones were surrounded by the impressions of its skin, left in the sand that covered the specimen's body before the soft tissues decayed. "Shall I ever experience such joy as when I stood in the quarry for the first time, and beheld lying in state the most complete skeleton of an extinct animal I have ever seen, after forty years experience as a collector!" Sternberg wrote of the find.

For the first time, scientists had the chance to study more than a dinosaur's bones. They were able to determine, for example, that the *Edmontosaurus*'s skin was not composed of overlapping scales—as is a snake's—but of a combination of larger scales and small bumpy ones called "tubercules."

But it was the pattern of the scales that aroused the most interest and led to generations of speculation that continues in full force today. The scales, it turned out, were not spread in even patterns across the dinosaur's body, as Sternberg pointed out in a description of the specimen: "Small octagon scales a quarter of an inch in diameter formed a diamond-like pattern about three inches apart, in longitudinal and perpendicular rows, the interspace filled with minute impressions of smaller scales, some no larger than the head of a pin."

Why was this discovery so interesting? Because it provided the first clues that dinosaurs may have sported far more vivid colors than the dull greens and grays that most early restorations gave them. In modern reptiles, varied scale patterns often show a corresponding color pattern. The *Edmontosaurus* mummy allowed the public, and even some paleontologists, to speculate far more freely about dinosaur coloration than ever before. "My thought in the matter is that at least some of the dinosaurs were probably neutral in color and they were probably lighter on the belly than on the backs," Barnum Brown wrote in 1936. "Such creatures as *Stegosaurus* may have been quite highly colored on the spines especially."

Sometimes it is not the dinosaur itself but the traces it leaves behind, that can teach us about its behavior. This was never truer than in the case of the great Glen Rose dinosaur tracks.

In March 1924, a commercial postcard found its way to the desk of paleontologist Walter Granger at the Museum. On one side it showed a photograph labeled "DINASAUR TRACKS, GLEN ROSE, TEX." On the other was scrawled the following note, written by a man named E. G. Sicard: "This card may be of interest to you."

Interest was too mild a word; Granger was excited. Dinosaur tracks were rarely discovered, and these ones looked like they might be real. If so, Granger wrote to Sicard, they represented "remarkably fine ones." By fortunate coincidence, the department's W. D. Matthew and George Gaylord Simpson were planning to be in Texas during the summer of 1924 and, Granger wrote, might be able to visit Glen Rose to take a look at the tracks themselves.

We know that Matthew and Simpson did take a collecting trip to Texas in 1924, but it seems that they never visited Glen Rose. Nor did any other Museum collector. Amazingly, the correspondence between Granger and Sicard seems to have been filed away, and soon no one in the department recalled that rare and important dinosaur tracks were lying in Texas, waiting for discovery.

Then, in a stroke of luck, a Museum paleontologist named Roland T. Bird entered a New Mexico trading post in 1938 and spotted some dinosaur footprints for sale. Though he concluded that these were fakes, he was shown some others that seemed real. They came, he was told, from an area near the town of Glen Rose, Texas.

Bird traveled immediately to Glen Rose, where he found the tracks to be well known—in fact, they were a source of civic pride, with one excavated footprint placed directly outside the town courthouse. Actually, the residents of Glen Rose were a bit surprised at his enthusiasm over the tracks, Bird recalled: "Yes, the natives said, looking me over carefully, there were lots of them up along the Paluxy River."

When he visited the river, Bird saw a remarkable assemblage of trackways of theropod dinosaurs, made during the early Cretaceous in what must then have been an expansive mudflat. This was a spectacular find, but it was about to get even better. "I noticed a large pothole not far away that seemed oddly out of place," Bird wrote. "Could anything that big possibly be a track? Could it be . . . and a wild thought occurred . . . possibly sauropod?"

It was. Bird had discovered the first footprint of the group of enormous plant eaters, the sauropods, which include the famous *Apatosaurus*, *Diplodocus*, *Barosaurus*, and many others. But even this wasn't all. "Suddenly filled with a wild thrill that I hardly dared to accept, I got up and looked around," Bird wrote. "A full twelve feet away was another pothole. . . . It, too, was a gigantic footprint."

Standing there, feeling as if the dinosaur that had left these incredible tracks might walk back into sight at any moment, Bird was elated. "There come rare moments in the lives of all of us when we see things that we do not actually believe," he wrote in a joyous letter back to the Museum. But he knew what he had found, and so did the equally excited curators back home.

The trackway that Bird chose to excavate and ship to the Museum (where it is now on display) was the most fascinating of all: It seemed to show a huge sauropod hurrying across the mudflat ("full of the business of going places," in Bird's words), closely pursued by a large theropod, apparently a relative of the famous carnosaur *Allosaurus*. Could this be a hunt in progress, evidence that the great carnosaurs hunted the even greater sauropods?

Probably not. Analysis by trackway experts Martin Lockley and Adrian P. Hunt shows that the evidence of a hunt along the Paluxy is controversial at best. "Based on the overall trackway picture, we surmise that twelve brontosaurs passed, probably as a herd, followed somewhat later by three theropods that may or may not have been stalking—but that certainly were not attacking," they write in their 1995 book *Dinosaur Tracks.*

Another trackway unearthed by Bird seemed to show only the forefeet of a sauropod. Bird interpreted this as evidence that the dinosaur was swimming, using its forefeet to push off while its body, rear feet, and tail floated in the water. This image confirmed a widely held theory at the time that sauropods were swamp dwellers who used water to help support their enormous weight.

Again, however, recent analysis by Martin Lockley and others has shown that Bird misinterpreted the evidence. In fact, it appears that these trackways were merely poorly preserved. Since many sauropods invariably leave deeper prints with their forefeet than hindfeet, all that survived for Bird to find were the last faint tracks of what had once been the prints left by all four of the dinosaur's feet.

Still, Bird's discoveries were magnificent, and they and other trackways *do* tell us a lot about dinosaur behavior. Bird's trackways were the first to reveal that some dinosaurs, including sauropods, traveled in herds, and that adult and juveniles traveled together. "It really looks as if a whole herd of sauropods had passed there in a bunch," Bird wrote to Barnum Brown from the Paluxy in 1940. "They were all headed the same way, like sheep, a suggestion of pushing and shoving on the far end, where two or three individuals jostled one another."

Most of all, trackways give us an unmatched glimpse of dinosaurs as active, living creatures, not just preserved bones. This excitement gripped Roland T. Bird, who described one trackway as a "sauropodian barnyard where a wallowing good time was had by all." And it continues to grip anyone with the slightest interest in the lives and habits of dinosaurs today.

The above finds and others have helped us gain some insight

into dinosaur behavior, but few of these insights are without controversy. As Museum paleontologists Mark Norell, Eugene S. Gaffney, and Lowell Dingus ask in their 1995 book *Discovering Dinosaurs*, "What do we really know about the dinosaurs?" The safest answer to that question is: We know nothing but what we see in the bones. Anything else is pure speculation.

Still, since the earliest days of dinosaur discovery, speculation—about dinosaur behavior, color, and diet—has been hard to resist. Step into the Museum's towering Roosevelt Rotunda, and you'll see an exhibit based on speculation: The sauropod *Barosaurus*, rearing up on its hind legs to defend its young from a marauding *Allosaurus*. "Could this have taken place? Sure," say the authors of *Discovering Dinosaurs*. "Is there objective evidence that scenes like this actually took place? No."

Trackways have shown that young and adult sauropods did travel together, and at least one trackway—a late Cretaceous site in Bolivia—seems to depict a herd of carnosaurs trailing after a group of sauropods. Unfortunately, no footprints or other evidence show that *Barosaurus* was even capable of rearing onto its hind legs, much less to protect its baby from a predator.

Not that scientists haven't tried to demonstrate that such behavior was possible. Norell, Gaffney, and Dingus describe the back-and-forth arguments resulting from biomechanical studies of sauropod skeletal structure. These studies seek to answer such questions as whether the hind legs could support the upraised body's weight and whether a heart of any size could have pumped blood to the brain of a sauropod in that posture.

But biomechanical predictions of animal behavior aren't very conclusive and don't even work well when applied to modern-day animals. "Living animals often exhibit unexpected capabilities," the authors point out. "For instance, given only one skeleton to examine, could you envision the circus antics of modern Asiatic elephants—rearing upright on their hind limbs, standing on their head, or walking on their front feet?"

In the absence of objective evidence, they conclude, the *Barosaurus* and *Allosaurus* mount "remains a spectacular, thought-provoking possibility." Such possibilities—always accompanied by the chance that the next great find will either prove or disprove them—are what make the unraveling of the dinosaur record and the study of dinosaur behavior such an intoxicating experience.

FOSSIL FISHES: WINDOW TO OUR ORIGINS

I like to say that everything interesting in evolution took place before fins evolved into limbs—that is, before fish developed the ability to leave the water and enter the land.

—John Maisey, fossil-fish specialist and Curator in the Division of Paleontology, in 1996.

With the opening of the Hall of Vertebrate Origins in 1996, the Museum is giving due to the fascinating extinct creatures that provide among the most important clues to the evolution of life on earth today, but which remain far less well known than the dinosaurs. Here are the aquatic plesiosaurs and ichthyosaurs and the magnificent flying pterosaurs, alongside early salamanders and ancient turtles. And here, too, are fossil fishes, the backboned animals that lie at the very root of the cladistic family tree that includes all vertebrate life on earth.

Fossil fishes have long intrigued curators at the Museum, especially after Bashford Dean supervised the purchase of the Jay Terrell Collection in 1900, giving the Museum its first large assemblage of fossil fishes. "As to these ancient fishes: There can be little question that in all of their forms, large and small, they were ravenous and shark-like in habits," he wrote. "And the large *Dinichthys* [now called *Dunkleosteus*] . . . was certainly a dangerous neighbor, easily the master of all other kinds of animals living in this time."

Today, John Maisey shares Bashford Dean's fascination with ancient fishes and their evolution. But Maisey and other modern ichthyologists know far more than scientists did in Dean's time, as a series of important discoveries has given us a far more complete and intriguing picture of fish evolution than was possible a century ago.

One of the most exciting finds was of a primitive fish called *Sacabambaspis* (a member of a group called "ostracoderms") in Bolivia. This small fish shows that the origin of fish, and therefore the origin of vertebrates, dates back at least as far as the late Ordovician period, about 450 million years ago. According to Maisey, the circumstances surrounding this crucial find provide an object lesson in how preconceptions can bedevil even the most eminent scientist.

"A paleontologist was exploring these Ordovician exposures with his students, and one of the students found an interesting fossil fragment that looked like fish bone to him," Maisey says. "But his teacher scoffed, saying it was just a piece of shell—common in the Ordovician—and threw it away. After all, it couldn't be a fish fossil, since everyone knew that fish didn't live in the Ordovician."

The enterprising student, trusting his own instincts instead of his teacher's, retrieved the specimen. When it was studied by a paleontologist with a more open mind, the fossil proved the student right, changing scientific conventional wisdom about the extraordinarily ancient origins of the fishes. "Once they realized that fish did actually live in the Ordovician, they had no trouble finding more *Sacabambaspis* fossils," Maisey comments. "In fact, the paving stones and curbstones of the nearby town of Saca-bamba are taken from the same Ordovician exposures and con-tain the same fossils—you can say that the streets are paved with *Sacabambaspis.*"

While Maisey is fascinated by the earliest stages of fish evolu-tion, much of his own recent research has focused on fishes that lived about 110 million years ago, during the Cretaceous period. In particular, he has studied the fossils of the Santana Formation in Brazil, where shales and limestones protrude from a dramatic upland area called the Araripe Plateau. Take one look at the fos-sils retrieved from the Santana Formation, and it's clear why a fossil-fish specialist would devote years to their study: The San-tana specimens may be the most finely preserved fossils ever dis-covered anywhere.

Scientists have known about the Santana Formation's richness since the early 1800s, when two members of the Academy of Sci-ences in Munich, J. B. von Spix and C. F. P. von Martius, were given a geological collection from northeastern Brazil. The collec-tion included beautiful fossil fishes of many kinds.

In the years following, other scientists—notably eminent pale-ontologist Louis Agassiz—described further specimens from the region and made attempts to unravel the area's complex geology. The most important of these scientists, Maisey says, was Profes-sor Rubens da Silva Santos, who beginning in the 1940s described a variety of new Santana fish species, discovered the formation's first tetrapods (terrestrial vertebrates such as crocodilians), and gathered other crucial geological and paleontological data.

This groundbreaking work and subsequent excavations and study—much of it with the support of Museum benefactor Dr. Herbert R. Axelrod—have allowed paleontologists to determine that the fossils of the Santana Formation come mainly from two levels of strata (called "members"), one a few million years older than the other. The earlier fossils occur in strata representing a lacustrine (freshwater) habitat, known as "the Crato Member." The younger fossils occur in deposits that were laid down in a lagoon or other brackish environment, now called "the Romualdo Member."

"It appears that the lacustrine environment became hypersaline—leading to the disappearance of many fish species—and then became lagoonal," Maisey says. "At no time, however, did conditions become those of a typical marine environment, as you'd find in the open sea. We know this because typical ocean invertebrates, including ammonites and corals, have never been found in the Santana Formation."

Between them, the Crato and Romualdo Members have yielded abundant fossil fishes, along with spectacularly well-preserved specimens of plants, insects, frogs, pterosaurs, and even parts of a dinosaur so well preserved that its soft tissue, including blood vessels and muscle fibers, became fossilized and can now be studied. But it is the fossil fishes of the Romualdo Member (at least two dozen species of more than a dozen families) that have given Maisey an unmatched opportunity to study the feeding behavior and other habits of animals that have been extinct for more than 100 million years.

How is it possible to study the feeding behavior of extinct fishes? Because the Romualdo Member specimens are so well preserved that, in many cases, the contents of their stomachs were fossilized along with them. By analyzing the dozens of specimens in which food is detectable in the stomach (or, more rarely, in the pharynx, perhaps indicative of a fish that choked on its last meal), one can learn something about what Maisey calls the "trophic hierarchy" of these fishes—what the rest of us might call the "food chain."

What Maisey was looking for was more than the obvious

answer. As he wrote in a 1994 article in the journal *Environmental Biology of Fishes*, "Small fishes were eaten by bigger fishes, then as now, but who was eating who, and how popular was the menu?"

Study of Santana specimens shows that a medium-sized fish named *Rhacolepis* feasted upon small shrimps similar to the modern genus *Mattea*. One newly described genus and species, thus far found mainly in *Rhacolepis* stomachs, was so clearly an important food source that it has been named *Paleomattea deliciosa*. *Rhacolepis* also ate smaller fishes, including *Santanichthys*. As Maisey points out, we can learn about the behavior of the prey species as well: "When several members of one species are found in a single *Rhacolepis*, it suggests that the prey species swam in schools."

Two larger fish, *Notelops* and *Cladocyclus*, both ate *Rhacolepis*, but, according to Maisey, since these two predators have very different body and mouth shapes, they may have adopted quite different techniques while hunting. "The upturned, terminal mouth in *Cladocyclus* suggests it came up from beneath its prey before striking, whereas *Notelops* may have borne down upon its prey at high speed," he writes.

One of the most abundant fishes in the Santana Formation is *Vinctifer*. Having no large teeth—only fine serrations along its jaws—it may well have filtered plankton and other microorganisms through its elaborate trapping structures called "gill rakers." Support from this theory comes from the fact that, despite study of more than 120 *Vinctifer* specimens at the museum, none has been found with anything in its stomach—not surprising if the preferred food was so small and easily digested. An important recent discovery—of larval, planktonic brachyuran crabs in the stomachs of fishes called *Tharrhias*—indicate that the Romualdo Member did, in fact, host a planktonic community, used as a food source by at least some fish species.

The exquisite preservation of the Santana fossil fishes may give us insights into more than just fish feeding habits. Careful skeletal analysis of *Rhacolepis* have revealed that their vertebrae contain "growth rings," much as trees do. As in trees, these rings allow scientists to determine how many years *Rhacolepis* lived, and to correlate aging with growth. Maisey is collaborating with fish ecologists with the Ontario Ministry of Natural Resources, and with ichthyologists at the University of Guelph, Ontario, using these new analytic techniques to garner more behavioral data from the fossils.

Further, researchers have found at least two *Rhacolepis* females containing fossilized oocytes (developing eggs). "These specimens have allowed us to make initial studies of oocyte structure," Maisey says. "In combination with the growth data contained in the vertebrae, they've also allowed us to say, 'This *Rhacolepis* was preparing to breed when it died toward the end of the biological spring season of its fifth year.' It's pretty neat to be able to do that with a fossil."

Clearly, Maisey could occupy the rest of his career studying the Santana fishes. ("With a few exceptions, you could teach a course in comparative ichthyology using just these fossils," he says.) But he is also interested in a broader perspective: He is using the Santana fossils—and fossil deposits of the same age in Venezuela, Colombia, and Mexico—to help paint a clearer portrait of the immense geological and biological changes going on in this stage of the Cretaceous period.

"This was a very critical time in the history of northeastern South America," he explains. "It was just after the separation of Africa from South America, and there was still close physical continuity between the two continents. These organisms were living right at the axis of this final separation. I'm interested in seeing if we can detect any impact of this event on the living world of the time."

Maisey believes he has been able to correlate at least one interesting phenomenon with the shifting of the earth's tectonic plates that caused the separation. "We know that the activity along the fault lines began in the south and moved northward, creating a series of rift basins, which filled up with lakes," he says. "In a number of the basins we've examined, there appears to be a progressive south-to-north change in the distribution of fish. At first you've got freshwater lake deposits with fish faunas in them, and then a bit later these same areas are filled with marine deposits, while farther north the basins are still freshwater."

Maisey pauses, and it is clear that he has a vivid image of a fascinating scenario in his mind's eye. "It's kind of nice to imagine these lakes developing and the fish somehow being shoved further north until they ran out of places to go," he says. "Of course, all of this is very preliminary—which is why it feels as if we've barely begun our research."

The Turtle's Skull

While John Maisey studies the life histories of fossil fish, ancient turtles are the specialty of Curator Eugene S. Gaffney. For many years Gaffney has worked to untangle the relationships and evolution of those fascinating reptiles, which first appeared in the Triassic period, at the same time as the earliest dinosaurs.

While it would seem to make sense to study turtle origins through analysis of the shells (the feature, after all, that distinguishes turtles from all other reptiles), the truth is that turtle skulls, in particular the ways their structure changes over time, have the capacity to provide great insights into the evolution of turtles.

The Museum's W. D. Matthew recognized this more than seventy years ago, writing in 1924, "I venture to remark that a more careful search for skulls of extinct chelonians [turtles], and less reliance upon the characters of the carapace and plastron [upper and lower shells] might perhaps aid in clearing up the real affinities of both fossil and recent members of the order." As early as 1975, Gaffney began taking Matthew's advice, developing a phylogeny and classification of turtles based largely on skull characters.

Two decades later, he continues to fill in the gaps in our understanding of how such an unusual group of reptiles evolved. In an article in *Nature* (May 5, 1994) announcing the discovery of an important new find in Africa, Gaffney and coauthor James W. Kitching point out that "the turtle skull is so highly modified that turtle origins are difficult to resolve without evidence about order of character acquisition." Until recently, the evidence of such order has been lacking: A large gap in both time and skeletal features existed between the late Triassic turtle *Proganochelys* (the most primitive form known) and more recent turtles.

Gaffney and Kitching's announcement in *Nature* was of a specimen that helps bridge the gap: *Australochelys*, an early Jurassic turtle from South Africa that is the most ancient African turtle known. *Australochelys*, which belongs to a new species, genus, and family, shared many primitive characters with *Proganochelys*, but not all. It's the differences that have led paleontologists to rethink the evolution of turtles.

"Previous turtle phylogenies suggest that most of the typical chelonian skull features evolved after turtles split into the two major groups, the Cryptodira and the Pleurodira," the authors write. "But this skull demonstrates that important cranial reorganization unexpectedly took place before the origin of the modern turtle groups."

Gaffney and Kitching speculate that the surprising skull

changes may reflect evolution of adaptations for hearing among these early turtles. What *Australochelys* shows for certain is that many more pieces are needed before the puzzle of turtle evolution is nearly complete.

CHILDS FRICK'S MYSTERIOUS TROVE

The beauty of the Frick Collection is that it has large population samples of large animals, extinct elephants, camels, rhinos from a particular place and time. We need to study population dynamics, variability within a species, and the course of evolution not only in rats and mice, but in large animals, too. Only the Frick Collection allows us to do this work, which is both important and a lot of fun.

—*Malcolm McKenna, Frick Curator in the Department of Vertebrate Paleontology.*

It is a truism with a strong grounding in fact that the better you are at self-promotion, the more likely you are to be remembered by future generations. Carl Akeley was not only a brilliant preparator and visionary conservationist but also a prolific teller of his life story. Roy Chapman Andrews was perhaps the only man who could have organized and run the Central Asiatic Expeditions, famous for the discovery of dinosaur eggs, *Velociraptor*, and a slew of other invaluable finds. But it was the spirit of adventure that Andrews embraced and publicized that made him immortal.

Then, on the other hand, we have Childs Frick. Son of the powerful, strong-willed industrialist Henry Clay Frick and a multi-millionaire himself, the younger Frick devoted most of his professional life to fossil mammals and also, with rare exceptions, to keeping himself and his wide-ranging collectors as invisible as possible to the general public, and even to other paleontologists. "I think Childs Frick and his work deserve to be far better known," says Malcolm McKenna. "But he didn't make it easy, since he was such a retiring person. I came to the Museum in 1960 to work on his collection, and even I only met him once before his death in 1965."

In a short 1975 biography of Frick, published in the journal *Curator*, paleontologist Theodore Galusha—one of Frick's leading collectors before joining the museum—gathered some of the facts about the man who spent his money so freely to increase our knowledge of mammalian evolution. According to Galusha, Frick was fascinated by natural history, and after attending Princeton chose to enter a career in science (much to the displeasure of his autocratic father, who thought Childs should have chosen business or finance).

After a stint collecting big-game mammals in Africa for the Museum and other institutions, Frick became more and more fascinated by mammalian paleontology. He joined the Museum in 1919, eventually taking on positions as both a research associate in Vertebrate Paleontology and as a Museum trustee. Almost immediately he began to finance collecting trips to sites dating from the Miocene and Pliocene epochs with lesser efforts devoted to collections from the Pleistocene and Oligocene.

At the same time, Frick began to establish research funds to help other Museum expeditions. "By 1932 he had set up, or mainly supported, twenty-seven other funds in the American Museum of Natural History for various other projects," Galusha writes. In addition to vertebrate paleontology, Frick "contributed generously to many other fields, including geology, biology, medicine, comparative anatomy, natural science education, forestry, anthropology, herpetology, and conservation. . . . His support in these and other fields of science was done unobtrusively; as a result few men—even his closest acquaintances—knew, or even guessed, how broad was the scope of his patronage of scientific research."

Establishing his own laboratory at the Museum, hiring his own collectors and preparators, Frick began what must rank as the most ambitious excavation of mammalian fossils in history. Here are the reports from a single field season, taken from an article by Frick in a 1929 issue of *Natural History*:

> The investigation of the difficult Miocene beds to the north of Barstow in the Mojave Desert, California, was continued for the eighth consecutive winter by Mr. Joseph Rak and assistants. . . . Work in the Hopi Indian Agency was resumed in the early spring by Mr. John C. Blick, assisted by Messrs. Charles Falkenbach and Joseph Rooney. . . . Researches were carried on in the Miocene, Pliocene, and Pleistocene to the North of Santa Fe, New Mexico. . . . The Pleistocene exposures along the Niobrara River near Hay Springs, Nebraska, were visited during midsummer by Messrs. Rak and Falkenbach. . . . The exploration of beds of Devil's Gulch-Valentine Pliocene affinity, in the vicinity of Ainsworth, Nebraska, was continued for the second summer by Mr. M. F. Skinner. . . . Exposures in the neighborhood of Elephant Butte and Benson, Arizona, have for a second time yielded Mr. Rak, while en route to California, a small but useful collection. . . .

"Every year, Frick would have teams in comparatively warm-weather sites like Barstow, California in the winter, and in colder areas like Nebraska and Wyoming in the summer," Malcolm McKenna comments. "A few years ago, some of us sat down and figured out that 1500-person-years went into collecting Frick specimens—and that doesn't include the paid collectors' wives, who often worked as hard as their husbands."

Nor did Frick focus only on the lower forty-eight states. In one extremely ambitious multiyear joint project with the University of Alaska, he sent a team headed by long-time Museum fossil hunter Peter Kaisen to remote regions of that great territory, which had only recently been opened up by mining interests and by the arrival of commercial airplane travel. ("This was Mr. Kaisen's first aerial travel and he pronounces it to be the ideal way to get somewhere and back again with comfort, speed and safety," reported the *Farthest-North Collegian*, the university newspaper, in 1930.)

Kaisen and other collectors brought back enormous assemblages of Pleistocene fossils. The 1930 collection included three tons of specimens, while the 1938 haul weighed a stunning eight tons, with 8,008 specimens packed into seventy-nine crates. "Besides the usual mammoth, superbison, caribou, and horse fossils, this year's collection includes such rarer finds as the mastodon, musk-ox, elk, moose, bear, lion, sabre-tooth tiger, camel, wolf, fox, wildcat (probably lynx), ground squirrels, and field mice," reported the *Collegian*.

"There was such a huge influx of specimens in the 1930s— much of it collected with the help of the Works Progress Administration—that the attics and crannies of the museum were bulging," Malcolm McKenna says. As a result, the Childs Frick Corporation (which Frick had created to oversee the business aspects of his enterprise), financed the creation of additional preparation and storage areas at the Museum, to be used by Frick Laboratory personnel.

Amazingly, Frick was so reserved, and wished his collectors to remain equally so, that no one knew how large his trove was. "Nearly nothing was published about his specimens, and although Frick's collectors were allowed to go to meetings, they couldn't present papers about their work," McKenna comments. "Frick's attitude was, 'Let's put away our specimens until we have a huge collection, and then we'll be able to study it more rationally.' Unfortunately, he frequently waited far too long, and his became virtually an unstudied collection."

Not surprisingly, the reticence of the Frick team caused extensive misunderstandings and jealousy among other collectors and local officials near the sites where the team worked. "For example, there were rumors that Frick collectors dynamited quarries to destroy whatever fossils they hadn't taken," McKenna says. "What they actually did was 'button up' the mouths of their quarries, partly to prevent anyone from getting killed if an overhang collapsed and partly to protect the fossils until they came back the next year."

Another common complaint was that the Frick collectors were pulling fossils out of the ground without mapping where they were found or recording the geologic strata. This, too, proved unfounded, McKenna says, "Actually, the data gathered by Frick's collectors were better than data kept by researchers from ninety percent of universities."

Some of the most bitter misunderstandings originated within the Museum. George Gaylord Simpson, the brilliant, famously opinionated Museum paleontologist whose theories of mammalian evolution are still influential today, was infuriated at the inaccessibility of the Frick Collection. "Simpson believed that specimens should be made available very rapidly to the scientific community—a belief that Frick obviously did not share," McKenna explains. "My wife, Priscilla, says that there are times you have to 'rise above your principles.' Simpson was never able to do this, never able to unbend enough to get along with Frick—and as a result he never got to see the Frick Collection, despite the fact that they were at the Museum together for thirty years."

Despite Frick's dicta, some of his leading collectors did manage to share some of their most important findings with other Museum paleontologists. "Morris Skinner and others would conduct what we called 'Sunday School,' inviting young scientists up on Sundays to teach what they knew, when they were sure Mr. Frick wouldn't be coming to the Museum," McKenna recalls. "They were concerned with continuity, they knew the separate Frick system had to come to an end eventually, so they would transfer their knowledge to us with the ultimate goal of integrating the collection."

When Childs Frick died in 1965, his massive trove—loosely estimated as containing between 250,000 and 500,000 specimens—belonged to the Childs Frick Corporation, which had no responsibility to donate the collection to the Museum. As it turned out, the Frick Corporation did choose to give the specimens to the Museum. In addition, along with the funds contributed by the Museum trustees and federal grants, the corporation also financed the construction of the ten-story Frick Building, which now contains the DVP offices and the endless crates, cabinets, and shelves that house the world's finest collection of vertebrate fossils.

"Private support of research in vertebrate paleontology on the scale provided by Childs Frick will probably never again appear," Theodore Galusha lamented at the conclusion of his 1975 eulogy for Frick. "His legacy will be perceived only dimly by the scientists of the future, but each time paleontologists publish the results of their research on the Frick Collection, their contribution will stand as a monument to Frick's profound regard for natural history and, in particular, to his love for vertebrate paleontology."

In Search of Ancient Kangaroos

Malcolm McKenna brought Paleontology Curator Richard Tedford aboard in the early 1960s to oversee and analyze the Frick Collection. ("The best decision I ever made," McKenna comments.) In the decades since, Tedford has done invaluable work on Frick's trove, but he has also carved out an important niche for himself: discovering and studying the bizarre, fascinating extinct mammals of Australia.

One of the most remarkable sites explored by Tedford is Lake Callabona in South Australia. Described by Sir E. C. Stirling, the scientist who first excavated it in 1893, as a "veritable necropolis of gigantic extinct marsupials and birds," this site has been visited by only five expeditions in the century since its first discovery. Only two have made extensive collections: the original South Australia Museum party led by Stirling and a joint Smithsonian Institution, American Museum, and South Australia Museum expedition in 1970, of which Tedford was a member.

What makes this Pleistocene site so remarkable? Tedford and coauthor Roderick Wells of Flinders University, Adelaide, South Australia, explain in a 1995 *Bulletin* describing *Sthenurus*, a huge extinct kangaroo found there. "Like the other large-bodied vertebrates at Lake Callabona, the *Sthenurus* species were mired in the clays while attempting to cross the floor of the lake during low-water and dry times."

The bogged-down animals would perish, and then would be quickly covered by clay and other sediments. As a result, the accumulating skeletons—many found still articulated, and some so well preserved that skin impressions are visible—give paleontologists an almost unprecedented look at the life around the lake between approximately 200,000 and 700,000 years ago.

The authors identify a total of three kangaroo species of varying size belonging to the genus *Sthenurus*, all of which lived simultaneously in the region. A combination of morphological work and comparison with living kangaroo species allow the authors to speculate on the living form and habits of *Sthenurus*—and also to acknowledge that much must remain guesswork. "The overall impression our functional speculations have produced is that *Sthenurus* was a bulky, browsing kangaroo," they report, but add: "Just how the three species coexisting at Lake Callabona partitioned this broad feeding niche beyond utilizing plants of different height is difficult to understand."

THE CALL OF THE GOBI

I don't believe that the golden age of exploration is something that we have to look back on, something that has passed. I feel very fortunate that there are still places like the Gobi Desert, where you can make important finds—discoveries that can still revolutionize our view of vertebrate evolution.

—Michael J. Novacek, Museum senior vice-president, Provost, and Curator of vertebrate paleontology, on the spectacularly successful recent expeditions to Mongolia.

Howling winds. Dangerous sandstorms. Blisteringly hot days and frigidly cold nights. The constant threat of sandblindness, of injuries sustained far from any doctor or hospital, of illness or death from tainted or absent water.

All these risks characterize any visit to the Gobi Desert. So why on earth would generations of Museum paleontologists brave such conditions to spend months tracking across this forbidding, nearly inaccessible wilderness?

For a very simple reason: That's where the fossils are. During the past seventy-five years, Museum expeditions to the Gobi have uncovered a treasure of nearly unimaginable dimensions: mammal and dinosaur skeletons of unmatched variety and preservation, countless dinosaur eggs, embryonic dinosaurs, and even dinosaurs perched on their nests like modern birds.

What's so remarkable about the richness of the Gobi is that it was so unexpected. When the Museum's Roy Chapman Andrews began to plot his first fossil hunt of the region in 1920, many supposed experts scoffed at the very notion that this "bowl of sand" might contain more than an occasional scrap of bone.

Neither Andrews nor Museum President Henry Fairfield Osborn was daunted by disparaging remarks, any more than they were cowed by the Gobi's harsh conditions and armed bandits. Interestingly, however, Osborn didn't send Andrews to Mongolia for dinosaur bones but rather for the remains of early humans. Osborn was already gripped by a set of controversial and increasingly unsavory racial theories that led him to believe that modern Caucasians descended not from African ancestors, but from light-skinned, plains-dwelling humans in Asia. He hoped—expected—Andrews would find confirming evidence of this in the Gobi.

Scientists have in fact found the fossils of human ancestors in Asia, early humans who themselves descended from hominids native to Africa, birthplace of the human race. But Andrews's series of Gobi exploits (collectively called the Central Asiatic

Expeditions [CAE]) between 1922 and 1930, did not find what Osborn hoped they would. Instead, they became perhaps the most famous fossil hunts of all time because of the dinosaur and nonhuman mammal fossils they uncovered.

More than three-quarters of a century later, the litany of important finds under the auspices of the CAE is still stunning. Andrews's team, most importantly paleontologist Walter Granger, were the first to discover the theropod dinosaurs *Velociraptor* and *Saurornithoides*; the bizarre, beaked *Oviraptor*; the early horned dinosaur *Protoceratops*; armored *Pinacosaurus*, and others. They found extremely important specimens of the small mammals that coexisted with the dinosaurs in the Cretaceous, as well as such spectacular later mammals as the giant early rhinoceros *Indricotherium*. And they found dozens of dinosaur eggs, many neatly arranged in nests that the scientists believed belonged to *Protoceratops*, whose fossils were abundant in the area.

And they did all this despite the harsh conditions. In a note added later at the end of his truncated journal from the 1923 expedition, Andrews commented: "I had to give up writing and reading at this point for the rest of the summer as I became nearly blind at times from the sand glare." Yet Andrews, Granger, and the others clearly had a wonderful time on these expeditions. "It was fossil hunting *de luxe* and we laughed & sang for our hearts were light," Andrews wrote with typical enthusiasm after the discovery of *Indricotherium*, the 1922 expedition's first major find and the one that proved that the Gobi was more than a bowl of sand.

The Central Asiatic Expeditions came to a halt after the 1930 trip, stopped by political strife in China and the Great Depression back home. But this was not to be the museum's last foray into the Gobi, not if Malcolm McKenna could help it.

From the time he was a child, McKenna had planned to be the paleontologist who returned to the rich fossil exposures of the Gobi, and once he arrived at the Museum he began to make efforts to reopen connections with the hardline Mongolian government. He had to wait until 1990, when the political situation in Mongolia finally eased, to see his dream become reality.

The new series of expeditions have been a joint venture between the museum and the Mongolian Academy of Sciences. Different scientists have gone along during different expeditions, but the core group has included museum paleontologists Mike Novacek, Malcolm McKenna, Mark Norell, Luis Chiappe, and James Clark (now with George Washington University), Museum preparator Amy Davidson, Perle Altangerel of the Mongolian Museum of Natural History, and Demberelyin Dashzeveg of the Mongolian Academy of Sciences.

If anyone associated with the new expeditions worried beforehand that all the important fossils had been removed by Andrews or during more recent Russian, Polish, and Mongol expeditions, their concerns were unfounded. The finds have been exceptional, perhaps the most spectacular series of discoveries ever from any single region. They've even surpassed the haul brought back from the CAE.

Thus far, the researchers have collected fine specimens of *Velociraptor*, the theropod made famous in *Jurassic Park*; a thus-far undescribed new genus of troodontid dinosaur; *Ingenia*, a relative of *Oviraptor*; and other dinosaurs. Additional specimens have included the highest concentration ever found of Mesozoic mammal skulls and skeletons; a superb variety of beautifully preserved lizards, including *Estesia mongoliensis*, a possibly poisonous relative of modern monitor lizards; and the bizarre Cretaceous bird *Mononykus*, further proof (if any was needed) that modern birds are actually theropod dinosaurs in feathers.

While the '90s team had great success excavating some of the same sites Andrews had visited (including the Flaming Cliffs of Shabarakh Usu, home to *Velociraptor*, *Oviraptor*, *Protoceratops*, and the famed dinosaur eggs), perhaps the richest site they have yet visited, a place called "Ukhaa Tolgod", was missed by the Central Asiatic Expeditions and subsequent fossil hunters.

It's not hard to understand why no one bothered to stop at Ukhaa Tolgod, says paleontology division chair and Curator Mark Norell. "We'd driven past it ourselves," he says. "It's not a really spectacular place, not like the Flaming Cliffs, where you can see these wonderful exposures through binoculars. Ukhaa Tolgod just has some brown hills—that's what the name means in Mongolian—and we knew we'd get there eventually mainly because we wanted to be systematic and check every outcropping."

The year that the party chose to stop at Ukhaa Tolgod was 1993, largely because one of the trucks got stuck in sand and they decided to make camp. "I was looking over this flat area, nothing spectacular—except I could see white flecks on the ground, dinosaur bones eroding out," Norell recalls. "I also found lots of eggshells, nests of what have traditionally been called *Protoceratops*. But then I noticed one egg lying there, and I could see all these white flecks of bone inside it."

Picking up the smaller of the egg's two pieces, Norell could tell immediately that the fossilized embryo did not belong to *Protoceratops* but to a theropod dinosaur. "Theropods have distinctive ankles and feet, and I could see a theropod foot sticking out," he says. "Basically, that was it: I saw the egg there on the ground and we picked it up."

As the specimen was being prepared back at Museum, it soon became apparent that the embryo was an unborn *Oviraptor*, or at least a member of the family Oviraptoridae. This was a remarkable discovery, not only because it proved that the so-called *"Protoceratops"* eggs actually came from a far different dinosaur, but also because they cast a fascinating new light on the discovery of the type *Oviraptor*, unearthed at the Flaming Cliffs in 1923 by George Olsen, an assistant on the CAE.

That specimen was famous for being discovered sprawled upon a nest of *"Protoceratops"* eggs; in fact, its full name, *Oviraptor philoceratops,* can be translated as "Egg thief with a fondness for ceratopsian eggs." Understanding that this association might have been misinterpreted, Henry Fairfield Osborn, in his initial description of the specimen, warned that the name "may entirely mislead us as to its feeding habits and belie its character." But neither he nor any other reputable paleontologist of the time suggested that the reason *Oviraptor* may have died atop the nest was that it was brooding its own eggs.

No reputable paleontologist would have had the nerve to suggest that dinosaurs might sit on their eggs, as modern birds do. But one man did make such a suggestion at the time: Roy Chapman Andrews—adventurer, expedition leader extraordinaire, but a mammalogist, not a dinosaur specialist. In his unpublished 1923 field journal, Andrews reports the exciting find this way: "The second 'clutch' included five eggs much larger than the first. . . . Just above them lay the pelvis & one hind limb of a small clawed dinosaur [*Oviraptor*]. It was some achievement not only to find the eggs but also the dinosaur sitting on them!"

It seems that Andrews heard about the specimen and immediately imagined a mother dinosaur sitting on her eggs. He may have had the enthusiastic amateur's ability to see past the dogma held dear by the experts, or he may have just been joking. Whatever was the case, he was wiser than he ever knew, as was shown by a discovery made at Ukhaa Tolgod in 1993, just a few days after the embryo turned up.

"I was walking in another area near camp when I found these big claws weathering out of a hill," Norell says. "I could tell that it was a big theropod, but it looked like most of the skeleton had weathered away, so we weren't even going to collect it."

In a twist that demonstrates vividly how many successful finds hinge on seemingly casual decisions, the explorers finally did decide to excavate the specimen—or rather, to let Luis Chiappe do it. Chiappe had recently been badly injured when a teapot boiled over onto his foot, and he had been growing increasingly frustrated being confined to camp while the wound slowly healed.

"So to give him something to do, we said, " 'Okay, Luis, you can go excavate this skeleton,' " Norell remembers. "So Amy Davidson and he were working on it. Then one day Mike [Novacek] and I were some distance away, and suddenly we see Amy driving the truck toward us. We thought something had happened, but she was saying, 'You have to come see this!' Then we knew they'd found something exciting."

What they'd found was an adult *Oviraptor* sitting on a nest of unhatched eggs. Further, the parent dinosaur was sitting in a classic brooding position: Its legs were folded accordion-style, its body was located in the center of the nest, and its arms were wrapped back around the nest to cover or protect the eggs. Substitute wings for arms, and you have the brooding position adopted by today's surviving dinosaurs, the modern-day birds.

In 1995, the team visited Ukhaa Tolgod once more and unearthed another beautifully preserved nesting *Oviraptor*, again in a brooding posture atop twenty eggs. A Chinese-Canadian expedition has also reported finding a less well preserved specimen, again an adult brooding eggs, arms wrapped around the nest.

It is certainly possible, Norell says, that the type *Oviraptor* specimen, originally accused of raiding the nest of "*Protocer-*

atops" eggs, was actually also brooding. "But we'll never know," he adds. "They removed the skeleton first, then the eggs, so we don't know exactly how the animal was positioned over the nest."

In tandem, the embryo and the nesting *Oviraptors* provide one of the most exciting glimpses we've ever had into the behavior of dinosaurs. For Novacek, Norell, and the Museum's other paleontologists, these finds—when combined with the systematic analysis—are even more exciting for the clues they give to the evolution of behaviors among modern birds.

Oviraptor, along with such other small theropods as *Velociraptor* and *Troodon*, belong to a subgroup of theropods known as maniraptorans. Birds belong to the same subgroup; they are, in fact, the last surviving relatives of these small, predatory dinosaurs. The mere fact that 80-million-year-old dinosaurs brooded their eggs provides proof that the evolution of this form of nesting behavior is an extraordinarily ancient development.

It is at least possible that, like modern birds, *Oviraptors* were warm blooded and sat on their eggs to keep them from getting chilled during cold desert nights. On the other hand, a cold-blooded *Oviraptor* might have brooded its eggs in the Gobi to keep them cool, shading them from the blistering daytime sun. Later, as birds evolved a more advanced, warm-blooded metabolism, this brooding behavior may have been adapted to the new use of keeping eggs warm in cool, or even frigid, environments.

Further clues to the behavior of *Oviraptor* and other dinosaurs depends on future finds, and the museum intends to continue sending parties to the Gobi for as long as they're allowed to. "There are still a lot of areas we've never visited," Norell says. "Of course, the further out we go, the further we are from water. We'll have to depend on wells—if we find that a well is dry, we'll be in trouble."

Novacek and McKenna both point to another reason why a large-scale series of explorations at this time are a necessity. "We know that if we don't explore a region this year, by next year private collectors may have gotten there and taken out the most valuable fossils," Novacek explains.

McKenna is particularly fascinated by the Gobi mammals from the Tertiary period, but he has had to put most Tertiary collecting on hold while the expedition focuses on Mesozoic exposures. "I can understand this, because collectors love to get their hands on the Mesozoic material, particularly the dinosaurs," he says. "There's no time like the first time for collecting this material, and things are already beginning to change. Even now, you can buy dinosaur eggs on the streets of Mongolia's cities. Who knows what will be for sale next year, if scientists don't find it first?"

Under the Gobi Flag

Expedition, a guidebook of the Museum's treasures, has this to say about the tattered American flag flown by Roy Chapman Andrews during the Central Asiatic Expeditions in the 1920s: "The Gobi Flag thus stands not simply for the achievements of a single expedition, but for the quest for knowledge, insight, and understanding that is the impetus for all expeditions, and informs all of the Museum's activities, both in the public eye and behind the scenes."

The flag—shredded by a Gobi sandstorm that pitted the windshields of the expedition's trucks so badly they had to be removed—also stands as a potent symbol of the dangers faced by Museum explorers as they travel the world in their quest. But, as Roy Chapman Andrews showed in a stunning 1926 letter from

Peking, the expedition's staging area, only two options existed: Acknowledge the dangers and confront them, or give up and go home. For him, for all the Museum's scientists, the choice was obvious.

"I have never seen China in such chaos," Andrews wrote. "I got caught in the middle of it while over at the railroad station. An airplane at that particular moment happened to be bombing the station and dropped two shells within thirty yards of my motor car. I jumped out and took cover under a freight train just in time to escape the bombs which dropped within ten feet of the car. If it had not been for the steel wheels of the train I would have been riddled with steel fragments."

Andrews went on to lament that the Central Asiatic Expedition plans had been completely disrupted by the fighting in China. Some of the equipment was already in the Gobi, guarded by one member of the expedition but, as Andrews added, "I have not been able to communicate with him for ten days and do not know if he is alive or dead."

Then, at the very end of this remarkable letter, Andrews made a statement that might well serve as the credo of all explorers who have braved bandits, wars, illness, and other grave threats to teach us about the world we live in. "Still, I expect everything is all right and that eventually we will get off into the desert," he wrote. "I am not worrying, since it does no good."

8 The Front Lines of Conservation

THE WAR TO SAVE THE BIRDS

> All lovers of architecture regard the destruction of the Parthenon of Athens by Turkish cannon in the year 1687 as an act of barbarism. Yet it would be possible for modern archaeologists and architects to restore this temple of Greece to a large measure of its former beauty and grandeur. It is far beyond the power of any men however, of all the naturalists of the world, to restore a single forest, a tree or flower, a bird or mammal, even a single vanished individual, let alone a vanished race: once lost, the loss is irreparable.
>
> —*Museum President Henry Fairfield Osborn,*
> *in the* American Museum Journal, *1912.*

More than any other branch of science, the study of birds at the American Museum of Natural History has been inextricably linked to conservation. From its earliest days, Museum ornithologists held to a belief, as Henry Fairfield Osborn also wrote, that when "an ax or a bullet penetrates the delicate living tissue, replete with this long history of contact with sunshine, oxygen, water, and soil, a temple is torn to pieces."

How could they think otherwise? Ornithology at the Museum was born into an ecological war zone. The nineteenth and early-twentieth centuries, which saw an explosion in the popularity of bird study and bird-watching alike, were also witness to the decline or disappearance of some of the United States's most spectacular birds. The passenger pigeon, once the most abundant bird on earth; the beautiful Carolina parakeet, the only parrot native to most of the United States; the great auk, the "penguin" of the northern seas; the far-wandering Eskimo curlew; the heath hen, a northeastern grouse that had once fed generations of Pilgrims—all were already gone or on the road to extinction by the turn of the century.

Worse, by 1888, when Joel Asaph Allen, curator of the Department of Ornithology and Mammalogy, brought twenty-six-year-old ornithologist Frank M. Chapman on board as assistant curator, it seemed that still more species were destined to disappear forever. Uncontrolled hunting of ducks, geese, and shorebirds for ravenous urban markets was wreaking havoc on populations throughout the country. It's difficult today to look at photographs of hunters of the time, as they stood proudly over piles of dozens or even hundreds of birds that represented a single day's haul.

Chapman was an extremely practical man, and, like most scientists, he didn't disapprove of hunting on moral grounds. For him, though, logic demanded that hunting of ducks and other birds be placed under some form of control. "Every student of the subject is sure that the continuance of a supply of game birds is to be had only by increased protection of those remaining," he wrote to a man who questioned his position. "In brief, the whole matter seems to me a very simple economic question. Will we use our capital or will we so conserve it that it will yield an annual interest?"

No such logical formula applied, however, when it came to another threat to dozens of bird species in the United States and abroad in the years surrounding the turn of the century, the madly popular fashion of using bird feathers to decorate expensive hats and gowns. "Ah, those were the halcyon days of the feather trade!" wrote ornithologist T. Gilbert Pearson, secretary of the National Audubon Society, in 1916. "Now and then a voice cried out at the slaughter, or hands were raised at the sight of the horrible shambles, but there were no laws to prevent the killing nor was there any crystallized public sentiment to demand a cessation of the unspeakable orgy."

Even as a young man, Frank Chapman was well aware of the mass destruction of birds for fashion. At about the time he joined the Museum, he undertook a survey to identify the feathers on the hats of the women he passed on an afternoon walk—an odd and grisly kind of birdwatching, indeed. In two days, he spotted thousands of feathers belonging to more than forty species, ranging from warblers and sparrows to owls and gulls.

It infuriated Chapman that birds were dying for something as frivolous as women's fashion. In a 1910 speech reprinted in the *American Museum Journal*, he pointed out how important insect-eating birds were to the health of North American forests. "Insects cost a loss to our forests of $100,000,000 a year," he said. "A tanager eats moth caterpillars at the rate of 2,100 an hour. A Maryland yellowthroat ate 3,500 plant lice in forty minutes. . . . Chief among the enemies of birds and therefore the forests is woman." Looking at photographs of Chapman, with his steely eyes and determined mouth, it's easy to imagine how uncomfortable any expensively dressed woman in the audience must have been.

Chapman knew that not all women were slaves to fashion, as he showed when suggesting a new Museum endowment to long-time benefactor Mrs. Frank K. Sturgis. "Now, the idea that occurs to me in connection with the proposed new fund is that it be devoted solely to the preparation of birds which are fated to early extinction as a result of their slaughter for millinery purposes and that it be contributed to only by women," he wrote in a 1905 letter to Mrs. Sturgis. "It would, therefore, stand for all time a silent but eloquent protest against a custom which is condemned by every high-minded thoughtful woman." The fund, named for Mrs. Sturgis, went on to support departmental research for several years.

Chapman was not alone in his efforts to stem the tide of the feather trade. The scientific establishment in the late 1800s and early 1900s was filled with fascinating, eccentric men who raised loud voices in defense of the birds. In lectures, newspapers, announcements by the National Audubon Society and American Ornithologists Union, and the pages of magazines like *The Auk* and *Bird-Lore* (founded by Chapman), the public heard from such prominent naturalists as Elliot Coues, George Bird Grinnell, William Dutcher, Theodore Roosevelt, and John Burroughs.

These men rarely saw eye-to-eye on anything having to do with birds (watching them argue in print and in public over issues ranging from bird classification to protective coloration was like sitting in on a decades-long family squabble) but they all agreed that North America's birds were in deep trouble. "I would like to see all harmless wild things, but especially all birds, protected in every way," Roosevelt wrote to Chapman in 1899, expressing a typical opinion. "I do not understand how any man can fail to try to exert all influence in support of such objects, as those of the Audubon Society."

Among the birds that Chapman feared were fated to early extinction by the feather trade, none were closer to his heart than the herons and egrets. During breeding season, many species of these long-legged wading birds develop gorgeous, flowing plumes, called "aigrettes" in Chapman's time. In an era when a fashionable woman might wear a gown embroidered with whole blackbirds or a hat topped with sparrow wings, the delicate white or gray aigrettes were in great demand—great enough to be worth the taking of human life.

In the early 1900s, Chapman was determined to visit the egrets and herons on their nesting grounds. While once that would have been easy (in earlier years, rookeries could be found in several southern states), by this time North America's last known large breeding colony, Cuthbert Rookery, was located on an inaccessible island in a swamp bordering the Florida Everglades.

But even the hard-to-reach Cuthbert Rookery was not free from the predation of the plume hunters. In 1904, while attempting to visit the site, Chapman found out that the rookery had been "shot out" while Audubon Society Warden Guy Bradley (assigned to guard the nests) was away. In speeches and articles, Chapman decried this brutal slaughter, earning himself the enmity of both the plume merchants and the politicians who profited by the feather trade.

Worse was yet to come. In 1905, Chapman was prevented from visiting the rookery by a fire that destroyed his gear. If he had succeeded in reaching the site, he likely would have lost his life, for that same summer, Bradley was murdered by a plume hunter who had staked out the rookery and Bradley's home. Bradley had long predicted his own murder, but had been unwilling to abandon the rookery even in the face of countless threats.

If any unnecessary death can be said to have meaning, Guy Bradley's did. The man who shot him, despite admitting the act, went free ("No jury in the region would convict him," according to a contemporary newspaper account), but the publicity surrounding the case—stoked by the outrage expressed in public by Chapman and other early conservationists—finally focused the American people's attention on the ravages of the plume trade.

Laws protecting birds had already been on the books, but these were routinely reversed, breached, or ignored in many states. But now, gradually and with many setbacks, both the states and the federal government began to pass and enforce laws that protected not only egrets, but other threatened bird species as well, from the depredations of overhunting. By 1912, Henry Fairfield Osborn was able to write, "In every part of the English-speaking world the principle of conservation is taking firmer hold on public opinion, as shown both in expression in literature and action in legislation."

Today, Guy Bradley's sacrifice and Frank Chapman's unceasing efforts of a century ago are commemorated in the Cuthbert Rookery habitat group in the Hall of North American Birds. When the display was unveiled in 1910, the *American Museum Journal* announced the opening by pointing out that the rookery "is unprotected and the birds, rare now, are liable to meet extermination in the near future." It is a pleasure, now that egrets and herons are common once more, to realize that the editor's crystal ball was cloudy that day.

A Friend of the Devil

An ongoing controversy within every major environmental organization is the debate over how much to cooperate with what is perceived as "the enemy." In recent years, the Wilderness Society has been criticized for being too friendly to hunters, the Nature Conservancy for working with large corporations, and the Sierra Club for not attacking government logging policies vociferously enough.

As a little-remembered 1911 controversy shows, negotiating

the thin line between intransigence and capitulation has always been a tough job for those groups dedicated to protecting wildlife. In that year, the leadership of the National Association of Audubon Societies, which included Curator of Ornithology and Mammalogy Joel Asaph Allen, decided to accept a gift of $25,000 from the Winchester Repeating Arms Company and a cadre of other gun and ammunition manufacturers to establish a "national game protective organization."

The gift (to be followed by four others on a yearly basis) came with no strings attached. "As we have pointed out to you, no one can possibly be more vitally interested in legitimate game protection than the manufacturers of sporting arms and ammunition," said a Winchester vice president in a letter to Society Secretary T. Gilbert Pearson, "for if the game is exterminated there would be a very large decrease in the demand for their products."

Having accepted the gift on June 2, 1911, Society officers were stunned by the immediate outcry, both within their organization and from the press and public. The *New York Times* was particularly unrelenting. On June 4, after Pearson attempted to explain that the gift did not commit the Society to any policy regarding the use of guns, the paper quoted unnamed members of the organization as saying "that the statement smacked much of interposing the stable door of careful consideration on the gun manufacturers after the horse of independence has been stolen."

In a June 5 editorial, the *Times* was even more scornful. "What they have always wanted was to sell guns, any kind of guns, to anybody," the editors said of the gun makers. "The plain and obvious truth is that the Audubon Societies, by taking this money, have almost if not quite forfeited whatever right they ever had to the honorable name they appropriated. The thing is distinctly scandalous."

Not surprisingly, the Audubon leadership folded under this onslaught, reversing their decision and refusing the money. Wrote the seventy-two-year-old (and chronically frail) Joel A. Allen to Frank Chapman on June 20, "The matter finally got on my nerves & temporarily affected my health, but it is all over now."

ROBERT CUSHMAN MURPHY'S MYSTERIOUS ISLANDS

Three tiny, bare, splintery rocks are there . . . yet small as they are, their name is known to the farthest ports of the world, and their share in making fortunes and in abetting tragedies, in debauching not only men but governments, has given them a place in history all out of proportion to their size.

—*Curator Robert Cushman Murphy,*
on the guano islands of Peru.

Frank M. Chapman continued his work for the Museum until his death in 1945, but he never again sought the degree of public attention that he'd captured during his battles with the plume trade. Instead, he, like all the Museum's biologists, looked to establish as complete a collection of specimens as possible, and then to intensively study the collections to gain a clearer understanding of bird classification and other puzzles.

From the beginning of his career, Chapman had collected and studied the birds of tropical America. In his later years, he chose to spend increasing amounts of time on Barro Colorado Island in the Panama Canal (the home he called his "Tropical Air Castle").

Here he collected and studied the birds of Barro Colorado, while also helping introduce the flora and fauna of Central America to a wider audience.

Other Museum ornithologists chose different horizons. James Chapin, along with mammalogist Herbert Lang, undertook a spectacularly ambitious expedition to the rain-forests of the Belgian Congo in Central Africa. The expedition began in 1909 (when Chapin was just nineteen) and did not end until 1915. By this time, the scientists had collected tens of thousands of specimens of birds, mammals, fish, and reptiles and amphibians, many of which were new to science.

Chapin spent years studying the glorious bird collection, eventually producing a monumental, four-volume monograph entitled *Birds of the Belgian Congo*. This classic work, filled with invaluable descriptions and other insights into the classification and relationships of that region's fascinating avifauna, still serves as the bedrock for modern studies of the birds of Central Africa.

Like countless ornithologists before and since, Ernst Mayr—a curator in the department for many years—has long been fascinated by the birds of Oceania, particularly New Guinea. Himself a veteran of expeditions to that inaccessible tropical island, Mayr spent years studying the enormous collections sent back by the Museum's Whitney South Sea Expedition during visits to a slew of South Sea archipelagoes during the 1920s. Today, Mayr is celebrated for his seminal ideas on speciation, distribution, and evolution—theories that developed directly from his work with this massive collection.

Ornithologist Robert Cushman Murphy chose to study the oceanic and island birds of a vastly different region, the cold waters off the coast of South America. The book that resulted from his wide-ranging travels, *The Oceanic Birds of South Amer-*

ica, is another classic of bird classification and behavior. But of all the places he visited, Murphy was most famous for his trips to a small group of islands located just off the coast of a country few Americans had ever visited.

The country was Peru and the islands called the Chinchas— three tiny islets where the numberless nesting seabirds left behind a nitrate treasure: excrement, called "guano," that for centuries was the finest fertilizer available. And Murphy, with chiseled handsomeness, a colorful writing style, and a voice as authoritative as a newsreel announcer's, was just the scientist to tell the Chinchas' story to the general public.

For thousands of years before the arrival of human settlers to the Peruvian coast, cormorants ("guanays"), boobies, pelicans, and other birds nested by the millions on these small coastal islands. Feasting on the abundant anchovies and other small fishes that teemed in the cold Humboldt Current nearby, they left behind guano that over the course of time rose in mounds more than one hundred feet in height.

With the arrival of pre-Columbian civilization to the Peruvian coast, the guano islands were discovered and exploited for the first time. "From afar the heaps of manure appear like the peaks of some snowy mountain-range," wrote Garcilasso de la Vega, historian of the Inkas, in his *Royal Commentaries* (1609). But despite this seemingly inexhaustible wealth, the native Peruvians well understood that a permanent supply of guano depended on the protection of the birds that provided the valuable product. "In the time of the kings, who were Incas, such care was taken to guard these birds in the breeding season, that it was not lawful for any one to land on the isles, on pain of death, that the birds might not be frightened, nor driven from their nests," wrote de la Vega.

The Spanish conquest put an end to all such careful administration, although the islands themselves were left relatively untouched until about 1840. When large-scale guano mining resumed, the Spanish acted with amazing greed and shortsightedness, viewing the birds not as an essential basis for an ongoing guano industry but as an obstacle to mining. Birds were driven away from their nesting sites or slaughtered wholesale, as if the plunderers believed that the guano would never run out.

"The hills are said to have been seven score higher in those days—built up above the level of the bedrock with the excrement of birds!" Robert Cushman Murphy wrote in the journal of his 1919–20 expedition. "And the flat top of North Island, now occupied solely by a dense colony of guanays, is said to have been a town of eight thousand inhabitants. No trace now remains except the corpses of the coolies, wrapped in their blankets, mummified by the guano, and with a coin beneath their tongues."

A contemporary glimpse of the Spanish assault on the Chinchas was recorded by the writer Clements Markham in his *Travels in Peru and India* (1862). "The three Chincha islands, in the bay of Pisco, contained a total of 12,376,100 tons of guano in 1853, and, as since that time 2,837,365 tons have been exported up to 1860, there were 9,538,735 tons remaining in 1861," he reasoned. "In 1860 as many as 433 vessels, with a tonnage of 348,554, loaded at the Chincha islands; so that, at the above rate, the guano will last for twenty-three years, until 1883."

Twenty-three years was a shockingly short time to exhaust a resource that had taken thousands of years to develop, but Markham's prediction actually was hopelessly optimistic. In truth, the guano of the Chinchas, which at its height had brought as much as $30 million annually to the nation's rulers, was virtually exhausted by 1870, just eight years after Markham wrote. Peru was confronted with the humiliating prospect of being unable to supply enough guano to fertilize its own fields, much less export any of the precious product.

Remarkably, even these decades of disgraceful actions didn't drive the guanay cormorants or other guano birds into extinction, and with the collapse of the guano industry came relaxation of the pressure on the Chinchas. The bird populations—and the supply of guano—gradually increased, and by early in this century enough existed to restart the guano industry.

The question facing the Peruvian government at this time was simple: Repeat the mistakes of the nineteenth-century rulers, and quickly exhaust the supply for immediate gain, or look back further, to the intelligent (if draconian) management techniques of the Inka? Or, as Murphy put it in a 1940 article for *Natural History*, "Now if the heedless human animal can act so adversely upon the world of life, not to mention his own interests, it should be equally plausible that by using his brain he should be able to bring himself into harmony with Nature."

Fortunately, the Peruvian government chose the latter course, instituting a Guano Administration to oversee a sustainable harvesting of the Chincha Islands' "crop." Under the early leadership of Don Francisco Ballen, a Peruvian scientist and life member of the Museum, true stewardship of the islands and their resource began.

By the time Murphy made his first visit to the Chinchas in 1919, great flocks of cormorants and other seabirds were once again nesting on the islands. "It looks from my point of view as though the hillside was covered with as many pairs of webbed feet as there is room for," he wrote in his journal as he sat among the guanays, "and yet new birds have been dropping by the hundreds every minute, and over the ocean to the north, south, and west, the endless black files are still pouring in toward the three islands."

Murphy was involved with developments on the guano islands for the rest of his life, and was able to see that the birds enjoyed continued careful management and protection. Today, the guano industry still harvests the islands' treasure, while the development of synthetic fertilizers guarantees that never again will there be such a mad rush to plunder the "three bare, splintery rocks," site of this unique interplay of fertile ocean, voracious seabirds, and human enterprise.

THE LURE OF PARADISE

It is perhaps not too much to say that paradise birds are the most beautiful of all living creatures and that, short of man himself, bower birds are the most bizarre. Seafarers of old when they first encountered the glorious birds of paradise took them to be wanderers from a celestial paradise; and in 1872 the first naturalist to encounter a skilfully constructed bower complete with its mysterious garden and attractive furnishings, attributed it to the inventiveness of man. . . . What manner of creatures are these to have inspired such a wealth of superstition and scientific wonder?

—*E. Thomas Gilliard, in* Birds of Paradise
and Bower Birds, *1969.*

New Guinea is a land unlike any other on earth. Plunging valleys are clothed in misty forests so dense that entering them is like stepping into a darkened room. Soaring snowcapped mountains seem jagged enough to have been created only yesterday. Indigenous peoples have been so isolated from each other that seven hundred different languages, a quarter of the entire world's total, are spoken there. Bizarre plants and animals thrive here, yet are found nowhere else on earth. Is it any wonder that by the 1920s

Museum scientists from several different departments would have been eager to visit this remarkable island?

Eager, but also a bit hesitant. At the same time that Robert Cushman Murphy was exploring the tumultuous life of the guano islands, even more ambitious ornithological exploits were underway across the world: the Whitney South Sea Expedition. This extraordinary twenty-year survey, begun in 1920 under the leadership of chief collector Rollo Beck, sent back tens of thousands of specimens and observed little-known birds in their native haunts on the remote and virtually unvisited islands of Micronesia, Melanesia, and Polynesia.

Yet for years after the Whitney Expedition began, there seems to have been no serious discussion at the Museum of the Whitney explorers visiting New Guinea. The British Lord Walter Rothschild had long been financing his own ambitious collecting trips to the island, and the Whitney organizers had no interest in duplicating his effort. But then, in 1928, Museum trustee Leland C. Sanford decided that a visit to the inaccessible New Guinea highlands might be a good idea and that Rollo Beck would be the man to make the trip.

After eight years as leader of the Whitney Expedition, the fifty-eight-year-old Beck and his wife, Ida (who had accompanied him on many of his expeditions), were prepared finally to head home to California. The Becks were worn out, ready for retirement, but they could not refuse this final summons from Sanford, who had funded earlier Beck trips and helped organize the Whitney Expedition.

So the stalwart Becks headed out again, enlisting local hunters to collect a few representatives of every species they could in several scientifically unexplored areas. But it's clear from reading their letters and journals at the time that both husband and wife were tired of the adventurer's life. "Collecting in New Guinea has drawbacks in plenty to offset the gorgeous colored birds and butterflies that are to be found," Rollo wrote in an August 1928 journal entry. "Mrs. Beck went out with me one day and after consuming her midday meal by the side of a tiny stream, she discovered that an inch-long leech had been feasting copiously on her blood while she had been feasting on sardines."

Ida Beck, one of the many remarkable nonscientist wives who have accompanied Museum collectors on their adventures was worried about her aging husband. "I am thankful for strength to help him by having properly cooked food, dry clothing and hot drinks when he comes in wet and tired," she wrote in a touching letter to Robert Cushman Murphy near the trip's conclusion, adding that "it is with true gladness that we are about to start on the homeward trail, for my body cries out for comforts and my mind the companionship of friends, books and pretty things."

Others may have not have realized the strength it took Ida Beck to spend so many years away from home, tending to her husband's needs, but Murphy certainly did. In recognition of her role, he named a new bird for her, *Acrocephalus caffer idae,* the long-billed reed warbler, a native of the Marquesas Islands.

Despite their lack of enthusiasm, the Becks' New Guinea expedition provided the Museum with a host of important bird specimens. The trip's greatest find was a spectacularly beautiful new species, *Sericulus bakeri,* the fire-maned bowerbird, also known as "Beck's bowerbird."

Rollo Beck must have known he had found something special when he collected his first "Madang goldenbird" (as he called *S. bakeri*), but when questioned by excited scientists back in the States, he was unclear about exactly where he'd collected this previously unknown bird. All he seemed to recall was that it and other specimens collected later had lived near Madang, northern New Guinea's principal port.

The ornithologists back home were frustrated. "It hardly seems possible that a new bird of such conspicuous coloration would be found so close to Madang," pointed out the New York Zoological Society's Lee Crandall, who had done research in New Guinea. "Beck is a collector pure and simple, and when I talked with him he could give me very little information about the bird, except that he remembers shooting one." In addition, Beck's field notes—which might have allowed scientists to deduce exactly where the specimens had come from—were soon misplaced, not turning up until 1960.

One person determined to find the home of *S. bakeri* was E. Thomas Gilliard, a Museum ornithologist closely associated with the study of New Guinea's birds. Gilliard had first visited New Guinea as a member of the United States infantry during World War II, and had sworn never to return. He did go back on a Museum assignment in 1948, however, and fell in love with the island's beauty, its people, and most of all its birds.

During the 1950s and 1960s, Gilliard visited New Guinea many times, usually with his wife, Margaret, who both kept camp and contributed greatly to his research. By all accounts, no one who talked to Gilliard about the birds of paradise or bowerbirds failed to share his passion for them. Even today, his enthusiasm and generosity of spirit shine through in his writings and the words of those who knew him.

When Gilliard visited the Madang region in 1956, no scientist or collector had seen *S. bakeri* since Beck's 1928–29 expedition. During this trip, Gilliard spent many fruitless days in search of this nearly mythical bird. "I walked 100 miles in rain following Beck's cold trail," he commented after one unsuccessful effort.

But then, in a 1958 trip to the Adelbert Mountains northnorthwest of Madang—many miles from where Beck's comments placed the bird—Gilliard's longtime wish was finally fulfilled.

Before he actually saw the bird alive, local hunters in his employ collected a male and female for him. Knowing how much this beautiful bird meant to the American scientist, the hunters (named Boure and Rambur) prepared a special presentation. Wrapping the gorgeous male in a leaf and putting it in a bag, they placed the female on top of it, and concealed this specimen with a pair of catbird bowerbirds, themselves belonging to a rare species that was new to Gilliard's collection.

"As I unpacked the bag, I noted the catbirds and a queer looking bird which I thought just might be the female of *S. bakeri,*" Gilliard wrote in his journal that evening. "Lo! I got down to the female, and it was *S. bakeri,* the long lost species. After much jubilation and backslapping, I reached casually into the sack and pulled out the leaf-wrapped bird, expecting to find a fruit-pigeon or something and then saw the reddish-gold of the nape of the male *S. bakeri.* I have never had a bigger thrill."

As it turns out, the fire-maned bowerbird is not uncommon in a narrow altitudinal range in the Adelbert Mountains. As with so many of the island's beautiful birds with restricted ranges, you simply have to know where to look for it, says Mary LeCroy, a research associate in Ornithology. "You really can't miss *S. bakeri,*" explains LeCroy, who worked with Gilliard until his death in 1965 and who shares his fascination with New Guinea and its birds. "It's like a splash of orange in the trees."

While collecting was an important part of Gilliard's job (as it is for every Museum ornithologist), his true passion lay in studying the unique behaviors of the living birds of paradise and bowerbirds. How could it be otherwise? Many male birds of paradise, cloaked in stunning plumes and frills, engage in displays that include raucous calls and odd leaps and wing movements; some even hang upside down at the climax of the display. Bowerbirds don't behave in such spectacular fashion, but instead construct complex structures (the bowers) on the ground out of leaves, grass, and other vegetation, then decorate them with colorful objects such as shells, stones, and flowers, and engage in more modest courtship demonstrations to woo any nearby female.

None of these behaviors was easy to film or record, but Gilliard was determined to try. Some of his greatest frustrations came when he was attempting to film the display behavior of shy and wary bowerbirds. "People go in today with their video cameras, but Tom had to rely on a pair of car batteries to power a sixteen-millimeter camera, and hire someone to pedal a pedal charger to charge the batteries to run the camera," LeCroy says. "Then, the humidity was so great that the emulsion on the film would swell and jam the camera in a very short time, so he'd have to stop and dry out the film and start all over again. But he was determined to get the behaviors down on film, so he did."

Even in the face of declining health (suffering from eye trouble and recurrent bouts with malaria, he last visited New Guinea in 1964, just a few months before his death) Gilliard persisted in his efforts. The results can be seen in *Birds of Paradise and Bower Birds*, an influential book published posthumously in 1969, and many other important works on classification and evolution. Another lasting testament is the presence of beautiful New Guinea and Philippine habitat groups in the Museum's Whitney Hall of Oceanic Birds, which include many specimens and much background material collected by Gilliard himself.

Today, the fascination with New Guinea that began with Rollo Beck continues in the research of Mary LeCroy, who studies bird-of-paradise behavior, and in the work of Curator Joel Cracraft, who is attempting to untangle the complicated evolutionary relationships that exist among the many species in this remarkable family. For ornithologists, the appeal of New Guinea is simple, according to Mary LeCroy. "Once you've been there, you want to keep going back," she says, "because there's always so much more to learn."

The Most Defiantly Faithful and Honest People I Know

Today, it's easy to fall into the trap of seeing early explorers and collectors as "Great White Male Hunters" who used local people merely as porters as they traveled to the heart of "uncivilized" lands—and in many famous expeditions that was undoubtedly so. But most of the Museum's scientists (and their patrons) well understood that a successful trip depended not only on the cooperation of the local inhabitants but on their knowledge as well. This was particularly true in New Guinea, home to such inaccessible forests and impassable gorges that familiarity with the local landscape and its wildlife was absolutely essential.

When Museum trustee L. C. Sanford chose to send Rollo Beck to New Guinea in 1928, he said in a letter, "I hope that whenever feasible you will make it a point to utilize native collectors.... Many of the natives of New Guinea are keen observers with a surprisingly wide knowledge of the fauna in their own districts with native names for practically all of the birds."

Trusting the local people enough to accept their help wasn't always easy. At the dawn of his distinguished career, ornithologist Ernst Mayr made a collecting trip to New Guinea's Arfak Mountains in 1928–29. In an article for *Natural History* entitled "A Tenderfoot Explorer in New Guinea," Mayr praised both the locals' knowledge and marksmanship, but said that they were "very touchy and have many taboos that must be respected."

Mayr couldn't keep himself from violating one of these taboos, however, as he found during a lunar eclipse one night:

> The moon became more and more covered by shadow, it grew darker and darker, but the natives showed no signs of interest or excitement. I asked them if they had no myth about it. . . . Not getting any response to my questions, I really became quite excited in my efforts to get some information about their belief.
>
> Suddenly one of the men slapped my shoulder in a fatherly fashion and said soothingly:
>
> "Don't worry, master, it will become light again very soon."
>
> That cured me and I never again tried to acquire any information that was not given willingly.

E. Thomas Gilliard, who visited New Guinea for the Museum many times, had no doubts about the character or skills of the men he worked with. Along with calling them "defiantly faithful and honest" in the field journal of his 1948 expedition, he described the residents of the villages in the Owen Stanley Range as "the most moral people I've encountered. The five Koraris I trained, Mari-uri, Someri, Yai, Arua and Kiva displayed an amazing knowledge of plants, animals, birds, geographical features. In fact, I never ceased being amazed at their store of knowledge."

For Gilliard, working in New Guinea must have been a relief in some ways. As he pointed out during a 1955 episode of the popular American Museum-CBS television series *Adventure,* the New Guinea villagers "didn't think of me as a lunatic with a butterfly net," unlike typical Americans of the time.

POSTCARDS FROM THE EDGE

There will always be pigeons in books and museums, but these are effigies and images, dead to all hardships and to all delights. Book-pigeons cannot dive out of a cloud to make the deer run for cover, nor clap their wings in thunderous applause of mast-laden woods. They know no urge of seasons; they feel no kiss of sun, no lash of wind and weather; they live forever by not living at all.

—Aldo Leopold, from a 1946 speech to the Wisconsin Society for Ornithology.

Many of the American Museum of Natural History's exhibits give the visitor a vivid, almost eerily lifelike glimpse of the world outside. The mountain gorillas in the Akeley Hall seem to be taking a moment's rest from the gentle actions of the day in their highland home, while the cormorants and other birds of the guano islands seem likewise caught for an instant in their endless cycle of feeding and nesting.

But, as the great conservationist and essayist Aldo Leopold well realized, sometimes a museum can do little more than remind the visitor that a creature once lived, but lives no more. Stop a moment and gaze at the solitary dodo standing in its showcase or at the handful of faded passenger pigeons perched on a dusty branch, and you must struggle to imagine what it was like to see these creatures alive. Today they exist only in our mind's eye.

One of the most important roles of any museum of natural history is to lend a voice to the voiceless, and by choosing the dodo and the passenger pigeon as treasures the American Museum has done just that. Another important task is to highlight stories that have not ended so sadly, or have not ended at all, as the fascinating and encouraging tale of another treasure, the peregrine falcon, demonstrates.

Perhaps most vitally of all, a natural history museum must also take a hand in influencing the future by teaching us more about the world we occupy and the creatures we share it with. This last, crucial role is now being undertaken by Museum ornithologists, more than two dozen researchers whose work spans the globe. The edge delineated in these "postcards" encompasses both the edge of survival that far too many bird species still teeter on, and also the boundaries of knowledge that museum scientists work to expand.

The Passenger Pigeon: Whirlwind in the Sky

Has there ever been a more famous extinct species than the passenger pigeon? Today, we remember this pigeon so well because it was both native to North America and remarkably large and handsome ("slate color, like weather-stained wood . . . a more subdued and earthy blue than the sky," said Henry David Thoreau). But mostly it lives on in our memories because it was once the most abundant bird on earth, and then—in such a brief time—it disappeared forever.

As early as 1605, the explorer Samuel de Champlain wrote of vast flocks of what was then called the "wild pigeon." Cotton Mather was so amazed by their abundance that he guessed that "the wild pigeons on leaving us repair to some undiscovered satellite accompanying the earth at a near distance."

But hard by the reports of the pigeons' abundance are descriptions of the vast quantities being killed for food. Writing in the 1630s, the New England historian William Wood is already describing "the shouting of people, the ratling of Gunnes, and pelting of small shotte" that greeted a flock of pigeons flying overhead.

Even as those along the east coast were being extirpated, the passenger pigeon was still present in staggering numbers elsewhere. In his classic *American Ornithology* (published in volumes between 1808 and 1814), Alexander Wilson describes a Kentucky flock that, at his very conservative estimate, included 2,232,000,000 birds.

One breeding site described by Wilson was several miles in breadth and stretched for forty miles, with every tree furnished with as many as ninety nests. When the young squabs were fully grown but before they left the nest, local people told Wilson, "the noise in the woods was so great as to terrify their horses, and that it was difficult for one person to hear another speak without bawling in his ear."

This was the moment—when the oily, succulent squabs were at their fattest but still helpless—that every hunter for miles around would descend on the nesting site. Using guns, clubs, poles, nets, and bare hands, the hunters (frequently entire families) would kill thousands of birds. Hundreds might be killed in a single shot with "swivel guns" filled with birdshot.

The last great (and most famous) nesting area was located near Petoskey, Michigan, a site that in 1878 contained more than 100 million birds. The hunting was relentless, and millions of pigeons were shipped by train to the east at a wholesale price of no more than twenty-five cents per dozen.

Petoskey, 1878, marked the last time passenger pigeons were ever seen nesting in such large numbers. From then on the pigeon population apparently declined steadily, although smaller nestings were reported in Michigan at least until 1881, and as late as 1883, a pigeon flight in Texas took three and a half hours to pass overhead. But these were clearly the last rivulets of a once-vast sky river that was now running dry.

The last remaining passenger pigeon, an old female named Martha, died in the Cincinnati Zoo at 1:00 P.M. on September 1, 1914—fewer than forty years after the Petoskey nesting that boasted more than 100 million birds.

Why did the passenger pigeon, whose flocks had once seemed

inexhaustible, become extinct so rapidly? Habitat destruction was one cause. Depending on untouched old-growth forests for nest sites and for beechnuts and other foods, the pigeon could not overcome the disappearance of these forests by the late nineteenth century.

Another reason was perhaps best expressed by the great Massachusetts ornithologist Edward Howe Forbush in his *A History of the Game Birds, Wild-Fowl, and Shore Birds of Massachusetts and Adjacent States* (1912): "The whole history of the last thirty years of the existence of the Passenger Pigeon goes to prove that the birds were so persistently molested that they finally lost their coherence, were scattered far and wide, and became extinct mainly through constant persecution by man."

Forbush writes with a logic that is irrefutable. "It is often asked how it was possible for man to kill them all," he writes. "It was not possible, nor was it requisite that he should do so, in order to exterminate them. All that was required to bring about this result was to destroy a large part of the young birds hatched each year. Nature cut off the rest."

As Forbush—but far too few of his contemporaries—realized, no species can long survive if its young are destroyed year after year. No living creature is immortal; most, in fact, have only a limited number of years in which they are both sexually mature and fertile. For a comparatively short-lived bird like the passenger pigeon, a single failed breeding season was a serious, but surmountable, setback. To suffer season after season of breeding failure pronounced a death sentence on the species.

"Our grandfathers, who saw the glory of the fluttering hosts, were less well-housed, well-fed, well-clothed, than we are. The strivings by which they bettered our lot are also those which deprived us of pigeons," Aldo Leopold said in 1946. "Perhaps we now grieve because we are not sure, in our hearts, that we have gained by the exchange."

Dead as a Dodo

The extinction of the passenger pigeon, it has been said, "went off like dynamite." Another famous disappearance, that of the dodo—the large, flightless relative of the pigeons that lived only on the island of Mauritius—happened just as rapidly, but with far less fanfare. The dodo was never widespread. It never thundered across the sky like a living whirlwind, never inspired flights of fancy by writers and historians. Like far too many other species, particularly those that evolve in isolation on predator-free islands, the dodo thrived until the arrival of humans, then slipped quickly and helplessly into extinction.

The dodo was first "discovered" by Dutch sailors in 1598, but it almost certainly had been known to the Arab traders who plied the Indian Ocean islands as early as the twelfth century. These merchants must have stopped at Mauritius and its neighboring islands of Reunion and Rodriguez (which harbored close relatives of the dodo, doomed to extinction as well). Perhaps they even killed a few dodos for food. But there was no trade to be had on an uninhabited island, no crop or other treasure worth staying to gather, so the Arabs would have been quickly on their way, leaving the dodo in peace.

With the 1598 arrival of a fleet of eight Dutch ships, however, the dodo's eons of peace came to an end. Admiral Jacob Corneliszoon van Neck and his men soon noticed the flocks of odd, flightless birds. In his journal of the voyage, van Neck described them as "larger than our swans, with huge heads only half covered with skin, as if clothed with a hood. . . . These birds lack wings, in the place of which three or four blackish feathers protrude."

The first Dutch explorers found the taste of dodo meat unpalatable, even dubbing the birds *walghvogels*, or "disgusting birds." The Dutch sailors who soon followed van Neck's expedition, however, were less choosy, killing and salting dozens of the birds to provide food for the long sea journeys.

Today, the word "dodo" is a synonym for stupidity, taken from the birds' supposed inability to detect and evade danger. But, as Andrew Kitchener, a curator at the Royal Museum of Scotland, put it in a 1993 article in *New Scientist* magazine, "If you've never met a predator before then why bother to flee club-wielding sailors?"

The dodo was no match for such attacks. Still, the species might even have been able to survive human depredation if not for the deadly cargo that accompanies sailors wherever they travel: rats, dogs, pigs, and other animals.

These creatures, all predators or opportunistic feeders, found a ready source of food in the dodo's vulnerable ground nests. The dodo had no way to defend its eggs from the assaults made by these introduced hunters. As a result, the last dodo died, unnoticed, sometime in the mid- to late-1600s, less than a century after Admiral van Neck and his men first recorded its existence. Its flightless relatives, the "white dodo" and the "solitary," which occupied the neighboring islands of Reunion and Rodriguez, followed soon after.

The dodo disappeared so quickly, with so little fanfare, that not a single complete skin or stuffed specimen now exists. (The Museum specimen is a model.) Today, only history books, a few reconstructed skeletons, and the lessons the dodo helped teach us about the fragility of island life, keep this bird from being completely forgotten.

The Peregrine Falcon: Back from the Edge

The headlong rush toward extinction has almost as many guises as there are species that become extinct. The destruction of the passenger pigeon (and the nearly simultaneous, and only marginally less effective, assault on the bison) most closely resembled a full-scale war. Conversely, the death of the dodo was more like an afterthought, so little remarked upon that years passed before anyone paid it any notice.

But the forces that push some species toward the edge are even more insidiously effective than the rats that nibbled at the dodo's eggs. The story of the magnificent peregrine falcon provides a perfect example.

Starting soon after World War II, ornithologists and amateur birdwatchers became alarmed at the steep decline in the populations of some of North America's most spectacular birds of prey—including the osprey, bald eagle, and peregrine. The birds were abandoning nesting sites they'd occupied for generations; even more disturbingly, their reproductive success rates were plummeting. Observers reported seeing more broken eggs than healthy babies in most nests.

It was clear that a calamity was taking place, one that might actually result in the extinction of one or more of the affected species. But what exactly was happening?

As we now know, insecticides, especially DDT, were causing the birds to lay eggs with such thin shells that they broke when the parents tried to brood them. From the late 1940s and through the 1950s and much of the 1960s, in Europe and the United States alike, health and agricultural authorities were engaging in massive spraying of DDT and related insecticides to destroy mosquitoes and plant pests. These toxic chemicals were reaching the peregrine and other birds from concentrated amounts stored in the tissues of pigeons, fish, and other prey species.

Although DDT was not pinpointed as the direct cause of the peregrine's quick slide toward extinction until the 1960s, the effects of pesticides on countless bird and animal species were well known to many leading scientists by the 1950s.

From then onward, the battle over DDT was fought all across the country. A typical scenario—scientists warning of disaster, authorities pushing ahead regardless—was recounted in 1995 by Richard P. Harmond in the *Long Island Historical Journal*. It involved Ornithology Curator Robert Cushman Murphy, who lived most of his life on Long Island, New York.

In 1957 the U.S. Department of Agriculture decided that the best method of fighting the gypsy moth was to spray 3 million acres of the northeastern United States with DDT. Murphy and other Long Island residents filed suit, charging (accurately) that DDT was "a cumulative poison such as will inevitably cause irreparable injury and death to all living things."

Named chairman of an emergency Committee Against Mass Poisoning, set up by the New York Zoological Society, Murphy pointed out in court that, far from eradicating the gypsy moth, spraying actually killed off the insects that controlled the moth— along with fish, crabs, birds, and whatever else the DDT came in contact with. In a case that ended up before the U.S. Supreme Court, Murphy and his fellow homeowners eventually lost the battle, and the spraying took place.

Murphy lived to see the publication of Rachel Carson's *Silent Spring* (1962), with its overwhelming indictment of insecticide use, and to witness, if not to participate in, several other attempts to ban DDT. The year before his death in 1973, he was to see the Environmental Protection Agency finally outlaw the use of DDT in the United States. (Unfortunately, the insecticide is still exported to other countries; in early 1996, researchers were shocked to find DDT residues in the flesh and eggs of albatrosses on remote Midway Island in the South Pacific.)

Typically, Robert Cushman Murphy had a cogent, clear-headed response to the battles he'd witnessed. "Americans have often employed science and technology arrogantly," he told the *New York Times* in 1971, "forgetting the precept of the Eliza-bethan, Francis Bacon, that 'nature is not governed except by obeying her.' "

For the peregrine falcon, bald eagle, and osprey, the banning of DDT came almost too late. By 1972 the falcon had disappeared from the eastern United States, and was nearly gone from the rest of its traditional North American range. Scientists estimated that a mere thirty nesting falcon pairs survived in the entire lower forty-eight states at the time. The plight of the eagle and osprey was nearly as dire.

But species are resilient. They've been tested through millions of generations of evolution to overcome all but the most unforgiving assaults. Slowly, gradually, as remnant DDT levels declined and eggshells grew thicker, the populations of eagles, ospreys, and falcons recovered until, one by one, each was removed from the Endangered Species List.

The peregrine's story may be the best of all. As is shown in the diorama in the museum's Hall of North American Birds, the falcons choose to nest on high, rocky aeries, such as those found on the Palisades overlooking New York's Hudson River. Unfortunately, hilltops usually feature sensational views, which makes them popular with people as well as falcons. So even as the peregrine recovered from the effects of DDT, its population was under threat from habitat loss.

Fortunately, the bird had a guardian angel: the Peregrine Fund, established in 1970 by Tom Cade, an ornithologist at Cornell University. Since then, the fund has captive-bred dozens of falcons; released them into the wild in suitable locations; and—perhaps most importantly—helped establish the birds in cities, where bridges and buildings provide replacement "cliffs" for vanished natural nesting sites.

Today, peregrine falcons nest in New York City, Baltimore, Chicago, San Francisco, and other cities across the country. Observant urban residents can be rewarded by a glimpse of a blue-gray adult flying overhead or a brown-and-white immature falcon swooping down on powerful, angled wings toward its favorite food, the pigeon. Even if you never see one, it's encouraging to realize that nature and the unnatural world can sometimes still coexist so comfortably.

A Rain-Forest in Manhattan

In the midst of the Museum's bustling Hall of Biodiversity, a refuge from the eye-catching video screens and interactive computer terminals, stands a very different kind of exhibit, a meticulous recreation of a patch of African rain-forest. Even though it is located thousands of miles from the forest that inspired it, this walk-through diorama captures some of the quiet mystery of the world's rain-forests, home to the greatest diversity of plants and animals on earth.

Ornithology Curator Joel Cracraft, Associate Director of Exhibits Willard Whitson, and more than two dozen other Museum employees traveled to the Dzanga-Sangha rain-forest in the Central African Republic to prepare for the exhibit. They brought along more than six thousand pounds of supplies, including plaster and rubber to make impressions of leaves and tree bark; video cameras; walkie-talkies; and hundreds of bags, boxes, and other containers to be used to transport specimens.

The Dzanga-Sangha is one of the richest environments in Africa, home to lowland gorillas, chimpanzees, forest elephants, a slew of monkeys and smaller mammals, and a breathtaking abundance of fascinating birds, reptiles and amphibians, insects, and plants. It is also, like rain-forests everywhere, threatened by human activities ranging from clear-cutting to mining. Fortunately, the government of the Central African Republic has set aside both a national park (where no hunting, mining, or clear-cutting is allowed) and a forest reserve, where local people can still follow their traditional lifestyles. Large-scale exploitation is forbidden.

This means that visitors to the Hall of Biodiversity who take the time to explore the stunningly crafted diorama (whose trees hold 411,000 model leaves!) will be learning about a place where the rain-forest's diversity is still protected—not merely getting a last look at a vanished wilderness.

RESEARCH TODAY: PIECING TOGETHER THE PUZZLE

A prerequisite to making any decisions concerning the preservation of populations, species, or higher taxa is knowledge of their existence. Creating such knowledge is a dominant part of the research of systematists, and few other workers are sufficiently skilled to undertake such studies.

—*Ornithology Curator George Barrowclough, in* Systematics, Ecology, and the Biodiversity Crisis *(1992)*.

Current classifications of birds usually state that the world harbors about nine thousand bird species, give or take a few hundred. For the ornithologists working at the Museum today, each one of these nine thousand species is like a separate piece of a gigantic jigsaw puzzle. There is just one place to put each piece to create an accurate phylogeny of the birds—a true picture of each species', each genus's, each family's, relationship with every other in the class Aves.

But the jigsaw-puzzle analogy is accurate only as far as it goes, because ornithologists face an even more difficult challenge. They must determine whether each piece, each species, has been accurately defined. One supposed species may actually be composed of birds belonging to several; conversely, three or more species may be "lumped" together under a single name.

As George Barrowclough and many other Museum scientists point out, achieving a better definition of what constitutes a species does more than allow us to understand the dimensions of the puzzle. It also gives us a sense of where the areas of greatest diversity are, what ecosystems harbor the most species of birds and other animals. Without that knowledge, we are severely limited in knowing where to devote limited conservation resources to best effect.

The only way to approach such challenges, Barrowclough says, is to undertake careful, systematic study of as many species as possible. To do so, Museum ornithologists have long utilized the department's vast collection of specimens, while adding to the collection during expeditions to areas little visited by previous generations of scientists.

Curator François Vuilleumier, for example, has focused on the little-studied birds of Patagonia, in Argentina and Chile. His goal is an ambitious analysis of biogeography and speciation of the birds in this fascinating region, which lies between the Argentine coast to the east and the Andes Mountains to the west.

Frequently, Vuilleumier and others must bring back species already collected during previous expeditions. "In the past, collectors would save only the skin, and sometimes a few bones." explains scientific assistant Paul Sweet, who has collected specimens in Venezuela, Argentina, and elsewhere. "To learn what we need to know about relationships between species, we need to preserve as much of the skeleton as possible, and even the soft tissue when we can."

With a sufficient supply of specimens, curators can attempt far more complex analyses than ever before. Curator Joel Cracraft's work on birds of paradise, for example, involves a team of researchers and ongoing study of skeletal anatomy, along with DNA sequences gathered at the Museum's Molecular Systematics Laboratory. "My laboratory research attempts to unravel the evolutionary history of the birds of paradise in order to understand the evolutionary changes that took place in their morphology, behavior, and ecology," Cracraft explained in the *American Museum of Natural History Environmental Journal*, a 1993 publication.

But not all curators have chosen to focus on exotic birds from distant lands. Curator George Barrowclough's nearly two decades of research into the relationships among different populations of juncos (small, ground-feeding sparrows native to North and Central America) is a perfect example of the role systematics can play in studying birds far closer to home.

As birders well know, juncos' regional populations generally resemble each other, but they also feature subtle differences in eye and back color, presence of wing bars, and other characteristics. In the past, these differences have caused scientists to divide juncos into six or more different species. Today, following discovery of some interbreeding junco populations, only two species are recognized in the United States (plus another in Mexico and Central America).

For Barrowclough, the juncos presented an ideal systematic challenge. "Even using traditional classification techniques, people have had a lot of questions about the relationships between different junco groups," he says. "Are the yellow-eyed ones a different species from the dark-eyed ones? And how about widely separated populations of yellow-eyed birds?"

Until relatively recently, Barrowclough's in-depth systematic study of juncos would have depended largely on microscopic analysis of bones and feathers. Now, with the greater availability of a technique called "electrophoresis," scientists can actually study the makeup of proteins in a bird's tissues. He is also studying junco DNA sequences, the foundations of life that can reveal more certainly than ever before the similarities and differences among junco populations.

Using these techniques, Barrowclough is certain that those who lumped different groups of juncos together have classified the birds incorrectly. "After working with them all these years, I can tell that there are about fourteen different species of juncos," he says.

For Barrowclough, though, his years of work on juncos have a greater purpose. "I like juncos—they're great birds," he says. "But this project has been designed to show how to study complex cases, how to put multiple sets together of genetic data, plumage color, and other characteristics. Once we've mastered the techniques, we can use them anywhere, even in the tropics, where diversity is far greater."

How powerful are these new genetic techniques? Barrowclough has recently employed them to study the spotted owl, the bird that has become famous as the living embodiment of the old-growth forests of the Pacific Northwest. Outside this region, the spotted owl is also found in geographically distinct populations in other mountainous areas in the western United States and Mexico, making it a challenge to study.

By using exquisitely sensitive DNA sequencing, Barrowclough and his coworkers were able to determine, for example, that a bird in one mountain range might not be closely related to one a few miles away, but to another owl hundreds of miles further off. In essence, DNA sequencing allowed him to create a "flow chart" depicting the movement of generations of spotted owls across their range, an extremely important finding that may allow far more effective protection of the species in the future.

When more widely used, such techniques will allow systematists and conservation scientists alike to understand when species are truly threatened with extinction, as why as well. As Barrowclough wrote in "Systematics and Conservation Biology," his contribution to *Systematics, Ecology, and the Biodiversity Crisis* (edited by Niles Eldredge, 1992), "A prerequisite to making any decisions concerning the preservation of populations, species, or higher taxa is knowledge of their existence. Creating such knowledge is a dominant part of the research of systematists, and few other workers are sufficiently skilled to undertake such studies."

Ernst Mayr, the ornithologist-evolutionist who employed systematic study as the springboard to his brilliant work on evolutionary theory, took a philosophical view of the role of systematics. "In this day and age, science is no longer conducted merely for its own sake. . . . When optimistically inclined, [the scientist] will say that he is helping to build a better world; when pessimistically inclined, he will say he is trying to prevent a further deterioration of this world," Mayr wrote in 1988. "But he cannot do this unless he has a sound understanding of Man and of the world in which he lives. And it is precisely the study of diversity and of evolutionary history which has made a major contribution toward the development of a *new image of Man.*"

9   Stories of Human Diversity

INTRODUCTION: A HISTORY OF VANISHED TIMES

The Department is carrying on its work in many directions. It is constantly adding to its collections, and is contributing to the advancement of science by numerous publications based on its expeditions. The work that the Department has to do is extensive and at the same time most urgent, because the native races and their remains are disappearing rapidly before the advances of our civilization.

—*Anthropology curator Franz Boas, in the*
American Museum Journal, *June 1902.*

Anyone who sets foot in the American Museum of Natural History recognizes immediately the central importance of its anthropology collections. In many ways, the extensive displays devoted to human origins; to Inka, Aztec, and other pre-Colombian kingdoms; and to living Asian, African, and North and South American peoples, provide a compelling endpoint to the stories told in other halls about the history of the earth and the organisms that populate it.

These anthropology collections are the result of more than a century of intensive, ambitious fieldwork. Beginning in the

1890s, the Department of Anthropology sent a succession of extraordinarily talented archaeologists, ethnologists (the people who study the origins and functioning of extant human cultures), and collectors to the world's remotest corners. Yet anyone visiting the Museum during its earliest years would have had no inkling of the extraordinary efforts to come.

The Department of Anthropology was first established in 1873, a mere four years after the founding of the Museum itself. *The Annual Report* for that year trumpeted the event, saying that "this new department promises to be one of the largest and most interesting features of the Museum."

Official claims aside, the newly established department, under the leadership of Museum founder Albert S. Bickmore, was little more than a repository for the first anthropological items obtained by the Museum. These early collections included objects from such widely diverse locales as New Zealand, the Arctic, Puerto Rico, and Fiji.

Remarkably, even these haphazard acquisitions gave the Museum one of the finest collections of anthropological objects in the world. By the early 1890s, however, the Museum's administration was no longer satisfied with merely relying on gifts and purchases as a substitute for actual research and collecting in anthropology.

On a comparatively small scale at first, the department began enlisting anthropologists to undertake expeditions. The first took place in 1891 when Carl Lumholtz explored the archaeological sites of northern Mexico and the Sierra Madre, and others followed in the next few years. But it was not until 1894, when Museum President Morris K. Jesup hired Frederick Ward Putnam as curator of the department, that the department changed radically.

Frederick Ward Putnam, perhaps the greatest visionary in the history of early American anthropology, saw what the science *could* achieve and set out to fulfill his vision. That vision, as described by Clark Wissler, one of the brilliant anthropologists hired by Putnam, was simple and direct: "Professor Putnam's idea was to make the Museum an instrument of field research, to go out with trained men, collect, and study the evidence of man's antiquity on the ground."

Putnam came to the Museum already occupied with a host of other responsibilities. In just the few years before joining the Museum, he had also helped establish the Field Museum in Chicago, organized and directed the department of anthropology at the University of California, and served as state commissioner of fish and game for Massachusetts. Remarkably, he assumed his role as chairman of the Museum's anthropology department on only a part-time basis; the rest of his hours were spent at the Peabody Museum at Harvard University, added to his long-time responsibilities as permanent secretary of the American Association for the Advancement of Science.

Still, Putnam clearly had enough time and energy left to reinvent the Museum's anthropology department, beginning with its name. Typically for the time, it had previously been referred to under several, seemingly interchangeable names, including the Department of Archaeology and the Ethnological Department. To Putnam, these various fields all belonged under a single designation, and the official Department of Anthropology was born.

Putnam's other early moves were far from semantic. "One of his strongest traits was his genius in interesting wealthy men in Museum development," Wissler wrote. "In almost equal measure he had a way of inspiring capable young men" to go into the field. Within a decade, these young men (and women) included many of the pioneers of modern anthropology, including Franz Boas, A. L. Kroeber, George Pepper, and Marshall Saville.

Just a few months after his arrival, Putnam sent Morris Jesup a note describing his philosophy. "In no department of human interest can the feelings of a people be so easily aroused and then led, as in that relating to man himself," he wrote. "How man came to be what he is, where and when he first appeared, how he has wandered over the earth in various lines of migration, and has developed this and that community, has discovered this and that art . . . are questions that everyone wishes to have answered." To answer such questions, he hired the brilliant young anthropologist Franz Boas. Almost immediately, Boas set out on the Jesup North Pacific Expedition, an amazingly ambitious ethnological survey that remains one of the great achievements in the Museum's history. (For more on this great adventure, see page 263.) With this and other efforts, Putnam instituted the spirit of exploration that lives on in vibrant, ambitious research now underway in the anthropology department.

Putnam also wrote, "An exhibition should be made of all the peoples of the earth in such a way as to show their particular character of race, variety, nation, tribe." By the end of his tenure at the Museum in 1903, he had laid the groundwork for the anthropology exhibit halls that today demonstrate the remarkable variety and complexity of human cultures past and present.

No one chapter—no one book—can do full justice to the marvellously diverse exhibits and research projects that have occupied the department during the past century. The sections that follow will focus on some of the treasures of the collection on exhibit, where they came from, and who brought them to the Museum. In addition, many of the objects provide a window to studies currently underway at the department. These studies will also be described, albeit briefly.

What this chapter can accomplish, in lieu of an encyclopedic discussion of human history, is to remind us of the diversity of human cultures, both ancient and modern, that created the objects on display. As Curator Emeritus Stanley A. Freed wrote in a 1980 article for *American Indian Art Magazine*, "[T]he existing collections are all that we will ever have of the artifacts that represent vanished times in the histories of hundreds of peoples." The collections, and everything written about them, must seek to ensure that these histories are not lost forever.

HUMAN PREHISTORY: GLIMPSES OF WHERE WE CAME FROM

I think to truly understand human origins, paleoanthropologists are going to have to abandon a *Homo sapiens*–centric viewpoint and look at human fossil remains with the same eyes as a scientist studying any other mammal group. Only by looking for patterns of diversity in the fossil record will we achieve a true definition of what constitutes *Homo*.

—*Anthropology Curator Ian Tattersall, 1996.*

The Mural of Primate Evolution, which adorns the Museum's Hall of Human Biology and Evolution, provides a vivid, scientifically accurate view of 50 million years' evolution of the group to which modern humans belong. Painted by Jay Matternes with painstaking scientific accuracy, using known fossil remains and logical anatomical guesswork, the mural provides a vivid look at our distant, ancient relatives.

Farthest to the right is the primitive, squirrel-like *Plesiadapis*, which lived in what is now Wyoming between 60 and 53 million years ago. Occupying the same territory about 48 million years ago was *Notharctus*, a more advanced primate with similarities to today's lemurs. Perfectly designed for an arboreal life, *Notharctus* roamed the rain forests that covered this part of North America at that time.

Aegyptopithecus, known from the Fayum region of Egypt, lived about 34 million years ago. It was one of the first of the higher primates, the group which in modern days includes the anthropoid apes (such as orangutans, chimpanzees, and gorillas) and humans—although it didn't closely resemble any recent higher primates. Far more apelike was the larger-brained *Proconsul*, which thrived in East Africa about 19 million years ago. Lastly, and farthest to the left, is *Sivapithecus*, with a face and jaw like a modern orangutan but a monkeylike body, which flourished in Pakistan and India only about 8 million years ago— just an eyeblink in the history of life on earth.

A glance at the mural's depiction of vignettes in primate evolution inevitably spurs one central question: Where do the origins of the human race fit into this panorama of primate life? This is a question that has intrigued scientists worldwide for more than a century, not least scientists at the Museum.

Perhaps the Museum's most prominent early investigator of human origins was William King Gregory (1876–1970). Trained as a classic scientific generalist, he seemed to be everywhere in the Museum during the first half of this century. As long-time Museum paleontologist Edwin H. Colbert wrote in the 1975 *Biographical Memoirs* of the National Academy of Sciences, Gregory was "renowned as a comparative anatomist; as a leading authority of the evolution of the mammalian dentition; as a vertebrate paleontologist; as a widely respected student of the fishes, both fossil and recent; as a contributor of much knowledge concerning the evolution of reptiles, especially the mammal-like reptiles of Permo-Triassic age; as a leader in the study of fossil and recent mammals; as an expert on various mammalian groups, especially the primates; and as a scholar with a worldwide reputation for his contributions to our concepts of the origin and evolution of man."

It was in his interest in primates, including humans, that Gregory made some of his most lasting contributions to science. As early as 1913 he began analyzing the relationships among living and fossil primates; his 1920 Museum *Memoir* on *Notharctus*, though dated, remains a triumph of close reasoning and open-mindedness.

From at least 1920 through the end of his long career, Gregory was particularly interested in "that portion of primate phylogeny leading to man," in Colbert's words. "It was his contention that early man was descended from brachiating ancestors, not unlike the modern chimpanzee, and he was an early advocate, perhaps the first such, of the theory that the then newly discovered australopithecines of South Africa were more closely related to the hominids than to the anthropoid apes."

Such theories brought Gregory into conflict with his long-time friend, Museum President Henry Fairfield Osborn. Osborn was an early proponent of evolutionary theory, at a time when the theory was far more controversial than it is today. But as he grew older, he became increasingly rigid in his views that humans and apes had evolved from separate families, and that the earliest humans had not come from Africa, but Asia.

It is little remembered today, but the original mission of Roy Chapman Andrews's great Central Asiatic Expeditions was to discover evidence of "Dawn Man"—the ground-dwelling, light-skinned human ancestor that (in Osborn's view) lived in Asia's high plains and developed into modern humans. In the wake of the CAE's world-famous discoveries (*Protoceratops*, *Velociraptor*, dinosaur eggs, etc.), that controversial mission was soon forgotten. But Osborn never let go of the idea that modern-day humans must have seen their first light in "Dawn Man."

Fortunately, Gregory and his theories survived Osborn and his. As historian Ronald Rainger says of Gregory in "What's the Use: William King Gregory and the Functional Morphology of Fossil Vertebrates," an article published in the *Journal of the History of Biology* (Spring 1989): "Emphasizing the importance of habit and function, he repudiated Osborn's interpretation of primate phylogeny, and indeed his entire evolutionary theory."

Today, all scientific discussions of human origins begin from the same ground zero: That, as Gregory realized, Africa is indeed where the roots of human evolution lie. This agreement, however, doesn't mean that scientists have learned everything there is to know about primate evolution and the placement of humans in that phylogeny. In fact, according to Curator Ian Tattersall, "We don't even have a firm definition of what constitutes *Homo sapiens*. So how can we claim to have a grasp on the relationships among ancient primates—including hominids?"

Tattersall's research illustrates both the goals and frustrations inherent in studying primate evolution through the fossil record. In one recent project, he and department research associate Jeffrey H. Schwartz (a professor at the University of Pittsburgh) collaborated with Vietnamese scientists in the study of Pleistocene period hominid and hominoid (ape) fossils found in caves in northern Vietnam.

"But these weren't the sort of caves you might find in Europe, filled with undisturbed cave-bear skeletons and signs of human habitation," Tattersall says. "Instead, they're solution cavities in a remarkable limestone landscape. The fossil material was all secondarily deposited—the animals died somewhere else, then got rolled on the ground, bashed by rivers, and ended up in the cave, cemented together by a very hard limestone matrix."

Not surprisingly, such rough treatment has tended to destroy all but the toughest fossils, meaning that most of the surviving specimens are isolated teeth. ("And most of the teeth have been gnawed by porcupines," Tattersall comments.) Yet even in reviewing these fragmentary fossils, the investigators have gotten some tantalizing clues to primate evolution and distribution during the Pleistocene.

Thus far, the researchers have discovered a mysterious new genus and species of hominoid ape (*Langsonia liquidens*), a new species of the orangutan genus Pongo (*P. hooijeri*), and four extinct subspecies of the living orangutan species *Pongo pygmaeus*

(*Pongo p. ciochoni, devosi, kahlkei,* and *fromageti*). As excitingly, the caves have also yielded teeth belonging to *Gigantopithecus* (a ten-foot-tall ape with teeth twice the breadth of a modern gorilla's), and at least one tooth belonging to an early human.

"Clearly, there was a very diverse hominoid fauna in this region during the Pleistocene," Tattersall says. "It would be wonderful to know more about what these animals looked like, but that will require finding fossils in a better state of preservation than the caves allow, and we simply haven't succeeded in finding such fossil deposits yet."

In another research project, begun in 1995, Tattersall and Schwartz are undertaking a close look at the classification of *Homo neanderthalis*, the Neanderthal. "Science doesn't have a decent definition of them, and there's still a lot of controversy over whether they're some strange variation on ourselves or something different," Tattersall explains.

Although scientists have been studying Neanderthal fossils for more than a century, few have studied the remains in the context of other hominids, Tattersall says. "Anthropologists tend to have a linear perspective—they use *Homo sapiens* as an endpoint and then project human features back into the past as far as they can," he explains. "But we come from a systematist's perspective—we're looking for evidence of diversity, not linearity, and that gives us a totally different viewpoint of what the Neanderthals were."

In studying Neanderthal specimens in museums across Europe, Tattersall and Schwartz found rich sources for future study as the project develops. "We were totally blown away by what we saw: some very obvious morphology that has never really been noted," Tattersall says. "And, of course, when we're done studying Neanderthal, we'll have to look at what we've found in the context of other hominids. I see this project as taking me to the end of the century," he adds. "At least."

ARCHAEOLOGY: KEYS TO OUR PAST

So, in short, the real equipment of an archaeologist is a scientific mind. As soon as archaeology ceases to strive for the mere collection of fine objects or curios, and turns to problems, it makes discoveries. We may justly take pride in the appearance of this new science, partly because our own Museum has played a conspicuous part in its inception, and partly because it will hasten the day when our archaeological exhibits can be made to tell the true story of man's career in the new world.

—*Anthropology Curator Clark Wissler, in the*
American Museum Journal, *February 1917.*

The Folsom Point and the First Americans

On the Museum's third floor, adjacent to the more extensive exhibits devoted to the life and culture of the Plains Indians, stands a modest, even old-fashioned display. It shows the cast of a skeleton of a bison, of a species (the label tells us) that has been extinct for ten thousand years. In close conjunction with the bones is a spear point, beautifully chipped by human hands out of stone.

It is easy to walk past this display without giving it a second thought. After all, more spectacular animal fossils can be found one floor up in the vertebrate paleontology halls, and the surrounding North American Indian exhibits are filled with spear points.

But this exhibit is different. When the original skeleton and associated point were first discovered near Folsom, New Mexico, in 1927, their discovery resounded like a thunderclap in the world of archaeology. For at the time conventional wisdom held that humans were only very recent inhabitants of North America, having arrived across northern land bridges from Asia no more than three thousand years ago. Experts scoffed at anyone who suggested that modern Indian culture had deeper and older roots.

The Folsom site was first discovered by a cowboy who noticed some old bones weathering out of the banks of the Cimarron River. The bones ended up in the hands of J. D. Figgins, director of the Colorado Museum of Natural History and a close collaborator with scientists at the American Museum. Figgins was interested enough in the specimens—an extinct bison and an ancient relative of modern deer—to send a Colorado Museum team to the site in 1926.

Now the finds began to get really exciting. Along with an abundance of fossil bones, the researchers found two projectile points and a chipped piece of flint associated with the skeletons. Figgins and Colorado Museum geologist Harold Cook were convinced that these finds proved that humans had settled in North America far earlier than previously believed.

Scientists at the American Museum were also convinced. But other experts were still skeptical, as Figgins noted at the start of an article in *Natural History*. "When we analyze the technical opposition to the belief that man has inhabited America over an enormous period of time," he wrote plaintively, "we find it is not only restricted to an individual minority, but it also appears to be traceable to the results of a too circumscribed viewpoint—a failure to appreciate properly *all* the evidence, and a seeming unwillingness to accept the conclusions of authorities engaged in related branches of investigation."

Clearly, even more indisputable evidence would be necessary to quiet the skeptics. In 1927, the American Museum's most famous fossil hunter, Barnum Brown, accompanied the Colorado researchers to the site. Remarkably, the site yielded up the evidence they were seeking, a spear point embedded between the ribs of a ten-thousand-year-old bison. Brown removed the last sediment above the point and saw for himself that there was no possibility of its having been introduced to the site after the burial of the bison's remains.

To Brown, this find—the one on display at the Museum—provided undeniable proof that Figgins and Clark were right. At a 1928 lecture before the New York Academy of Medicine, he held up a box containing the Folsom point and other artifacts from the site and said, "In my hand I hold the answer to the antiquity of man in America." Even the stubbornest doubters had to agree.

The Folsom finds, along with discoveries of artifacts from two other early cultures (Clovis and Goshen) proved that humans came to North America no later than about ten to twelve thousand years ago. But did they prove that no humans inhabited the continent *before* that time? This is a far more contentious question, and one that continues to be debated today.

Most of the hard evidence seems to support the idea that the Clovis were the first people to reach North America. But, according to Anthropology Curator David Hurst Thomas, that hasn't prevented the subject from continuing to be controversial. "Many archaeologists have begun to acknowledge, if sometimes only privately, that people might well have arrived in the New World as early as 40,000 years ago," he points out in a 1993 book entitled *The Early Americans*.

Evidence supporting this theory is inconclusive but intriguing. In a Pennsylvania site known as Meadowcroft Rockshelter, for example, archaeologists have used radiocarbon dating techniques that seem to show habitation nineteen thousand years ago. Another site, in southern Chile, is even more controversial: Layers of sediment deep below an early habitation appear to provide evidence of human culture that may be thirty-three thousand years old.

"Yet despite the findings from Meadowcroft, Monte Verde, and numerous other sites, we have no unequivocal, indisputable archaeological evidence that the New World was inhabited before Clovis times," Thomas writes. "The debate rages on. . . ."

The Folsom find wasn't the Museum's only important discovery in American archaeology, of course. As early as 1912, the Museum sent Curator Nels C. Nelson to excavate seven-hundred-year-old Indian ruins in the Galisteo Basin, south of Santa Fe, New Mexico. Here, and especially in the ruins of the Pueblo San Cristobal, New Mexico, which he excavated in 1914, Nelson developed a revolutionary new technique of stratigraphy. (Stratigraphy is the study of geology, fossils, or archaeological sites in the context of the age and composition of the rock strata in which they appear.)

In some European sites Nelson had studied, stratigraphy was easy, since the different rock strata were as easy to distinguish as the layers in a seven-layer cake. In the middens (ancient trash heaps) of the San Cristobal ruins, however, the site lacked such clear divisions, even though Nelson knew he was looking back through time as he dug down through a midden.

Nelson's solution was to create his own "nonvisual" stratigraphy that did not require distinguishable layers of rock. He divided a midden measuring three by six feet wide and nearly ten feet deep into one-foot vertical sections, then carefully catalogued the potsherds as to the level in the sections where they had been found. "It seems obvious to us today, but at the time Nelson's method was revolutionary," comments David Hurst Thomas. "This alone makes him perhaps the most important figure in early twentieth-century archaeology." Nor were Nelson's techniques scorned or ignored in his own time. As early as 1917, the Museum's head curator of Anthropology, Clark Wissler, was declaring these stratigraphic techniques "the new archaeology."

But Nelson wasn't done developing innovative techniques from his new stratigraphy. As described by D. R. Barton in a 1941 *Natural History* profile, Nelson believed that "every culture worthy of its name had its 'capital of fashion,' " representing the cultural center of a society at a given time.

"Wherever excavations penetrated deep enough to indicate that a ceramic 'capital' had once stood on that particular spot, Nelson obtained sample fragments from each stratum, thus charting the *vertical* evolution of styles," Barton explained. "Then shallow diggings were made at various distances away from the capital in several directions. These revealed a *horizontal* evolution of the same style which corresponded remarkably with the vertical gradation."

Nelson would repeat the procedure, moving further and further away from the capital until the potsherds resembled only those most primitive relics found deepest in the vertical excavation. "Here then, the outward spread of the culture by trade, conquest and other agencies might be assumed to have ended," Barton wrote of the technique, which Nelson dubbed his "Age and Area Hypothesis." "Once Nelson verified this working principle of Age and Area, anthropologists recognized that it applied not only to particular cultures but to hemispheres as well."

In recent years, David Hurst Thomas has continued the Museum's commitment to archaeological efforts in the American West. His research, too, covers New Mexico—including sites in downtown Santa Fe—but some of his most ambitious efforts have focused on an area known as Monitor Valley in Nevada, which contains the remnants of nomadic Indian civilization that first came to the area about six thousand years ago.

Here Thomas has been demonstrating the timelessness of Nelson's stratigraphic techniques, while also demonstrating how archaeology has changed in recent years. During more than fifteen field seasons in the Monitor Valley, Thomas has collaborated with nearly two dozen other scientists, including specialists in archaeology, ethnology, geology, paleontology, paleobotany, and other fields.

"Sometimes I felt like my job was simply to put the pieces

together, to manage logistics, and to keep the field team from killing each other," Thomas says. "But it was the only way to achieve my main objective, which was to look at this area from an ecosystem point of view—not just studying the habitations but truly understanding what life was like there at the time."

Even such a holistic and systematic approach did not prevent Thomas and his collaborators from almost missing a crucially important Monitor Valley site. In 1978, a forest ranger, exploring a barren, windswept meadow at eleven thousand feet below the peak of Mount Jefferson, found the remains of a rock enclosure, and told Thomas about it. When the archaeologist explored the meadow, he expected to find merely a shelter used by hunters seeking bighorn sheep at these high altitudes.

What he found instead was a stunning profusion of artifacts, including spear points and tools, many lying on the surface of the ground. When the scientists studied the site, they soon learned that about one thousand years ago this settlement—which Thomas named "Alta Toquima"—had been used not only by hunters but by entire families, as demonstrated by the presence not only of weapons, but of stones for grinding meal, and tools for making clothes. "The questions we can't quite figure out is why the families were there," Thomas says. "This is a very hostile environment, even in summer. There's no water. They would have had to carry everything in, just as we did."

One plausible theory shows the clues that an ecosystem approach can provide for the study of centuries-old lives. Using tree-ring analysis, radiocarbon dating, and other techniques, scientists have been able to identify massive droughts that, many centuries ago, gripped parts of the West for as much as two hundred years at a stretch. "The fact that these epic droughts occurred gave us a new hypothesis to consider: perhaps people sought refuge at Alta Toquima because a drought had devastated the lowlands," Thomas says. "Now we just have to see if we can test the hypothesis and find out if it's true."

Vanished Kingdoms of the New World

Since the earliest days of the Department of Anthropology, the ruined cities of extinct Mexican and Central and South American civilizations have intrigued Museum archaeologists. Before the turn of the century, Marshall H. Saville—the department's first full-time archaeologist—was exploring the ruins at Monte Alban, Palenque, and Mitla. Among the objects he helped bring to the Museum were a series of stone funeral urns from the state of Oaxaca, carved with magical figures of men and women with the features of bats, jaguars, and other animals.

The three-thousand-year-old Kunz axe, another of the Museum's greatest Mexican treasures, also came from Oaxaca. This magnificent object was owned by Tiffany gem expert and honorary curator George F. Kunz before being purchased by the Museum in 1891.

The axe, about ten inches in length and six inches wide, has been carved into a figure that is half-human, half-jaguar. Scholars speculate that it may represent a shaman who has transformed himself into a jaguar, the most powerful hunter in the jungles of Mexico's Gulf Coast. Its size and the artistry with which it was made (painstakingly chipped with stone flakes, then scored, perhaps with a piece of bamboo, to create the fine features) indicate it was most likely a ceremonial rather than utilitarian object.

No one can be certain what the axe was used for, because the cultures of the people who lived in the area three thousand years ago remain so mysterious. The Gulf Coast lowlands near where the axe was apparently found were inhabited by the Olmec people, an early culture that erected vast, complex ceremonial sites, including the ruins San Lorenzo and Tres Zapotes. The highland people who produced the axe might have been Olmec as well, or might have been a separate culture that traded with the Olmec Empire.

We may never know for sure. Sixty-five years ago, Museum anthropologist George C. Vaillant, an expert in ancient Mexico, wrote, "The Olmecs move like shadows across the pages of Mexican history." The same is largely true today.

The complex interactions among different ancient cultures that took place in the hills and valleys of Oaxaca continue to capture the attention of today's anthropologists. In 1993, Curator Charles Spencer began an ambitious field project, focusing on three large archaeological sites that were successively occupied between 700 B.C. and A.D. 200, the period in which the great state of Monte Albán emerged.

Monte Albán state was home to the Zapotec, a city-dwelling people who scientists believe had cultural affinities to the Olmec and the ancient Maya. Spencer's work, undertaken in cooperation with local authorities and Mexico's Instituto Nacional de Antropología Historia, has involved intensive mapping of the sites and controlled surface sampling throughout the area.

No extinct culture is more famous, more studied, or more haunting in its extraordinary extent and tragic fall, than the Inka Empire. At the time it was overthrown by Pizarro and the Spanish *conquistadors* in 1532, this extraordinary empire stretched from the Andes Mountains of Ecuador to Chile. No wonder that archaeologists have long sought to explore the ruins left behind by the Inka, and to learn as much as possible about their culture.

The Museum has on display several Inka objects, but none finer than the figurine known as the royal llama of the Inka, produced on the Island of the Sun, in Lake Titicaca, Bolivia. It was presented to the Museum a century ago by the archaeologist-adventurer Adolph

Bandelier, who spent extensive time collecting both artifacts and legends among the inhabitants of the Lake Titicaca region.

The llama's body is constructed of silver sheets carefully shaped and soldered together; the blanket is cinnabar; the diamond designs along the back may once have been inlaid with turquoise; and the blanket trim is gold. The wonderful elegance, humor, and energy that radiate from this sculpture are both marvelous and heartbreaking. It is heartbreaking because it reminds us of how the Spanish conquerors melted down most Inka gold- and silverwork, converting priceless artworks into blocks of hard currency for the treasury back home. Only luck allowed the royal llama to survive.

In life, llamas were important ceremonial (as well as utilitarian) animals for Inka royalty and priests. Every morning, Inka priests presided over the sacrifice of a live llama during a ceremony held at the Temple of the Sun. Museum experts believe that the royal llama figurine represents not an animal to be sacrificed, but a special white llama that the Inka ruler (called "Sapa Inka") kept as a pet or mascot.

Throughout the Museum's history, its archaeologists have returned often to Peru (the center of the Inka Empire), to study both Inka and pre-Inka civilizations. Perhaps most prominent among them was Junius Bird, whose famous excavations at Huaca Prieta, a large mound on the Peruvian coast, produced objects dating back five thousand years, long before the rise of the Inka—including many textile fragments that remain among the oldest ever found in the New World.

Today, research into the Inka continues under the guidance of Anthropology curator and Museum dean of science Craig Morris. In recent years, Morris has undertaken fieldwork in archaeological sites in Cotapachi, Bolivia and Chincha and Huánuco Pampa, Peru. In his writings and in conversation, he shows a particular interest in gaining deeper insights into the spread of Inka power from the center of the empire to its outer reaches. To trace this spread, he follows changes in styles of architecture, artifacts, and other objects over space and time—a focus that recalls Nels Nelson's Age and Area Hypothesis.

Among Morris's most intriguing conclusions is one that contradicts most definitions of how empires function. "It is becoming increasingly apparent that the Inka empire was not just a huge domain formed through gradual expansion by conquest, with a uniform general policy to turn each newly conquered territory into a replica of those conquered before it in order to create a relatively homogeneous state," he wrote as coeditor of the 1985 book *Andean Ecology and Civilization.* "In fact, the brilliance of the Inka achievement seems to lie in its ability to accept, use, and perhaps even foster variability."

Morris's studies of style variations in the empire bear out this contention. Huánuco Pampa was a major Inka administrative center. As such, its public buildings bore a close resemblance to those of Cuzco, the empire's seat of power. "The use of large numbers of small round structures for common residential buildings is one of the few highly visible characteristics that may be attributed to local architecture," he writes in *Style, Society, and Person* (1995). "However, the hands of the local masons who built Huánuco Pampa are also detected in other, subtle ways," including the placement of the stones and the material used to fill the gaps.

The buildings in villages located in the countryside outside of Huánuco Pampa show even less Inka influence. "One thing is evident in the villages of the Huánuco region: The Inka made no effort to build their own structures in the preexisting local settlements, nor did local builders often imitate Inka buildings," Morris writes.

Findings such as these are immensely revealing of the philosophy and strategy of the great Inka rulers as they extended their empire along the Andes. As Morris points out in *Andean Ecology and Civilization,* "The limited evidence to date does indeed suggest that some kind of master plan was in place by the time of Pizarro, but it was a plan that attempted to deliberately order and manage the ecological and cultural diversity the empire encountered, rather than reduce it to some easy administrative common denominator."

Such insights can only be gained by study of undisturbed archaeological sites, but for Morris and others the search for untouched sites grows ever more difficult. "Looting is a problem that grows worse every year," he says. "I have a colleague who was making plans to excavate a new site, but unfortunately he was overheard talking about it. When he returned to the site six months later, it had been bulldozed—which meant it could no longer be listed, registered, and protected. It was now a 'non-site.' "

Fortunately, Morris adds, interest and pride in their antiquities is increasing in the countries where the Inka once ruled. "Public consciousness has been raised, and people are now more protective of their archaeological history," he says. "There's a long way to go, but I'm encouraged."

ETHNOLOGY: LEARNING FROM RITUAL

By 1896, when the Department of Anthropology began to plan its first ambitious expedition, Museum ethnologist Franz Boas felt as if he were in a race against time. Much as Joel Asaph Allen, Frank M. Chapman, and other biologists sought to study and collect rare birds and mammals before their (seemingly inevitable) extinction, Boas felt that the cultures of indigenous peoples in North America and elsewhere were vanishing as well. If anything was to be learned of these cultures' rites and rituals, it would have to be learned soon.

Curator F. W. Putnam had convinced Museum President Morris Jesup to hire Boas. But it was the young ethnologist's enthusiasm and sense of urgency that helped convince Jesup to personally finance what remains one of the most important expeditions in the history of American anthropology: the Jesup North Pacific Expedition, a five-year exploration of the northwest coast of North America and vast expanses of the Russian coast, islands, and Siberia.

Jesup saw the expedition as providing the answer to a question that had long fascinated him: Did the Indian tribes of North America migrate from Asia thousands of years ago? Boas claimed that answering this question was the expedition's primary goal. "Among the great problems in anthropology, the one that stands out as of particular interest and importance to the American people is the problem of the earliest history of the native races of our country and their relation to the races of the Old World," he wrote in 1903.

But it is clear that Boas's true interests lay elsewhere. Most likely, he believed that the origins of North American Indian tribes clearly lay among the tribes of Asia, making a time-consuming search for proof unnecessary. Instead, Boas was fascinated by the similarities and differences among the cultures of the Kwakiutl, Haida, Gilyak, Tungus, Yakut, and other peoples the expedition intended to study. To learn about the unique aspects of each culture before its uniqueness vanished, he sent out a team of extraordinarily skilled field researchers, including Berthold Laufer, Waldemar Jochelson, Waldemar Bogoras, and himself.

Today, the volumes of anthropological data gathered by these men (and, in many cases, their wives as well) are still considered an invaluable record of cultural richness and diversity. One of the most haunting of the Museum's dioramas, the scene showing a shaman performing a healing ceremony in a Yakut village in eastern Siberia, is a classic example of a combination of art and anthropology. It gives a hint of the rites and rituals that fascinated Waldemar Jochelson during his time with the Yakut people.

Jochelson himself was a remarkable man. Born in Russia in 1855, he engaged in what were considered revolutionary activities as a student and was forced to flee to Berlin in 1875. During nine years in Germany and Switzerland, he honed his antigovernment opinions, writing for the journal *Forward* and other revolutionary publications.

In 1884 he attempted to enter Russia under a false name but was promptly arrested. He spent three years in solitary confinement and an additional ten years in northeastern Siberia before being allowed to leave Russia once more. But his Siberian exile provided its own opportunities: Jochelson spent the time studying the languages and cultures of the indigenous people. Once Boas convinced the suspicious Russian government to let Jochelson and his wife, Dina Brodsky, back into the country, they were an ideal choice to study the Koryak, Yukaghir, and Yakut tribes for the Jesup expedition.

The objects brought back by Jochelson and Brodsky (a physician in training, she also contributed immensely to the expedition's ethnological work) included three Yakut shaman's robes, one of which is worn by the shaman in the diorama. This shaman is in the process of healing a sick woman, attempting to wrest her soul from the evil spirits that have captured it.

On the robe's back are several iron and copper pendants and three iron disks, each of which has its own ritual meaning. One disk, Jochelson explained in a 1933 monograph published in the Museum's *Anthropological Papers*, is called the "ice hole" and "refers to the hole through which the shaman descends to the lower world, the world of evil spirits." The other two represent the sun and moon, which light the shaman's path as he descends into the lower world.

However evocative, the Museum's diorama cannot capture perhaps the most compelling aspect of a shamanic ceremony: The ritual itself, in which the shaman dances (pendants rattling and disks clanging), beats a drum, and chants as he draws the evil spirits from the patient's body. The force of the ritual taking place in the dark, smoky hut must have been powerful indeed.

A close look at the Yakut shaman diorama reveals a Russian Orthodox icon hanging on the wall. This shows that, even in Jochelson's time, the government was attempting to force the Yakut to abandon their traditional religious practices and adopt Christianity, and also that, at least in private, the Yakut were resisting the pressure.

It would be logical to believe that a century after the Jesup expedition, in an age of jet travel, worldwide television networks, and increasing urbanization, belief in spirits and shamans would have dwindled or disappeared throughout the world. Logical, but not true, as has been shown by current Museum ethnologists who have been studying cultures in South America, Africa, and Asia.

In recent decades, it has still been possible to find peoples on this earth largely unaffected by outside pressures, but such cultures grow fewer every year. In his fieldwork among the Kuikuru of central Brazil and other Indian tribes of the Amazon, Curator Robert Carneiro has had the rare opportunity to witness the daily life of some of these remarkable peoples.

The Amazonian societies studied by Carneiro had a deep understanding of their tropical forest environment. The Kuikuru, for example, "were able to name 191 different trees I asked about, but beyond that, they could cite a use—and often multiple uses—for 138 of these trees," Carneiro writes in an essay in *People of the Tropical Rain Forest* (1988). "Beyond identifying the names and uses of plants, Amazonian Indians understand their

roles in the web of forest life. For example, a Kuikuru can tell you
that the tapir likes the seeds of the *aku* tree, that monkeys eat the
fruit of the *inui* or *egeikajï*, and that the fruits of the *fingugi* are
relished by the toucan."

The peoples of the Amazon hold strong supernatural beliefs,
expressed through a rich mythology whose similarities span different cultures. "Shamanism continues to be a prominent feature
of virtually all Amazonian tribes," Carneiro writes in *Traditional
Peoples Today* (1994). "Above all else, the shaman (almost
invariably a man) is a healer, but he may also be asked to locate
lost or stolen objects, to divine the future, or to identify sorcerers.
In time of war, he may be expected to help his village by sending
evil spirits to attack the souls of its enemies."

The close connection between the Amazonian tribes and both
the natural and supernatural worlds has evolved over thousands
of years. As is well known, however, outside forces are threatening to destroy these vulnerable societies. In a few remote areas,
Carneiro points out, tribes live on with at least a semblance of
their traditional culture. "But the quickening pace of deforestation, road building, and economic development in general
throughout Amazonia poses a critical threat to their survival," he
warns in *Traditional Peoples Today*. "Unless these processes are
drastically slowed, it is likely that within a few decades no tribe
will remain with more than a vestige of the culture that, for thousands of years, allowed Indians to flourish in the world's largest
area of tropical rain forest."

The exhibits on view in the Hall of African Peoples give hints
both of the extraordinary cultural diversity to be found on that
great continent, and of the close ties those cultures maintain
to rituals and ceremonies. The African spirit-dancer figure,
dressed in a costume made of real snail shells and topped by a

carved wooden snail on its head, provides one example of the variety of characters to be found in many of these ritual performances.

This spirit dancer plays a part in the ceremonies of the complex Engungun cult, practiced by the Yoruba people of Nigeria. According to University of California, Berkeley, anthropologist William Bascom (who collected the costume for the Museum), the cult "is dedicated to the worship of Amaiyegun, the god who taught people how to make and use the costumes which mask their wearers, and thus saved the people of Ife when Death and his followers were killing them."

The spirit dancer, Marikoto, is not a figure of religion or war, but a trickster who entertains the audience. Bascom, who witnessed Engungun rituals, described Marikoto and other tricksters as having "elaborate costumes representing various animals in which they appear, amusing the spectators and astonishing them with rapid changes and magical disappearances; they also have numerous wooden masks with which they mimic various peoples and occupations."

The spirit-dancer costume, like those that fill the hall, shows the wonderful variety and vibrancy of African ritual. Just as importantly, it demonstrates the critical role that such costumes (and the figures they represent) can play in keeping a sense of cultural identity alive, even in the face of relentless pressures from the outside world.

Anthropology Division Chair and Curator Enid Schildkrout has traced the evolution of ritual among African peoples for many years. A fascinating example can be found in *African Reflections* (1990), in which she and coauthor Curtis A. Keim detail the lives, art, and rituals of the Mangbetu people of northeastern Zaire.

An understanding of the importance of ritual among the Mangbetu before the arrival of Europeans is essential to any

insight into their culture. "Two ritual institutions were central to
the Mangbetu community: *naando* and *natolo*," Schildkrout
writes. "*Naando* is a complex group of ideas and practices that
varies throughout the Mangbetu region. It is also the name given
to a substance made from the root of a forest plant (*Alchornea
floribunda*) that, when eaten, produces altered states of consciousness."

When eaten, *naando* also gave users the power to bless someone, to divine, and to heal. "In most Magnbetu areas, specialists
in the use of *naando* . . . belonged to a society that used the root
along with dancing, songs, and other rituals to discover hidden
things (such as witches), to foretell the future, and to bring a general blessing to people."

Natolo, too, was a ritual institution basic to the maintenance
of Mangbetu lineage. "Ancestors, *atolo* (sing., *natolo*), watched
over members of the living community and disciplined them
when they did not show proper respect," Schildkrout explains.
"If a person had an illness that persisted or a personal problem,
such as the inability to conceive, it was possible that an ancestor
was the cause or could help with a cure."

In reading these passages of *African Reflections*, it is impossible not to notice that Schildkrout is writing in the past tense. As
she reveals, those who practiced traditional Mangbetu rituals
paid a heavy price after the arrival of the colonial powers in the
nineteenth century, followed by Christian missionaries just before
1900. *Naando* and other ritual institutions were banned, and
magic whistles and other ritual objects were collected and burned.

But although they tried to instill Western beliefs (couched in
Mangbetu terms), the missionaries "failed to provide a completely convincing alternative to the Mangbetu understanding of
the world," Schildkrout writes. "The missionary view of reality
was alien in concept and accessible only through whites."As a

result, most Mangbetu continued to rely on more traditional practices and beliefs, but privately, although there was no doubt that missionary influence and economic and political pressures succeeded in weakening the long-held Mangbetu worldview.

"Today the result seems to be very mixed," Schildkrout says. Those who remember the persecution of the colonial period make sure that dedicated Christians are not present before expressing their beliefs. Such older informants, she concludes, "accept Western education as necessary for wealth and self-protection, but they remain uneasy about its effect on society."

When Curator Emeritus Stanley Freed and his wife, Ruth (an Anthropology research associate) first journeyed to the North Indian village of Shanti Nagar in 1958, they wondered if the villagers would share their insights with a pair of visiting Americans. "As it turned out, they were marvellously cooperative—I still look back on their openness with complete awe," Stanley Freed says. "People were always available for interviews, and most were very honest."

Acting as a husband-and-wife team had immeasurable benefits, he adds. "I think you get four times as much information that way."

During their initial fieldwork and on a return visit twenty years later, the Freeds found themselves fascinated by the study of ghosts and their relationship to village life. "The study of ghosts was not a planned project for the field trips of 1958–59, and 1977–78," they write in their 1993 monograph *Ghosts: Life and Death in North India.* "However, it reveals the value of long-term, holistic ethnography, which includes the study of culture, society, biology, psychology, ecology, history, and individuals within a community."

During the first visit, the Freeds learned about illnesses caused by ghosts and possession by ghosts. When they returned to the village in 1977, they found that it had been gripped by instances of ghost possession. They were fascinated by the seeming correlation between the rise in ghost possessions and stressful outside events, which included epidemics of malaria and typhoid, a murder, a possible suicide, an accidental death of a young girl, and a government-ordered, coerced sterilization program.

Among many other findings, their subsequent study showed them that, even in a more modern age, "Belief in ghosts is reinforced by ancient traditions, often embodied in sacred literature, and specific cases of ghost possession reflect the relations that the living had with the dead. Tradition defines the various types of ghosts, tells how the souls become ghosts, and explains their connection to illness and curing practices."

Curator Laurel Kendall has chosen to study religion and ritual in South Korea, a society that has undergone dizzying changes in recent decades, and where tradition would seem to be fighting a losing battle against modernity. "When I was a Peace Corps volunteer there in 1970, it seemed to be a largely rural society," she says. "But by the time I returned to do my dissertation research in 1976, it had become a majority urban society, with a newly visible middle class."

During Kendall's early visits, she was assured by her Korean contacts that shamanism—traditionally relied on for divination, to treat illness and carry messages from ancestors and other ghosts, and for many other purposes—had largely died out, except perhaps in the deepest recesses of the countryside. "But the truth was—and is—that the cities are home to many very active shamans," she says.

At first, the emergent Korean government and professional classes sometimes rejected such rituals, seeing this rejection as a sign of modernity, Kendall says. "But the use of shamans crept in through the back door, and has become a part of Korea's cultural identity to be embraced, not abandoned," she explains. "In fact, today the most numerous clients seem to be small businesspeople, who have profound financial anxieties."

In *The Life and Hard Times of a Korean Shaman* (1988) and many other works, Kendall provides a compassionate view of the challenges faced by shamans, most of whom are women. "In Korea, shamans *(mudang, mansin)* are both born and made: fated from birth to suffer until they acknowledge and accept their destiny, initiated, and then trained by a senior shaman to perform *kut*, less elaborate rituals, and divinations," she writes in a contribution to the 1996 book *The Performance of Healing*, edited by Carol Laderman and Marina Roseman. (*Kut* is an elaborate ritual designed to revitalize an entire house and household following illness, family quarrels, or financial loss.)

In the same article, an established shaman named Kim Pongsun tells Kendall about the travails of Chini, an initiate to shamanism. "If the initiation ritual fails, then the initiate has no professional standing as a shaman, she can't divine for clients. No food, no money, an empty belly, illness, she has to go through all that again," Kim Pongsun says. "Chini's all alone in the world."

Ironically, Kendall says, the intimacy and personal quality of each initiate and shaman's story is in danger of being drowned out by the commercialization of shamanic ritual. "In the 1980s, the government began to call shamans cultural treasures," she explains. "Where once we were afraid that shamanism would disappear, now Korean shamans are finding themselves being put up on a stage and performing as 'treasures.' Of course, they're still doing the real thing too—and it does show that shamanism is constantly evolving, and often in unpredictable ways."

MARGARET MEAD: THE BRIDGE

"Did anyone remember you?" people asked me when, in
1953, I said I had returned from Pere, the little Manus village in the Admiralty Islands where my husband and I had
spent seven months in 1928. "Did you remember anyone?".... To the 210 people of Pere village, we were the
kind of event that would be talked about again and again,
and as long as I tried to think and write about anthropological problems, the memory of the people—especially the
children, whom I studied intensively—would be sharp and
clear in my mind, each small figure etched sharply against
the background of the lagoon where their pile houses were
silhouetted.

—*Margaret Mead, in* Natural History, *1976.*

The beliefs held by Franz Boas, Clark Wissler, and other anthropology pioneers—that indigenous cultures were doomed to
extinction—gave them the impetus to perform risky, expensive,
and difficult fieldwork. The result of these efforts were collections
of artifacts, photographs, and—most importantly—volumes of
printed material that dutifully describes the habits of North
American Indians, Siberian tribes, and many other peoples. The
Museum and the history of anthropology are immeasurably
richer for their efforts.

In another way, however, this striving to document doomed
societies risked a research dead end. Unless Boas and the others
were willing to declare anthropology itself extinct, they would
have to accept that even the "purest" cultures would someday
be affected by the outside world and would be worth studying
anyway.

Today, of course, every ethnologist focuses on the evolution of culture, on the ways age-old rituals interact with influences both from within and outside the society. In doing so, every researcher owes a debt to the first anthropologist who followed this approach in her own research, Margaret Mead.

Mead (1901–1978) was visionary when it came to recognizing the value of longitudinal fieldwork, the study of a evolution of a society over generations. "She was the first to hold a baby in her arms as an anthropologist, and later to talk to the same person about his grandchild," says curator David Hurst Thomas. Adds curator Stanley Freed, "For most of us, you reach an age where you're simply too old to go back into the field. Margaret never got to be too old."

Mead's longitudinal approach was never more dramatic than in her research among the Manus people, residents of the Admiralty Islands off Papua New Guinea. With her husband, Reo Fortune, she first traveled to the village of Pere in 1928 (calling this visit "the best field trip we ever had" in her 1972 memoir, *Blackberry Winter*) and returned several times before her final trip there in 1975, just three years before her death.

During the initial 1928–29 fieldwork, Mead began to understand the rhythms of life among the Manus. She and Fortune witnessed rituals of childhood and of the transition of children into adults. And the visitors had been present at what Mead always considered perhaps the most important event in any society: "We had seen death, and without witnessing a death one cannot feel that one understands very much about a people," she stated.

During her half-century of visits to Pere, Mead watched the villagers confront the lure and dangers of the modern world. In 1953, "I found a people vigorously pursuing a course of modernization," she wrote in *Natural History*. "[I]t was to be a utopia constructed by adopting modern ideas—money instead of dogs' teeth, one God instead of ancestral ghosts and local place spirits, education instead of the trials of daring demanded by local warfare and headhunting, political unity instead of village feuds, and a rule of law instead of a rule of angry individual defense of rights and privileges."

By 1963, the rush to modernize had inevitably stumbled over some harsh realities. "Almost overnight the plagues of the modern world—crowding into cities, pollution from deposits of human waste in the sea, and juvenile delinquency—appeared, ten years out of the first proud modernization effort," she wrote. "The people had still not realized much economic progress because the island has few resources."

When Mead returned in 1971, she found that the dream of quick, seamless modernization had faded, and that the islanders "were beginning to ponder what was worth saving from the past before it was gone forever. The slit gongs, once abandoned for a gong made from a torpedo case, were back. . . . The old dancers were back also, in old costumes worn over modern dress, which looked unesthetic to our eyes, but not to theirs."

During her last visit in 1975, Mead was even more hopeful of the Manus's ability to balance the best of their own traditions with the most useful benefits offered by modernization. "The society was still distinctively Manus, but with a new sense of identity, ready to combine the old and the new," she wrote.

For Mead, the perspective gained by her years visiting with the Manus proved what she had suspected from the start of her career in anthropology—and what the invaluable insights gained by today's ethnologists confirm: "I realized how little we had been able to learn when we used to study a people only once, and how illuminating and unique was this opportunity to follow the same population—a microcosm of the world—for forty-seven years, as they fanned out into the wider world, but retained the core of their culture at home."

Index